THE VIRTUES OF HAPPINESS

OXFORD MORAL THEORY

Series Editor

David Copp, University of California, Davis

Drawing Morals
Essays in Ethical Theory
Thomas Hurka

Commonsense Consequentialism
Wherein Morality Meets Rationality
Douglas W. Portmore

Against Absolute Goodness
Richard Kraut

The Lewd, the Rude and the Nasty
Pekka Väyrynen

In Praise of Desire
Nomy Arpaly and Timothy Schroeder

Confusion of Tongues
A Theory of Normative Language
Stephen Finlay

The Virtues of Happiness
A Theory of the Good Life
Paul Bloomfield

Having It Both Ways
Hybrid Theories and Modern Metaethics
Edited by Guy Fletcher and Michael
Ridge

Motivational Internalism
Edited by Gunnar Björnsson, Fredrik
Björklund, Caj Strandberg, John
Eriksson, and Ragnar Francén Olinder

The Meaning of 'Ought'
Beyond Descriptivism and Expressivism
in Metaethics
Matthew Chrisman

THE VIRTUES OF HAPPINESS

A Theory of the Good Life

Paul Bloomfield

OXFORD
UNIVERSITY PRESS

OXFORD

UNIVERSITY PRESS

Oxford University Press is a department of the University of
Oxford. It furthers the University's objective of excellence in research,
scholarship, and education by publishing worldwide.

Oxford   New York
Auckland   Cape Town   Dar es Salaam   Hong Kong   Karachi
Kuala Lumpur   Madrid   Melbourne   Mexico City   Nairobi
New Delhi   Shanghai   Taipei   Toronto

With offices in
Argentina   Austria   Brazil   Chile   Czech Republic   France   Greece
Guatemala   Hungary   Italy   Japan   Poland   Portugal   Singapore
South Korea   Switzerland   Thailand   Turkey   Ukraine   Vietnam

Oxford is a registered trademark of Oxford University Press
in the UK and certain other countries.

Published in the United States of America by
Oxford University Press
198 Madison Avenue, New York, NY 10016

Library of Congress Cataloging-in-Publication Data
Bloomfield, Paul, 1962-
The virtues of happiness : a theory of the good life / Paul Bloomfield.
pages cm
Includes bibliographical references and index.
ISBN 978-0-19-982736-7 (hardcover); 978-0-19-061200-9 (paperback)
1. Ethics.   2. Happiness.   3. Conduct of life.   4. Virtues.   I. Title.
BJ1481.B63 2014
170—dc23
2013041300

CONTENTS

Acknowledgments   *vii*

Introduction   1

1. Getting Our Bearings   9
    1.1. The Problem   9
    1.2. The Diagnosis   16
    1.3. The Solution   28
    1.4. Common Dialectical Ground   42
    1.5. The Argument from Ontology   57
    1.6. The Argument from Epistemology   72
    1.7. Objections and Conclusion   79

2. Becoming Good   92
    2.1. The Paradox of Happiness   92
    2.2. The Most Important Thing in the World   96
    2.3. Taking Care of Yourself   114
    2.4. Beyond the Paradox of Happiness   125

CONTENTS

2.5. Developmental Practical Rationality   134
2.6. Immorality as Incomplete Development   146

3. Why It's Good to Be Good   153
    3.1. Human Nature and the Good Life   153
    3.2. Pleasure, Mood, and Self-Fulfillment   165
    3.3. Virtue   172
    3.4. Courage: Managing Danger   177
    3.5. Justice: Judging Fairly   184
    3.6. Temperance: Tempering Mettle   188
    3.7. Virtue, Luck, and Happiness   201
    3.8. Benefits of Morality   213
    3.9. Love Is Its Own Reward   215
    3.10. Wisdom   222

Bibliography   233
Index   245

ACKNOWLEDGMENTS

In the Preface to my first monograph, *Moral Reality*, I explicitly assumed that morality is "a practical endeavor tautologically aimed at the fullest possible flourishing of the highest and best aspects of our selves or our natures." I have always thought it is better to be a good person than a bad person, that courage is better than cowardliness, and self-discipline is better than being weak of will; that it is better to win fairly than to cheat and better to be wise than foolish. Growing up, these never seemed like "deep thoughts", but rather plain common sense. Richard Joyce reminded me while discussing his review of my book that the assumption that the moral life is better than the alternatives is far from obviously true, as a glance at the history of moral philosophy reveals it to be rife with skepticism for the idea that it is in a person's self-interest to be morally good. So, I've written this book in defense of the earlier set of assumptions, and I thank Richard for providing the initial impetus. I have attempted to make this book as metaethically neutral as possible, and I have certainly not assumed the sort of moral realism for which I argued in the earlier book.

The writing began during a leave from teaching granted to me by the University of Connecticut Humanities Institute. I am grateful to the Institute for its support and especially thank Richard Brown, its Director at the time, for many interesting and helpful conversations. During that year, I also benefited from conversations with my fellow fellows, especially Joel Blatt, Brenda Murphy, and Sharon Harris (in whose office I first saw Maxfield Parrish's *Dusk*—special thanks!). With further regards to UConn, I am lucky to be part of its Department of Philosophy, which has become my philosophical home. My colleagues have been wonderfully helpful, having heard and discussed much of the book with me during our weekly brown bag lunches, though special thanks go to Joel Kupperman, Don Baxter, Sam Wheeler, Lionel Shapiro, Tom Bontly, Marcus Rossberg, and Hallie Liberto. I have also benefitted from discussions with many UConn graduate students, some of who have since moved on: Jeff Wisdom, Alexis Elder, Daniel Massey, Kathy Fazekas, Michael Hughes, and Toby Napoletano. David Pruitt helped extensively, in his typically meticulous way, with the penultimate draft of the entire book. My debt to Michael Lynch, my compañero since graduate school, goes further: not just a dedicated friend and colleague, he is a veritable font of excellent advice, encouragement, and philosophical acumen.

I have presented material directly related to the book at the University of Nevada (Las Vegas), Union College, University of British Columbia, Bowling Green State University, and University of Miami, as well as at the MARGE Reading Group, the Arizona Colloquium in Ancient Philosophy, the Southern Society for Philosophy and Psychology, the Arizona Workshop in Normative Ethics, and the American Philosophical Association (Pacific Division). I thank the audiences for their comments and discussion.

I have been working on this project for enough years to be confident that I have forgotten helpful conversations I had along the way, at conferences, walking to restaurants, or later over coffee or drinks. So, I am grateful to many not mentioned here and I apologize to them for my poor memory. I do happily remember fruitful conversations with or receiving helpful comments from: Robert Audi, Neera Badhwar, Carla Bagnoli, Bob Barnard, Heather Battaly, Eddie Binder, Simon Blackburn, Ben Bradley, Tom Carson, Ruth Chang, Roger Crisp, Terence Cuneo, Stephen Darwall, Remy Debes, Daniel Dennett, John Doris, Jamie Dreier, Julia Driver, Stephen Finlay, William FitzPatrick, Margaret Gilbert, Michael Gill, Daniel Groll, Dan Haggerty, Chris Heathwood, Terry Horgan, Thomas Hill, Jr., Thomas Hurka, Paul Hurley, Rosalind Hursthouse, Robert Johnson, Richard Kraut, John Lemos, Don Loeb, Hal Lorin, Emily McRae, Diane O'Leary, Connie Rosati, Jacob Ross, David Schmidtz, Andrew Schroeder, Danny Scoccia, Russ Shafer-Landau, Walter Sinnott-Armstrong, Aeon Skoble, Matthew Noah Smith, David Sobel, Eliot Sober, Daniel Star, Michael Stocker, Judith Thomson, Mark Timmons, Raul Vargas, Pekka Väyrynen, Mark van Roojen, David Velleman, Steven Wall, Denis Walsh, Ralph Wedgwood, Eric Wiland, and David Wong. In 2008, I edited a volume called *Morality and Self-Interest* (Oxford University Press), and profited greatly from interacting with my contributors and from their contributions, though I thank Christopher Morris in particular, as he gave me valuable advice on that volume as well as very helpful feedback on a late draft of this book. I have had particularly helpful conversations with Valerie Tiberius, who merits special mention for her incisive comments on a late draft of the entire book. Julia Annas continues to be a wonderful support and inspiration for me, both in life and in philosophy, and I am deeply indebted to her.

I thank Peter Ohlin at Oxford University Press for his continued support and faith in the project. Wendy Katz helped me with editorial comments on an early draft of the first chapter. Ginny Faber, copyeditor extraordinaire, has my deep gratitude, and I thank Kate Nunn, Emily Sacharin, Molly Morrison, and Alison Williamson for their help with the book's production. Thanks at the end of it all to Casey Johnson and Andrew Parisi who helped with the final set of proofs.

My dearest friends are a deep well of common sense and the mere thought of them uplifts my spirits: Andre Ariew, Paul Beatty, Neil Carver, Jonathan Dekel-Chen, Nancy Goldfarb, Glendon Good, Bradly Jacobs, John Kolligian, Matt Lorin, Susan Mindell, Christian Rauh, Eric Siegel, and Raul Vargas. Special thanks go to my family, the Bloomfields, Greenfields, Meyersons, Barans, Michels, and Tarios.

Finally, I am most especially grateful to my wife, Sonia Michel, with and from whom I've learned more about love than I ever could have dreamt in my philosophy.

THE VIRTUES OF HAPPINESS

Introduction

Since its dawn, morality has always been on the defense; it has never stood up on its own.

We all learn early on that life is not fair: bad things happen to good people and good things happen to bad people. Why play fairly in an unfair world? And, as quick as that, morality can look like a game for fools.

We commonly think that we will be happiest if we can get our desires or preferences satisfied, if we can get "what we want out of life". And, as it turns out, sometimes the only or easiest way to get what we want is to lie, cheat, or steal. Because the most obvious reason to abstain from these is that we could be caught and punished, it may often look as if the only reason to abstain is for fear of getting into trouble. In fact, this fear is usually sufficient to ensure fair play. But the realization quickly follows that if we somehow knew we could not be caught, we would then have no reason to refrain from behaving immorally.

So, it has never seemed unreasonable to see morality as it was portrayed in Plato's *Republic* by Plato's older brother, Glaucon, who worried about how morality could be justified when it seems straightforward to think that it is

> a fact of nature that doing wrong is good and having wrong done to one is bad, nevertheless the disadvantages of having it done to one outweigh the benefits of doing it. Consequently, once people have experienced both committing wrong and being at the receiving end of it, they…decide that the most profitable course is for them to enter into a contract with one another, guaranteeing that no wrong will be committed or received. They then set about making laws and decrees, and from then on they use the terms "legal" and "right" to describe anything which is enjoined by their code. So that's the origin and nature of morality, on this view: it is a compromise between the ideal of doing wrong without having to pay for it, and the worst situation, which is having wrong done to one while lacking the means of exacting compensation. Since morality is a compromise, it is endorsed because, while it may not be good, it does gain value by preventing people from doing wrong.[1]

Morality is merely the best of bad options, a necessary evil, lacking adequate justification on its own merits. Thus, if only by dint of a ring of invisibility, we happen to be strong enough to fear neither paying for our bad behavior or being harmed by others, there would be no point to go on and not do what Glaucon calls "ideal": only fools sacrifice their own self-interest for no good reason. Philippa Foot succinctly presented this challenge by noting, "[I]f justice is not a good to the just man, moralists who recommend it as a virtue are perpetrating a fraud".[2] And Simon Blackburn has written:

---

1. Plato 1993, 358e–359a.
2. Foot 1958–59, 100.

This is the permanent chimaera, the holy grail of moral philosophy, the knock-down argument that people who are nasty and unpleasant and motivated by the wrong things are above all *unreasonable*: that they can be proved to be wrong by the pure sword of reason.[3]

In fact, demonstrating the unreasonableness or even the irrationality of immorality is not sufficient to justify morality. People who already accept morality might take comfort in the irrationality of immorality, but it is too easy to imagine self-consciously immoral people being nonchalant or even apathetic about irrationality, preferring to be irrational and get what they want to being rational and not.[4] They could even give a little sophistic hypothetical syllogism: "The most rational thing is to do whatever it takes to get what I want. Sometimes getting what I want requires me to be irrational. Therefore, sometimes the most rational thing to do is to be irrational." Or they might quote Whitman's "Song of Myself": "Do I contradict myself? / Very well then I contradict myself / (I am large, I contain multitudes.)" or perhaps Emerson's "Self-Reliance": "A foolish consistency is the hobgoblin of little minds, adored by little statesmen and philosophers and divines. With consistency a great soul has simply nothing to do. He may as well concern himself with his shadow on the wall."[5] As a result, the

---

3. Blackburn 1984, 222. More recently, Alison Hills has also called the justification of morality in the face of egoism, "the Holy Grail of moral philosophy" (2010, 1). She distinguishes between modest and ambitious arguments, where modest arguments are based on premises that egoists do not accept, while the ambitious ones are based on premises that egoists do accept. Hills' arguments there are explicitly modest; the arguments of the present book are meant to be ambitious.

4. Nozick 1981, 408, makes a similar point. This shows the limits of arguments against egoism by Nagel 1970 and Korsgaard 1996.

5. Whitman 2007, 67; Emerson 2010, 36.

arguments against immorality contained herein do not attempt to demonstrate its irrationality, but rather point out immorality's well hidden, self-defeating nature: being immoral keeps a person from being happy.

The book's setup and arguments are intended to show that living morally is not only justified but, indeed, is the only way of living that leads to happiness and the Good Life. If the arguments are not perfectly sound, they at least point in the right direction. The strategy of the book is to wed the ancient sense of "happiness" or "the Good Life" that we take from the Greek *eudaimonia* to a contemporary sense of "self-respect" derived from work by Kant. Starting with these conceptual tools, it follows that whenever immorality is disrespectful to its victims, it is to the same degree self-disrespecting to its perpetrators. Since all parties to the debate agree that people cannot be happy and live the Good Life without self-respect, the justificatory tables turn, and those who have attacked morality end up having to defend the misshapen position in which true happiness requires lacking self-respect.

There are two kinds of primary dialectical opponents. The first is typified by the egoist, or the immoralist, or any figure whose first priority is self-interest, or the interests of family, or a parochial community, when these interests are conceived and pursued without proper regard for morality.[6] Immorality on this view arises from improper partiality to the self or to what one happens to care about, and it is intended to capture both the large-scale immoralities performed for the sake of self, family, nation, or God as well as the small-scale and mundane immoralities found in the occasional insensitivity we may show to taxi drivers or waiters at the end of a

---

6. "Families, clans, friends, classes, nations, races,…can play the same role as the person of these egoists." Michael Stocker 1979, 744.

bad day. It is also intended to capture motives for immorality rang-
ing from malice to acting with mistaken rectitude. In all these cases,
people are in fact acting with improper partiality.

The second type of opponent can be thought of as "the moralist", captured well by *Out* in the following excerpt of a dialogue written by W. D. Falk:

> *In:*...One would hardly be a human being if the good
> of others, or of society at large, could not weigh with one as a
> cogent reason for doing what will promote it. So one has not
> fully learned about living like a rational and moral being unless
> one has learned to appreciate that one ought to do things out of
> regard for others, and not only out of regard for oneself.
>
> *Out:* No, you have still not got my point, I am saying that only
> insofar as you ought to do things—no matter whether for your-
> self or for others—for the sake of others, is the reason a moral
> reason and the ought a moral ought. Reasons of self-regard are
> not moral reasons at all, and you can forget about them in the
> reckoning of your moral obligations.[7]

According to the moralist, morality is conceptualized independently of self-interest and always trumps it. On such views, the prescriptions of morality are impartial, stringent, and overriding. The
problem, as we shall see, is that the moralist's full impartiality is just
as improper as the egoist's full partiality.

Importantly, both the egoist and the moralist assume that
self-interest and morality are characteristically, even conceptually,
set against each other. Defeating this assumption is the first important goal of the book: although there is at least a bit of truth to both

---

7. "Morality, Self, and Others," repr. in Bloomfield 2008a, 226.

sides, this assumption works against living well. On the contrary, the thesis to be defended is based on the idea that morality is conceptually set against making poor choices and living badly.

As for the plan of the book, the familiar place to start is with the question "Why be moral?" There is reason, however, to think that, as a place to start, this gets the valence wrong. Better to ask, "Why not be immoral?" If the opening worry is that morality may only be a necessary evil and that the only reason to be moral is the fear of being punished for acting immorally, the first task is to show why immorality is to be avoided even when it can be practiced with impunity. It is one thing to ask what the "payoff" is for being moral; it is quite another to ask what the harms of immorality are, especially when being immoral gets us what we want, can be so much fun, and a thrill to boot! Only once we are clear on the harms of immorality, on "why it is bad to be bad", will we be in a reasonable position to see the right motivations for being moral, and then to investigate the benefits that accrue to those who are good. And that is the outline of the book: the topic of why it is bad to be bad is taken up in chapter 1, what happens as people become good at valuing what ought to be valued is the topic of chapter 2, and the benefits are of being good, or why it is good to be good, are covered in chapter 3.

The book's main thesis is that living morally or virtuously is necessary and sufficient for people to live as happily as possible, given who they are and their circumstances. The basic argument for the claim of necessity amounts to the following hypothetical syllogism:

> Morality is necessary for self-respect.
> Self-respect is necessary for happiness.
>
> ———————————
>
> ∴ Morality is necessary for happiness.

The ultimate intent, however, is to defend the stronger claim: if the happiest life is the best life, then we never can live better or be happier than by living morally and virtuously, where this can be understood temporarily as judging wisely what is truly good and valuable as such, and then acting accordingly. This claim is not quite as strong as the infamous Stoic claim that virtue is sufficient for happiness, full stop. The present thesis is only that living as virtuously as possible will make one as happy as possible. Moral theory cannot change our place in our familial or historical milieux; it can only help us deal with what life presents to us. Given the sort of creatures we are, there is no guarantee of the Good Life for any human being facing all the manifold vicissitudes of reality. Perhaps, if we were gods, our happiness could withstand any and every misfortune and still be guaranteed. But we are not gods, and we have already noted how unfair life can be: the worst things can happen to the best people, and it makes no sense to say that the happiest of all possible human lives can be full of all the worst possible things. Nevertheless, we can defend the claim that living morally and virtuously is always the best we can do, regardless of the circumstance. There is no way of life that leads to a better outcome than virtue. We ought to expect that any morality fit for human beings to live by will not be merely formally rational but also downright humane, and therefore substantially tailored to the limitations imposed by the always fallible, mortal nature of Homo sapiens.

Chapter 1

Getting Our Bearings

1.1 THE PROBLEM

Imagine life is very hard where you are and that you hear from a reliable source about opportunities for a better life in the ports of the Northern Sea. You've heard it is a long way away, and you know that if you go, there will be no returning. But you decide to leave nonetheless, only to find that getting started poses a problem: you do not know which direction the Northern Sea is from where you are, and most people you ask say they have no idea either. Other people, though, some quite confidently, tell you that north is to the left when you face the sun at dawn. Others, however, equally confidently, tell you that the north is to the right. Neither opinion can be easily ruled out, though, obviously, both cannot be correct. So, you're stuck. You need to get your bearings to know which way is which, so starting requires figuring out who to trust and who not to trust, whose advice to take and whose to ignore.

For even marginally reflective people thinking about how they ought to live in order to be happy, the choice is much the same. Living one way or another is inescapable, and all but the most pathological of us want to live as good a life as we can, so naturally we want to know how to go about it. At various points, we will have to make choices, and what we ought to do in order to live well is sometimes far from apparent. These choices seem especially difficult when the mutually exclusive options are what we want to do, perhaps what is fun, desirable or expedient, or on the other hand, "the right thing to do", or what is onerous, or difficult but nevertheless wholesome or kind or good. Obviously, these options are not going to be equally effective in helping us live well: our choices will inevitably affect the quality of our lives. Some "authorities" who claim to know how best to live tell us to always follow our self-interested desires, whereas others tell us to "do the right thing". What we need is a theory to guide us through these decisions, but all the so-called authorities have their own theories about how to live. As in the preceding scenario, we need to know who's pointing us in the right direction, who to trust and who to ignore.

For convenience, let's call the question "How ought I to live?" "the Question". Now, without taking any substantial, normative position, we can answer the Question tautologically: one ought to live as well as one can. Let us name *living as well as one can* "living happily", "living a happy life", or living a "Good Life". Importantly, the phrase "the Good Life", as it is used here, is not the same as what is sometimes called "the High Life", and is it certainly not intended to conjure up hedonistic images of material luxury and ease. Rather, it is intended to pick out which human lives actually instantiate the property of *being well-lived*, which lives are truly *good* for creatures such as us. What counts as "goodness" for humans is what we will argue over after we agree on some schematic preliminaries. Whatever goodness turns out to be, no human can live perfectly, and probably only a few rare prodigies live excellently. The rest of us can nevertheless modestly strive to live as well as we can. When we are successful, we live the Good Life, for someone situated as we happen to be. In this way, we may simply stipulate that "the Good Life" and "the happy life" will (synonymously) refer to the sort of life we will live if we live according to guidance that constitutes the (or a) correct answer to the Question. The ancient Greek word for this kind of life is *eudaimonia*. Here, we at least have a name for what we are seeking, and this gives our thoughts about how to live a theoretical orientation, a goal or standard. Importantly, it gives us no more than a name; we would not want to beg any substantial, normative questions about what makes a life good by assuming, for instance, that the contented or pleasant life is better or worse than the exciting or adventurous life, or that it is better to have a lot of money rather than a little of it. These are the sorts of conclusions we are trying to reach, not places from which to begin. So, it is better if we all agree that each of us wants to live a good life and then argue about what that means, rather than to be unable to agree on even that much.[1] The stipulation is not of much practical help, but it does give our deliberations structure and brings out a tacit assumption behind the Question: all ways of living life are not equally good. The stipulation implies a standard which may or may not be met. We acknowledge the existence of a standard so that we can say there is a difference between success and failure, even though we do not yet know what counts as either. Even if there is no such thing as a perfect life, we still know that there are better and worse ways to live. The good ways lead in the direction of the Good Life, the bad ways lead away. The problem is that we may end up acting in hard to detect but nevertheless self-defeating ways if we cannot correctly get our bearings.[2]

---

1. The dialectical strategy of naming the happy life as the goal and making the substantial argument focus on what counts as "a happy life" comes from the Greek eudaimonists. For a fuller discussion, see Annas 1993.
2. This implies both a single "final end" and that we can make "all-things-considered" judgments. Aristotle has an argument for why there is a single goal of life, which assumes that reflection begins with an attempt to make sense of the arc of one's life, taken as a whole: this idea of unity is the starting point. With regard to doubts about all-things-considered judgments,

Among the authorities who would tell us how best to live, a prominent contingent tells us that we should do the "right" thing, we should live "morally", where this is understood from an impersonal point of view. These folks, let's call them "moralists", think that we ought always to do our duty, regardless of what we may want to do, and even when doing the right thing works against our self-interest. This need not imply that moralists are self-abnegating or think their interests matter less than the interests of anyone else; rather, they think that everyone's interests matter equally. Moralists simply think that morality always ought to trump self-interest or prudence, a notion captured by the traditional assumptions that morality is "overriding" and its demands at least somewhat "stringent".[3] Morality is supposed to have authority.[4]

Unfortunately, the moralists have not been able to say exactly why people should accept the authority of morality over self-interest. Some, most famously H. A. Prichard, argue that questioning the authority of morality is confused and demonstrates a lack of understanding of what it is to be obliged.[5] Earlier, Richard Price put the point in the following way:

> To ask, why are we obliged to practise virtue, to abstain from what is wicked, or perform what is just, is the very same as to ask, why we are *obliged* to do what we are *obliged* to do?—It is not

see arguments of Ruth Chang. For Aristotle, see 1998, 1094a1–24; for commentary, Annas 1993, 31–32; Becker 1998, 117–19; and Russell 2012, 15–22. See Chang's introduction to her edited volume, Chang 1998, as well as her 2004. For an example of the sort of problem Chang addresses, which features the tension between the values of morality and self-interest, see Copp 1997. These issues come up again briefly in §3.3.
3. For more on overridingness and stringency, see Scheffler 1992.
4. Much of the view of "moralism" is taken from a discussion by G. E. M. Anscombe which traces the history of this modern conception of *morality* to Judeo-Christian religion; see Anscombe 1958. T. H. Irwin has recently argued that the schism between morality and self-interest can be traced back to Scotus' rejection of Aquinas' eudaimonism. See Irwin 2008.
5. Prichard 1912, as well as Prichard 1952.

possible to avoid wondering at those, who have so unaccountably embarrassed themselves, on a subject that one would think was attended with no difficulty.[6]

Price's and Prichard's view is unsatisfactory, if only because self-respecting people have a legitimate concern for their own self-interest and this probity can impel them to ask if the demands of morality are conducive to self-interest or not; self-respecting people can always legitimately question authority, if only to acquiesce to it afterward with increased confidence in their rectitude.[7] Morality ought not to demand blind obedience. Others have appealed to rationality to explain moral authority, and yet others try to reduce it to a combination of sentiment (empathy or sympathy) and social pressure; but all this moralizing has yielded indecisive results at best.

Another contingent of the authorities, diametrically opposed to the first, may be called the "egoists". Egoists tell us that if our goal is really to live the best life possible, and if morality requires us to make sacrifices to the quality of our lives for the sake of others, then, whenever it is most convenient, we should forsake morality and pursue self-interest. They think the claim of the special authority of morality is a sham or a fraud; egoists, like Thrasymachus, Callicles, Machiavelli, Hume's Sensible Knave, Nietzsche, and Rand, pejoratively think of morality as purely conventional, the rules of "herd mentality". The egoists referred to here often do not subscribe to "ethical egoism", or the idea that *everyone* ought to look out first and foremost for themselves. Paradigmatically, the appeal here is to a non-universalized, solipsistic form of egoism in which the egoist prefers that everyone is not an egoist; someone like a free-rider who does not want everyone to try to ride

6. Price 1787, 180; for commentary and defense of this line of thought, see Wedgwood 2013.
7. See Schmidtz 2008.

13

freely.[8] Morality, on this view, is the means by which the mediocre keep down those who would otherwise dominate and flourish.

As such, the wise thing to do is to act morally (or as if we are moral) when it is in our self-interest to do so, while eschewing moral behavior when it suits our purpose. If we can ignore morality with impunity, there is no reason to not do so, since the only real reason to act morally is to avoid being punished for acting otherwise. As the challenge of Plato's "Ring of Gyges" story is meant to show, if we were to have a ring that made us invincibly invisible when we wore it, allowing us to act without fear of punishment, there would be no reason to sacrifice our self-interest either for the sake of others or in the name of morality. Only dupes, fools, and suckers really buy into the supposed special authority of morality; in the realpolitik, accepting that supposed authority is unwise and self-defeating.

So, we have, on the one side, moralists who say that the Good Life lies in one direction and, on the other side, egoists who say it lies in the opposite direction. The fundamental problem in answering the Question is that it requires us to articulate how morality is related to the goal of living as well as possible. The moralists say that the good and wise way to live is to be moral and that the bad, unwise, way to live is to reject morality; the egoists say the opposite. Both claim wisdom is on their side alone. One might think that the dispute between these two positions would have sorted itself out over the centuries, that it would become obvious which position is correct. But, given that we can conduct the experiment of our lives only once and that we humans like to think favorably of ourselves and the choices we make, neither side is capable of seeing the other

8. This sort of solipsism comes up again below, when the "formal" conception of *morality* is discussed in §1.3.

side's position as being as strong as their own. In the debate between moralists and egoists, the grass is not greener on the other side.

A final caveat before we proceed to a diagnosis of the problem: perhaps needless to say, the picture just drawn is a caricature, and the idea of correctly "getting one's bearings" is a metaphor. The positions of the moralists and egoists just described are polar opposites; in real life, the situation is complicated by the positions that lie in between. One nuanced picture involves an old metaphor from the Stoic, Hierocles, describing the way in which we are all encompassed by "circles of concern", with the circle closest to us representing self-concern; the next circle representing concern with immediate family; the next, concern with extended family; the next, concern with "fellow tribesmen" or those in neighborhood; then, concern with all fellow citizens; and the outermost circle represents the entire human race.[9] Adapting this picture somewhat, the pure egoist is concerned only with the innermost circle (full partiality to self), and the pure moralist is concerned with only the outermost circle (full impartiality). And here we can certainly find circles which fit the concerns of fanatics, sexists, racists, and narrow-minded people of any flavor you please; after all, most immorality is not perpetrated by ingenious villains or fanatics but by commonly selfish people or those who are simply callous, caring little for the needs of others. The picture may be further complicated by those who have tried to make morality less stringent than the traditional moralist holds (to be discussed more below). Whether we picture the situation as a problem involving bivalent compass directions or as Stoic "circles of concern", we can see the concerns of self-interest (prudence) and morality as diametrically opposed with a number of options between them and, for simplicity's sake, can treat the extremes as our basic options.

9. Long and Sedley 1987, 349.

1.2 THE DIAGNOSIS

The stalemate between the two positions has occurred because the moralists and the egoists share a conception of *morality* that is ultimately flawed, in which morality is primarily, if not wholly, an interpersonal, other-regarding, social phenomenon whose function, on the large scale, is to make communities (of the good) possible and on a smaller scale, is to guide us in our social interactions. Much of the point of morality is to solve certain coordination problems. True, each of us counts: we can count our own interests in our moral deliberations, and to this degree, morality, technically, is not wholly interpersonal. Moral thinking is *social*, however, since it only begins when the interests of others are given weight within an individual's deliberative procedures. And while there may be many ways to solve the requisite coordination problems, they cannot be solved if everyone demands that they be treated as a special case, to be given special consideration. To be sure, the continued existence of society is in each person's self-interest; but the familiar thought is that the existence of society comes at a cost to self-interest (or, in political terms, to the exercise of liberty), the idea being that the gains of living in society outweigh the costs of curbing one's self-interest to the demands of morality, which make society possible. (Hence, the compromise that purportedly constitutes morality, as described by Glaucon in the Introduction.) If one conceives of *morality* as fundamentally or even analytically *social*, then a division, a competition, is automatically established between "moral" considerations and what is in a person's "self-interest".

This pernicious "me versus the world" opposition is easy to see in even the briefest of glosses on the history of modern moral philosophy. Hobbes' state of nature aptly captures the opposition as a "war of all against all", where morality is a solution which works by setting itself against the individual's self-interest. A Hobbesian or "contractualist" view of morality holds that there is no morality without (or prior to) a social compact; contractualists and some relativists typically take morality to be a social artifact, a necessary evil justified by cost/benefit analysis but otherwise of no intrinsic value.[10] Kant famously saw good will and the moral action it inspires as being intrinsically valuable, and capable of providing a rational way out of the war of all against all. Nevertheless, he vigorously argued that morality is one thing and the happiness of the individual agent quite another; having good will for him involves a divorce of impartial rationality from self-interest and happiness. While Kant reserves a place within morality for dignified self-respect and duties to the self, his reasons for doing so have nothing to do with what makes an agent's life go well: self-respect is important because it is a rational demand of morality, not because it contributes to (or partly constitutes) the Good Life for the agent. The problem with servility as a character trait is not that it ruins one's life but that it is immoral and, as a result, one who is servile fails to live up to one's duty to morality itself. As Thomas Hill, Jr. writes:

> The essentially Kantian idea here is that morality, as a system of equal fundamental rights and duties, is worthy of respect, and hence a completely moral person would respect it in word and manner as well as in deed. And what a completely moral person would do, in Kant's view, is our duty to do so far as we can.[11]

Thus, we owe it to morality, not to ourselves, to maintain our self-respect.

10. Gauthier 1986; Harman 1975.
11. Hill 1973, 99.

True, Kant thought that we have self-regarding obligations, for example, the duty to improve ourselves and develop our talents.[12] But insofar as these improvements and developments have moral value, it is independent of any contribution they may make to our happiness. Despite the complexities of Kant's position on moral value and the value of the self, he undeniably accepts a dualism within us between, on the one hand, the empirical or phenomenal, from which all motive of personal happiness arises, and, on the other, the rational or noumenal, wherein is our free will and from which we derive our moral duties.[13] True, there has been much good contemporary work done on giving Kant's morality a more human face, as well as on his anthropological application of morality to human virtue in *The Metaphysics of Morals*.[14] Still, at the end of the day, Kant puts a premium on rationality and discounts happiness by making it orthogonal to rationality; his dualism is not "me versus the world" but "my rationality versus my happiness". As will become clear, the positive account of morality to be defended below does lean on some Kantian notions, though it has a more substantial conception of a well-lived and happy life at its foundation.

In chapter 4 of *On Liberty*, Mill defines "morality" in clearly social, other-regarding terms, sharply distinguishing it from prudence so eloquently that it merits extended quotation:

> Cruelty of disposition; malice and ill-nature; that most anti-social and odious of all passions, envy; dissimulation and

---

12. For an extended discussion, see Johnson 2011.
13. For more on tensions arising from this dualism, see Johnson 2002, and for more on Kant on happiness, see Engstrom and Whiting 1996.
14. For Kant with a human face, there is no better starting point than Herman 1993. For Kant's anthropology, see Timmons 2002.

   I am indebted to Donald Baxter and Valerie Tiberius for conversations regarding Kant on these points.

insincerity; irascibility on insufficient cause, and resentment dis-proportioned to the provocation; the love of domineering over others; the desire to engross more than one's share of advan-tages (the [pleonexia] of the Greeks); the pride which derives gratification from the abasement of others; the egotism which thinks self and its concerns more important than everything else, and decides all doubtful questions in its own favour—these are moral vices, and constitute a bad and odious moral charac-ter: unlike the self-regarding faults previously mentioned which are not properly immoralities, and to whatever pitch they may be carried, do not constitute wickedness. They may be proofs of any amount of folly, or want of personal dignity and self-respect; but they are only a subject of moral reprobation when they involve a breach of duty to others, for whose sake the individual is bound to have care for himself. What are called duties to ourselves are not socially obligatory, unless circumstances render them at the same time duties to others. The term duty to oneself, when it means anything more than prudence, means self-respect or self-development; and for none of these is anyone accountable to his fellow creatures, because for none of them is it for the good of mankind that he be held accountable to them.[15]

Famously, Sidgwick codified this point of view when he bap-tized as "the fundamental dualism of practical reason" the schism within our practical, deliberative capacities between the personal, prudential, or egoistic, on one side, and the impersonal, general, or moral (for him, utilitarian) point of view on the other. He acknowl-edges that the idea came to him from a discussion of Butler's about the opposition of self-love and conscience. Sidgwick concedes, in

15. Mill 1992, 75–76.

the final pages of *The Methods of Ethics*, that it is no more or less reasonable to take one's own happiness as one's ultimate good than it is to take the greatest happiness for the greatest number as one's ultimate good. This leads him to acknowledge a principled division, a "fundamental contradiction", within practical reason between oneself considered alone and everyone taken together.[16]

The dominant contemporary understanding of *morality* still conceives it this way.[17] To take just one clear example, Harry Frankfurt self-consciously embraces this approach when he writes, "Morality is most particularly concerned with how our attitudes and actions should take into account the needs, desires, and entitlements of other people", and adds the following in a footnote:

> There are other ways, of course, to construe the subject matter
> of morality. However, defining it as concerned with our relation-
> ships to others...has the advantage of making especially salient
> what many people find to be the deepest and most difficult issue
> with which moral theory has to contend: namely, the seemingly

16. See Sidgwick's 1907, 404n1, 507–9.
17. Recently, Derek Parfit in his 2011 explicitly endorses Sidgwick's presentation of and solution to "the profoundest problem", cast in terms of the dualism of practical reason 1:130–
   40. Other examples include Stevenson 1937, 31; Baier 1954 and 1958; Telfer 1968; Harman
   1975; Scanlon 1982 and 2000; Wolf 1982; Gauthier 1986; Nagel 1991; Kagan 1991; Hills
   2003; Darwall 2006; Joyce 2006; and Finlay 2008. For less stringent views, which are com-
   mented upon below, see Scheffler 1982 and 1992.
      Roger Crisp defends a "dual source view", which is close to the view defended here in
   many ways. However, it involves a rejection of the classification of the "should" in the question "How should I live?" as either moral or prudential. This is perhaps confounding from
   a theoretical point of view. More substantial problems arise as it comes out that moral education should eschew the dual source truth, as well as the result that caring more for one's
   children than for strangers ends up being "unsupportable in itself" on either of the two
   sources of reasons. See Crisp 1996 and 2006, esp. 143.
      For another critique of the social point of view, see Falk 1963 and 1986.

inescapable possibility of conflict between the claims of morality and those of self-interest.[18]

Most philosophers who work on *morality* understand it in this way. Other philosophers accept the divide and work on the other side of it, concerning themselves with individual self-interest, referred to as well-being, welfare, happiness, etc.; they, too, typically define what is good for an individual in a way which has no necessary ties to being moral and then go on from there to try to reconcile morality and self-interest as much as they can. As James Griffin says in *Well Being*, "The question is[,] Can we make morality less alien?"[19] From this typical starting point, philosophers working on well-being then articulate it with morality in one way or another.[20]

Answering the Question correctly, or satisfactorily defending morality and answering Thrasymachus et al., is impossible with this set of assumptions on board. Dealing with life's conflicts as if they were conflicts between morality and self-interest keeps us from seeing both the best resolution to them and how to argue against egoists like Thrasymachus. The truth about practical wisdom or rationality is supposed to be our answer to the Question, but the social conception of *morality* builds a dualism into the answer that is fundamentally irresolvable. Of course, there can be conflict between self-regarding considerations and other-regarding considerations (much more is said about this below). But the right or best way to approach this conflict is *not* to say that the nature of the values at hand are different, that moral considerations are purely other-regarding and therefore have a different sort of value

18. Frankfurt 2004, 7.
19. Griffin 1986, 130.
20. See Parfit 1984; Griffin 1986; Sumner 1996; Scanlon 2000; Darwall 2002; Crisp 2006; Tiberius 2008; and Haybron 2008.

and authority than self-interested, prudential considerations do: we ought not to conceive of the problem as one between different kinds of value, the moral on one side and the prudential on the other, or as one between different kinds of reasons with intrinsically different "weight".[21] To do so is a fundamental mistake.

Surely the subject matter of morality is partly concerned with reconciling self- and other-regarding considerations; but to call other-regarding considerations "moral" and give them special standing or authority in our deliberations, simply because they are other-regarding, is to approach *morality* in a backward, question-begging way. Self-regarding and other-regarding considerations often do need to be reconciled, but this does not, certainly by itself, imply that morality and self-interest are intrinsically at odds with one another. Morality is best thought of as the solution rather than as part of the problem.[22]

This problem arises not only for the most draconian and stringent moral theories, but also for those theories which try to be more "human". Many hybrid theories, most prominently perhaps that of Samuel Scheffler, recognize "the personal point of view" and build prerogatives into moral theory permitting the favoring of oneself or

21. Another way the psychological duality is sometimes cashed out is in the Platonic metaphor of the horse and rider in which the horse represents our emotions, appetites, and passions and the rider is our rationality. I think all forms of dualism in psychology are harmful. The point is not to adopt rationalism or sentimentalism, and then to sublimate the other side as much as possible. Rather, it is better to see these as not being in competition in the first place; it is best to integrate one's rational and sentimental faculties into a whole that has psychological integrity. These points come up again in chapter 3.

22. Some have insisted that the reconciliation of self-interest and morality must be a mistake, given that the former names an "indexical" concept, picking out an individual, while the latter does not. Wayne Sumner (1996) makes this conceptual point in terms of *well-being* and *perfectionism*. The point only stands, however, if morality lacks all indexical elements, which is exactly the point under contention. And on the contrary, we shall see that there are concepts, centrally *self-respect*, which will capture most of our attention, but also *integrity, self-trust, autonomy*, and others, which are inherently, undeniably moral and yet are also indexical.

one's loved ones, and so on, to a degree that is out of proportion to their importance from an impersonal point view.[23] Accommodating the personal is intended to lessen the tension between concern for the self and what might be called "pure moral concern". However, employing agent-centered prerogatives mitigates but does not eliminate the dualism of self-interest and morality: these theories will still entail obligations, the fulfillment of which will cause the egoist to balk. No one has ever suggested that agent-centered prerogatives would disarm Thrasymachian arguments against morality. At a more theoretical level, while agent-centered prerogatives do allow for some self-concern, nevertheless "agent-centered restrictions" on morality are required, limiting when the best overall consequences may be pursued: there are times when it is wrong to produce the best consequences when these are judged from a purely impersonal point of view.

The argument for this is quickly made. Standard cases of servile behavior, say the case of a servile wife or of an Uncle Tom, provide counterexamples to the claim that there are no valid agent-centered restrictions.[24] Even if the wife's willingly servile behavior maximizes familial happiness, it is morally wrong for her to engage in it: one is not morally permitted to carry out a self-disrespecting act in order to please others. Similarly, one is not permitted to disrespect oneself to prevent others, even many others, from similarly disrespecting themselves: one cannot be required by morality to be a "bad example". The justification for these restrictions is the notion that, without very special pleading, no one can be responsible for another person's self-respect: I am responsible for maintaining my own, and if, for example, others require my bad example to keep them from

23. Scheffler 1982, 1992.
24. For more on servility, see Hill 1973 and Hampton 1993a.

engaging in self-disrespecting behavior, it shows that they do not genuinely respect themselves in the first place. Therefore, I am off the hook (at least in this regard). There are times when one ought not to do what is judged best from the impartial point of view: thus, consequentialism is rejected.

If another theory of morality were inherently more human or humane than traditional or moderate moralism and also allowed its defenders to argue effectively against Thrasymachus, the Sensible Knave, and those of their ilk, then these would be strong points in favor of the alternative.

The present thesis is that the stalemate between moralists and egoists is attributable to both sides accepting a conception of *morality* as "purely" social and a conception of *practical rationality* that has a built-in schism between the demands of morality and those of self-interest. Both conceptions are equally confused and obfuscating. The dualism they imply has made it difficult to figure out the best way for humans to live.[25] It implies that each of us is essentially "a house divided against itself", since we are agents who are both self-interested and moral; the dictates of practical reason are therefore conceived as being at odds with themselves. If practical rationality serves two masters, morality and self-interest, then the war of "all upon all" is supplanted by a war of "self upon itself". Unsurprisingly, answering the Question will be difficult, if not impossible, given this inherent schizophrenia.

Accepting a dualistic theory of practical reason makes it inevitable that we must choose between morality and self-interest. Moralists say that "moral considerations", with their special authority, trump

---

25. The social conception of *morality* is undoubtedly the source of charges typically leveled against consequentialists and deontologists that their moral theories alienate us from what we think makes a life go well. See Stocker 1976; Williams 1973, 1981, chap. 1, and chap. 10 of his 1985.

"self-interested" or "prudential" considerations; whereas egoists, calling this putative authority "bunk" and feeling pleased with themselves for getting a free ride, say that only suckers pay the fare when no one is looking.

Naturally, egoists, as well as other critics of moralism, are quick to point to the absurdity of thinking that we ought to live as if we were as much strangers to ourselves as we are to real strangers. Insisting that we have a greater stake in our own lives than in the lives of others, egoists claim that sacrificing self-interest in the name of "morality" or "rationality" (much less "sympathy") is actually irrational. Egoists are not about to take that course; for an egoist, what is good for others or for society as a whole is always, at best, of secondary importance. As the egoists see it, being moral forces people unnecessarily to compromise the quality of their lives, and so the egoist chooses immorality when morality leads away from self-interest. On such a line of thought, immorality may seem a better answer to the Question than morality because immorality gives us permission to make looking after ourselves our first priority. Naturally, immorality starts to look good.

Moralists and egoists both see moral behavior as an often unpleasant necessity, with the egoists rejecting the necessity due to its unpleasantness and the moralists insisting upon it nonetheless. One consequence of this is that if morality is purely impartial and other-regarding, then our concerns about what is good for us from the first-person point of view, such as those that arise when we attempt to answer the Question, are not moral concerns at all. To a moralist this self-concern is immoral or nonmoral, while the egoist does not care either way.

The problem is that both sides conceive of living as well as possible as a forced choice between rotten options: moral concern and self-concern. It is hopeless to try to solve the problem of how to live best, given this fundamental duality in practical reason. Our only chance of solving the problem is to adopt a unified theory of practical reason and a conception of *morality* cast in terms of what truly leads to the Good Life (whatever it may be).[26]

Before we proceed, some terminological assumptions should be laid bare. As noted, "happiness" and "the Good Life" are meant to be co-referential: the happy life *is* the Good Life. "Practical rationality" is not narrowly defined, either in terms of prudence or self-interest, or in terms of morality or how to best manage social relationships, but is a much broader notion encompassing all the deliberative procedures by which people make practical decisions in their lives, from the quotidian to the monumental, from raising a roofbeam to making "life and death" decisions; it includes instrumental rationality but goes beyond it by allowing us to deliberate about which ends to pursue.[27] Like almost all practical endeavors, deliberative procedures can be performed poorly or well, with error or without; but when our practical rationality is functioning properly, when it is as it ought to be, it yields conclusions telling us to do what we (truly) ought to do. Practical rationality becomes moral when it is engaged in determining what to do in characteristically moral situations, that is, when the quality of one's life or the lives of others is at stake.

26. See §1.7 below for an objection to this diagnosis of the problem.
27. Chapter 2 has an extended discussion of this conception of *practical rationality*, or *phronesis*. As Annas says in explicating Plato's sense of *dikaiosyne* in *Republic*, "I shall use 'morality' for the area of practical reasoning carried on by an agent which is concerned with the best way for a person to live"; see her 1981, 11. See also her 1993 and 2011, and Bloomfield 2012. For other contemporary philosophers who conceive of practical rationality in this unified way, see Falk 1963 and 1986; Quinn 1994; Becker 1998; Foot 2001; Thomson 2003; and Setiya 2007, Svavarsdóttir 2008.
　　This does imply that almost all of our practical reasoning can have moral salience, since raising a roofbeam improperly can lead to the deaths of those living under it. Here I follow Scheffler's 1992 19ff, discussion of how brushing one's teeth can have moral salience.

There is also a metaethical neutrality in place with regard to the relation of "value" to "goodness". The verb "to value" describes what we do when we evaluate something or someone; the noun "value" is a reification of what is evaluated and valued. People can have bad values, which means they value things they ought not to value. When people have good values, they value what deserves to be valued or what ought to be valued; they value good things. When they have bad values, they value bad things. The neutrality just mentioned concerns the Euthyphro contrast: either X is good because we value it, or, we value X because it is good.[28] Presumably, nothing said hereafter requires one rather than the other.

We also speak of the "instrumental value" and the "intrinsic value" of things. Typically, when we say that X has instrumental value, if X is, say, a hammer, we presuppose that the hammer has properties by virtue of which it is objectively and pragmatically useful: we have not made a merely subjective judgment about the hammer's capabilities. We speak similarly of intrinsic value. Skeptics might balk at the idea of intrinsic value, but in the current debate, the parties agree that some people's lives (their own at least) have intrinsic, inherent, or non-derivative value. If there were no intrinsic value in the world, then self-respect would be unjustifiable. (More on this below.) A classical argument for intrinsic value is that if there were none, there would be no "point" to doing anything, only an infinite regress of doing A instrumentally for the sake of B, B instrumentally for the sake of C, and so on.[29] In any case, all self-respecting people think and behave as if (at least) their own lives have non-instrumental, intrinsic value, and this goes for the moralist as much as for the egoist.

28. Wright 1992.
29. This argument, noted above in §1.1, is Aristotle's, see 1998, 1094a, 1–24.

1.3 THE SOLUTION

So we have asked the Question, and what philosophy has primarily delivered so far is a debate between moralism and egoism. When set out in this fashion, it is not hard to see that neither side is fully correct in itself. Their positions are on opposite sides of a continuum, but both embody Sidgwick's dualism. We can transcend the stalemate easily enough, if we simply say that the answer to the Question is "morality", whatever it may happen to be. When morality is not defined in contrast to self-interest but rather as the content of our true, all-things-properly-considered judgments about what to do and how to live and what sort of person to be, things unfold rather more smoothly. When all self-regarding and other-regarding considerations are deliberated under the umbrella of practical moral reasoning, it becomes easy to see how interconnected, how inextricably bound together they actually are. We find no prejudice toward the impartial point of view, as we do in moralism, and none of egoism's prejudice toward the self.

The place to begin is by identifying *morality*, or the truth about morality (whatever that amounts to), or "Live morally!", as the correct answer to the question, "how ought I to live?", which will obviously include an answer to, "how ought I to treat others?" On this view, morality is whatever leads us to live the best lives we possibly can, all things considered, given who we happen to be and the circumstances into which we are born.

One way to comprehend this wide-scope sense of "morality" is through an identification of it with practical rationality, when the latter is conceived of properly and when we are engaged in answering questions about how best to live (cf. footnote 27 above). The true theory of practical rationality, as applied to the living of a life, constitutes the correct answer to the Question. If we say that "morality" is the correct answer to the Question, then the truth about morality, the truth about how one ought to live, is simply the truth about how one ought to reason practically and behave in order to live a Good Life. The true, correct moral theory is the true, correct theory of practical rationality as it applies to the issues involved in living as well as one can. (And, again, we have still kept everyone in the debate; no normative questions have been begged: all we are trying to do is "capture the debate" as it stands within a single argumentative framework. Worries about whether or not terms are merely being shuffled around are addressed below.)

We can understand the concept of *morality* at play here as one which William Frankena, building on work by W. D. Falk, called the "formal conception" of *morality*.[30] Frankena understands people's "moral values" as any overriding values they think ought to guide their practical decision-making. Only when people value what they ought to value (whatever that may be) can they be said to live by the "correct" or "true" morality. In this way, we can speak of a person's "moral character" as being either good or bad, and we can speak of a person's morality as being corrupted, depraved, or evil, as we speak of "Hitler's depraved morality". Thus, people's moralities are embodied by their practical rationality as the final and authoritative values and considerations that drive their behavior. Of course, people do not always behave as they think they ought, due to such phenomena as weakness of will, so they might not live according to "what morality says", even by their own lights. This is not a problem for the formal conception of *morality*, but it does help us to see the relations that obtain between how people behave, the moralities they supposedly accept, and what the truth about morality actually is. When we

---

30. See Frankena 1966a, 1966b; Falk 1963, reprinted in Bloomfield 2008a, as well as Falk 1986; also Bloomfield 2013.

drop the social conception of *morality* and understand it in this formal way, we begin to see more clearly how the truth about morality
(whatever it is) is the correct answer to the Question.[31]

Notice that on this view, anyone who gives us an answer to the
Question thereby gives us a theory of morality. This might upset the
egoists, who do not think they are giving us a theory of morality but
are rather telling us to do without morality. Such a response would
be a mere semantic confusion. If we call the moralist's traditional
answer to the Question "M-morality", then we can understand the
egoists' rejection of M-morality as false and their replacement of it
with a different theory of how to live, as a different "morality". Call
the egoist's theory of how to live "E-morality". The egoists think that
E-morality is the correct answer to the Question. In this sense, the
egoists give us a theory of morality just as much as the moralists
do.[32] As long as both moralists and egoists agree to not make any
assumptions up front, to not beg any normative questions about
the nature of the Good Life and how to live it, the egoists should
have no cause to dispute the theoretical structure we are erecting.
If we find that the argument genuinely leads to the conclusion that
the Good Life is the life of selfish egoism, then so be it. And if we

---

31. Very often, R. M. Hare is thought to be the prototypical formalist about morality. (Frankena
1966a, for example, writes this way.) This, however, is a mistake. Hare builds a normatively substantive element, i.e., universalizability, into the very concept of *morality*. So, on
Hare's view, solipsistic forms of egoism which are not universalizable, such as free-riding
or Thrasymachus' or the Sensible Knave's, do not count as "moralities", they are not in "the
moral game". Simon Blackburn concurs. The present dialectical strategy is to *not* beg the
question against these non-universalizable theories as proposed answers to the Question. It
is only by getting Thrasymachus et al. *into the game* that their position can be defeated. See
Hare 1981; Blackburn 1998; Bloomfield 2013.

32. In different ways, this is similar to some readings of Thrasymachus and Nietzsche.
Annas reads Thrasymachus as a eudaimonist in her 1981; loosely, she takes Socrates and
Thrasymachus to be arguing over the right answer to the Question. Similarly, but perhaps
more controversially, Philippa Foot reads Nietzsche in this way in her 2001.

find that the Good Life is the life of beneficent altruism, then, again, so be it.

So, the egoists are in the game. And this is a distinct dialectical advantage compared to the social conception of *morality*. Eliminating practical rationality's dualism and saying that morality is the answer to the Question allows those we would otherwise rule out as "immoral" or even "amoral" into the debate. We are in fact developing a defense of *morality* while starting with assumptions the egoist (or immoralist) will accept.[33] If the goal of normative moral theory is to answer the Question, then of course how we treat others will be a part of the answer; but there is no reason to begin by assuming that the social aspects of morality will exhaust the issue. Taken as a whole, morality is broader than the question of how we ought to treat others, encompassing not just the interpersonal but the intrapersonal too, since it is all part of figuring out a complete answer to the Question.

The moralists might not be happy about identifying morality as what leads people to live the best lives possible, given their view that the whole point of morality is to trump self-interest. But even they must admit that in real life our choices are often very complex and that the prescriptions of the moralists do not always square with common-sense morality, which does *not* always draw so principled a distinction between other- and self-regarding considerations that we may unequivocally say the former do and the latter do not count as "moral." "Moralist" is often a pejorative label precisely because of moralists' stringent view of morality's overriding demands. Common-sense morality may be somewhat moralistic, but it also recognizes that there are situations, for example, open and fair competitions, in which the morally right

33. See footnote 3 of the Introduction, regarding Hills 2010.

thing for people to do is to promote as strongly as possible their individual self-interests over the interests of others. At the very least, common-sense morality tells us that some self-regarding considerations are easily just as "moral" as other-regarding considerations. We can use two examples to illustrate.

The first example again concerns voluntary servility and is fairly simply sketched by Falk in "Morality, Self, and Others":

> It could be sound advice to say to a woman in strife with herself and tied to a demanding parent, "You ought to consider your-self, and so break away now, hard as it may be on the parent." One is then saying more than simply, "If you wanted to you would have a right to." One is saying, "I know you are shrink-ing away from it, but this is what you ought to do, and above all else." In form this is an ought through and through, and an overriding one at that, but its ground is not other-regarding.[34]

If common sense were fully committed to the social conception of *morality*, then we would not be able to say that the "ought" in the advice to the dutiful daughter is a moral "ought". Assuming that leaving is the right thing to do, the implication would be that the right thing to do, what she ought to do, all things considered, is to act immorally, which sounds odd. Of course, a moralist may insist that the "all-things-considered" ought at play here (what Falk calls the "ought through and through") is not a moral "ought", sim-ply because it is a case in which other-regarding considerations fail to trump self-regarding considerations. Or the moralists might stick to their guns and insist that the daughter stay with the parent because other-regarding duties always trump self-interest. The goal

34. Reprinted in Bloomfield 2008a, 240.

at this point, however, is not to adjudicate the issue. The goal is to gain a view of the situation from which the demands of morality do not *necessarily* weigh against what is best for the daughter simply because she could do more good for her parents by staying. The daughter should figure out the best thing to do tout court, when all the relevant considerations, whatever they may be, are given their due deliberative weight. The answer we arrive at in this way *is* the moral truth about what ought to be done. Self-interested considerations are neither less moral nor more moral than other-regarding considerations; they are all of a piece. In this way, we have done more than avoid begging normative questions: we have also eliminated the conceptual difference between what is morally best and what is best for us as humans trying to live as well as we can. If the values leading us to live the best life possible, the values we hold most dear, *are* the true moral values, then morality cannot require us to act against them. This conception of *morality* is not alienated from what makes a life go well; it is defined by what makes a life go well. It does not tell us what our values ought to be, only that we no longer need to see tension

(Con't from p. 32) A more fleshed-out example of the "dutiful daughter" is found in Hampton's 1993a, 163:

> There is a contemporary song by Tracy Chapman, which recounts the story of a young woman who faces a choice between living an authentic life of her choosing but abandoning her alcoholic father whom she loves, or serving the father but thereby accepting a life of poverty, drabness, and frustration. What ought she to do? If her love for her father is authentic and deep, she may choose to stay with him, and in those circumstances, that action would be self-authored. Indeed, to do anything else might mean she would be full of regret the rest of her life. Yet this decision will allow her few of the resources necessary to develop skills, talents, projects, and traits of character that are the mark of a well-developed self. Hers is a nasty choice, and in many respects, a deeply unfair one.

My views are in many ways similar to Hampton's.

between the Good Life, or what is best for us, and morality: if the moral values (whatever they might be) are what we value most in our lives, then that tension, between what we value most and morality, ceases to exist. Living as well as possible may require us to recognize that other-regarding considerations may trump self-regarding considerations that would otherwise hold sway; but it need not be that way: there may also be times when self-regarding considerations fairly win the day.

This is not to suggest that *morality* introduces some new "covering value" which, just by existing, can adjudicate tensions between self- and other-regarding considerations. Normative theory will have to do this work. The suggestion, to be filled out in subsequent chapters, is that *virtue* is most fit to carry this normative burden, an idea that is easily seen only, however, after the interrelations between self- and other-regarding considerations are explicated, as they are in arguments to come.[35]

No one has ever denied that morality tells us that we ought to be fair to others. What has not been appreciated properly is the way in which morality tells us that we ought to be fair to *ourselves* because we ought to be fair to everyone and we are included in the scope of "everyone". Morality does not say, "be fair to everyone except yourself"; it says, "be fair to everyone including yourself." This

---

35. This is not to imply that either consequentialism or deontology are incompatible with thinking of self-regarding considerations as being within the scope of "morality", or understanding the truth about morality *as* the truth about living as good a life as possible. One could view either of these two normative theories as the single correct strategy for living as well as possible. In fact, however, there are reasons to think that virtue theory, consequentialism, and deontology, when considered as strategies, can be integrated with each other, so one need not choose between them: there are lessons to be learned about living as well as possible from each of these normative theories. On such a view, practical wisdom would be partly constituted by knowing which strategy to deploy when. This comes up again at the start of §3.10, for a development of these ideas see *Moral Reality*, chapter 2.

self-regarding aspect of morality cannot properly be accommodated by the social conception of *morality*. Morality must be not just consistent with, but also committed to the idea that, as adults, we are *more* responsible for ourselves than we are for others and that, at least, everyone has a right to self-defense, for example, or a right to protect their self-respect. It is in any case undeniable that at the deepest levels we can only be responsible for our own actions and that we cannot be responsible for others in the same way. "Being fair to ourselves and to others" does not imply that we should treat ourselves and others in the same way. We are not to ourselves as we are to others, and we are certainly not strangers to ourselves, and morality ought to build this valence into its deliberative procedures. Morality (or perhaps more precisely in this case, justice) demands that we be fair "all things considered". And fairness to ourselves requires, at least sometimes, our favoring ourselves, especially when we clearly deserve it and most especially when it is not at the expense of others—but sometimes, as the dutiful daughter example shows, even when it is at the expense of others. These are not morality's grudging concessions to the demands of nonmoral self-interest; they are the origins and essence of morality itself. Falk writes, immediately after the dutiful-daughter example quoted above, "One cannot love one's neighbor as oneself if one has not also learned to accept one's own wishes as a proper object of respect and care, as one's own wishes are the paradigm of all wishes. There is a profound sense in which charity begins at home."

Perhaps an actual, and complex, social example will help to make the point, even though on one level it is another story of a dutiful child and the "abandoning" of a parent. Consider the case of Herbert Freeman Jr., a victim of the devastation that followed the breaking of the levees in New Orleans after Hurricane Katrina. After bringing his aged mother to the Superdome and watching her die, he was, days later, pressed by the National Guard to get on a bus before paying his final respects to her. He tells the story choked with evident filial piety, as follows:

> My mother died in September on the first and she had to stay out there in the heat for four days; because I left on the fourth, and she was still there. I wanted to go and be with her. The National Guard told me I had to get on the bus, and they all had AK-47s [*sic*]. He told me he was doing his job. I said, "Well, let me, let's go back there just to see her before I leave," and he said, "No, you're not going to do anything. You're going to get on this bus and stay on this bus." Just like that. So, I had to make a decision whether to go against authority and get myself in trouble, or to just, you know, leave it alone and I could handle it a little better later on. You know. So, I prayed to myself and the voice within me told me just to get on the bus, don't do anything, just stand still, and watch my salvation.[36]

Freeman's story is just one of a multitude of tragic stories to which one could point. The relevance for us is the variety of considerations he faced at the moment of making the decision: there were self-interested considerations regarding maintaining his integrity and self-respect; familial, filial considerations; other-regarding social considerations of other evacuees, considerations about the use or abuse of power, about whether or not Freeman merited special treatment, and/or whether or not his going back to pay his last respects to his mother would have had any effect on the provision of aid to other victims. What is crucial is that what Freeman was faced with was, in the most general sense, a *moral* problem, and therefore

36. My transcription, from Act II of Lee 2006.

all the relevant considerations ought to count as "moral consider-ations." It would be invidious to separate out some subset of the considerations and confer upon them the status of being "moral" while withholding this status from others, most especially if we then give these purported "moral" considerations special author-ity or deliberative weight. When situated within a complex real-life example, the distinction between what is self-interested and what is moral seems both academic and artificial. It is easy to imagine varia-tions on the scenario in which resisting authority and not getting on the bus is the right and moral thing for Freeman to do; and it is just as easy to imagine other variations in which it would have been wrong to not get on the bus.

The answer for what Freeman ought to do which comes from the social conception of *morality* is clear: it is to say with the mor-alists that Freeman only does the right thing if he lets the "moral" considerations trump the "self-interested" ones; or to say with the egoists the exact opposite for the opposite reasons. There is a sense in which both options beg the normative question against Freeman. We are not going to properly discern what he ought to do just by attending to which considerations moralists and egoists label by the terms "morality" and "self-interest." Rather, we ought to acknowl-edge that Freeman's decision concerns (roughly) whether or not to stand up to authority for the sake of his filial piety and that, regard-less of what the right or correct answer to what he ought to do is, the decision he makes lies squarely within the provenance of morality. If he does the right thing, whatever it may be, he does the moral thing. The formal conception of *morality*, backed by a unified conception of *practical rationality*, gives just this result.[37]

---

37. One might object that we must retain a distinction between moral and prudential value in order to explain why we think it is prudentially good for the clearly guilty Mafioso boss to be found innocent, and why we think this is a morally bad result: because it is morally bad

Furthermore, common-sense morality recognizes that certain concepts have moral salience even though what they range over may be completely private and unsocial. In particular, whatever theories of *self-respect, integrity, hypocrisy,* and *servility* we adopt will attend to intrapersonal relations; and any theory of morality that fails to mention these reflexive relations ought to be seen as incomplete. It is hard to understand the moral import of many psychological phenomena, such as Stockholm Syndrome or narcissism, without attending to the self-regarding aspects of morality.

On top of these intrapersonal relations, self-regarding virtues like courage or temperance (self-discipline) are commonly on the list of cardinal moral virtues, and almost everyone can see suicide as always a morally laden choice of existential proportions, even for Robinson Crusoe alone on his island. Even the most private sexual matters may have moral salience. Regardless of how modern moral philosophers have cut up the territory, common sense does not see morality as being purely public, social, or other-regarding.

Another way to see the point is by relating it to the basic moral emotions of shame and guilt. Many think that this difference somehow marks a distinction between "self-based" moralities and "social" moralities. One way to articulate these would be to see shame as what we feel when we let ourselves down, or when we do

---

to allow morally bad people to attain great prudential good in their lives. The response is that it is not necessarily bad for the Mafioso to avoid jail time. Consider that if the Mafioso truly repented and moved to Calcutta to work for the rest of his life with Mother Theresa's orphans, then we might not think it such a bad thing for him to not go to jail. If the arguments to come below are sound, then we harm ourselves whenever we perpetrate immorality, and we cannot truly be happy or genuinely live the Good Life if we are immoral, however much it may seem like having money and power and fame make a life go well. The unreformed Mafioso thinks that he is living a Good Life by avoiding jail and going back to his life of crime. But the point of the arguments to come is that the Mafioso is wrong: his "Good Life" is a fraud. These ideas were inspired by conversation with David Pruitt and in response to Zimmerman 2001, 152–53.

what makes us feel "ashamed of ourselves", while seeing feelings of guilt as appropriately arising when we let others down, or when we are "guilty" of something. Many do closely associate *guilt* and *morality*, which might seem to support a social conception of *morality*. The problem with this is that it renders shame as a nonmoral emotion, which seems wrong. Some, including Bernard Williams, think of shame as being primarily social because of its close association with embarrassment in front of others, and if so, then the situation is unclear.[38]

If we nevertheless think of shame as self-related and guilt as other-related, we may call both "moral emotions", and this does seem apt. One point to note in this regard is that while the acts for which we ought to feel guilt are ones that are properly called "immoral", those which merit shame are often not properly called this.[39] Of course, some shameful behavior is immoral, but not all of it is: certain instances of weakness of will, or not "standing up for oneself", or making a fool of oneself – all these may be things to be ashamed of but are not typically thought of as forms of immorality. If the dutiful daughter of oppressive parents fails to do as she ought and stays with them, it seems inapt to say she's done something immoral. This may seem to support the social conception of *morality*, but only if we questionably assume that all moral failings are strictly speaking "immoral". Shameful actions, on this view, manifest a different sort of moral failing, again typically ones in which we let no one down but ourselves, and calling them "immoral" seems unduly harsh, blaming, and condemnatory. Admonishment is not always a good way to improve people's behavior or strengthen their character; it may be more like rubbing salt in a wound. Regardless,

---

38. Williams 1993; see also Stocker 2008.
39. A number of people have pointed this out to me over the years, including Margaret Gilbert, Stephen Finlay, and Donald Bloomfield. I thank them all for discussion.

common sense acknowledges the weaknesses leading to shameful behavior as failings of a person's "moral character". By bringing both other-regarding guilt and self-regarding shame under the purview of *morality*, its scope encompasses a complete answer to the question of how to live.

Importantly: changing our conception of *morality* as suggested is not merely a semantic reshuffling of the same old problems. We have not simply swapped the name "other-regarding considerations" for "morality" and "self-regarding considerations" for "self-interest", and left everything else the same. Our new conception of *morality* has both normative and dialectical import. The normative aspect involves shifting the "authority" of "morality" away from the primacy of other-regarding social considerations. In the new conception, acting for the sake of self-interest over the sake of others is no longer automatically "wrong" from the moral point of view. We have made morality humane by eliminating the idea that only impartial considerations are inherently moral. To say that morality becomes humane is not to say that it will never be impartial; of course it will be, at least and certainly when justice requires it. The normative question then ceases to concern how to justify morality in the face of self-interest; rather, it concerns how best to articulate self- and other-regarding considerations within a well-lived life. This certainly changes the normative focus of inquiry and will often yield a different result than one deriving from the view that a wholly impartial and other-regarding morality always trumps all.

To put it another way, the only special status which now accrues to morality is that which comes along with being the output of an "all-things-considered" judgment (cf. footnote 2 of this chapter). "All-things-considered" judgments do not entail a particular decision-making process in which reasons trump or silence each other, or are weighed against each other, or are related to each other

in some particular lexical hierarchy reflected within the deliberation. However we ought to normatively commensurate the different values of these reasons, the fact is we do. The extension of the
moral considerations will be as wide as necessary to accommodate
all the relevant considerations *in situ*, from concrete and practical
facts on the ground to abstract principles, as determined by whatever the best theory of morality or practical rationality declares. The
"all-things-considered" judgment settles the matter as precisely as is
possible in the context. Crucially, "other-regarding considerations"
no longer have special authority as "moral" considerations. The
supposed "queerness" of moral properties, like *goodness*, as made
famous by John Mackie, was necessary for morality to have its characteristic overriding authority, its "to-be-doneness", or "practical
oomph" trumping self-interest or any other kinds of consideration.[40]
On the present view, the morally correct prescription for action has
only the authority of being the right or best thing to do, all things
considered; no "special" authority is required to trump self-interest
because self-interest is already figured in. If one lives morally, one
will live the best life possible: that fact constitutes all the authority
morality has and needs.

Morality actually constrains choice only to the degree to which
people have developed themselves to be constrained by it. So, good
people feel bound by morality, bad people do not. Moral motivation is not a special form of motivation and, given that it need not
override self-interest, there is no reason its motivation needs to be
special. Morally, there are ways we ought to behave; semantically,
there are ways we ought to speak; and epistemically, there are ways

---

40. John Mackie introduced the idea of morality's "queerness" in his 1977, in which he also
introduced the term "to-be-doneness". The overridingness of morality has been much discussed. See Scheffler 1992, Frankena 1966a, as well as Hill, Jr. 1973. The term "practical
oomph" comes from Joyce 2006, and is discussed further in his 2008.

we ought to think. And we can be motivated in these ways or not, we are constrained by them or not, depending on who we are and the values we have taken as our own. (This is discussed more in chapter 2.) For now, the only "special authority" morality retains on this view derives from the "all-things-considered" feature of moral judgment. In this sense, the dictates of morality are final and authoritative but are not metaphysically or psychologically suspect.

From a dialectical point of view, the conceptual change shifts the ground in the debate between defenders of morality and its historical opponents, such as Thrasymachus and the Sensible Knave. No longer is it automatically true that if one acts in one's own self-interest, then one acts immorally (or non-morally). If immorality ever "looked good", it was because it was trading on a draconian picture of morality in which one should always sacrifice self-interest for the sake of others. Given the alternative formal conception of *morality*, those who defend recognizably immoral actions in the name of self-interest have less dialectical leverage in defending their view of how to live. Not only does morality no longer work against self-interest, the conceptual change makes it easier to see arguments for why immorality is harmful to its practitioners, based on a dialectically neutral set-up. As mentioned in the Introduction, sound arguments for this conclusion have been thought of as the "holy grail" of moral philosophy. But before they are presented, we need to engage in a fuller discussion of this new dialectic.

1.4 COMMON DIALECTICAL GROUND

If the fundamental dualism of practical reason implies that we cannot answer the Question without subjugating either morality or self-interest to the other, a unified practical reason shows that a straightforward answer is possible. And by identifying morality as the correct answer to the Question and unifying practical rationality, we have recast the problem as one of how to properly integrate self-regarding and other-regarding considerations within the scope of *morality*. Since the deliberative process, when figured correctly, aims at a unified goal, we can expect that there will be inferential ties and implications between the self- and other-regarding (or intra- and interpersonal) considerations. In this lies the most important conceptual benefit of having a unified conception of *practical rationality*: it makes us see that how we treat others is inextricably bound up with how we treat ourselves, and vice versa. As we shall see, the *respect* involved in "respect for others" and "self-respect" is the same; having self-respect carries implications for respecting others. Once these relationships are appreciated, the Question becomes less theoretically complex, and moral problems quickly resolve to the handling of particular cases.

Before we go further, we must clarify how the positions formerly occupied by the moralists and the egoists should be understood given the formal conception of *morality* and the unified conception of *practical rationality*. By now, it should be clear that neither side was completely wrong or completely right. The moralists were right that other people should be considered in our deliberations about how to act, but wrong that moral thought is essentially and peculiarly social, impartial, and indifferent to self-interest. The egoists were right that we have a special relationship to ourselves that merits consideration in deliberations about what to do and how to live. Their mistake was to overestimate how much special consideration ought to be given to the things they happen to care about (whether this be self, family, religion, etc.). We have transcended these limited positions; we have not, however, ended the debate about how to live. We still need to correctly get our bearings. If the truth about morality is that it leads to happiness, we still need to know in which direction to head. We need to reconceive the debate and the way to do this is to think about the engaged normative values or conceptions of the *good* that were captured by the moralists and the egoists. The view to be defended is certainly closer to that of the moralists than of the egoists, but the conception of *morality* on the view to come is intended to be self-respecting, unified and humane, not "schizophrenic" in the least, and fully committed to being not just livable but the best way to live.

To simply recast the debate as being between "defenders of other-regarding considerations" versus "defenders of self-regarding considerations" is inapt since part of the point is in seeing how irredeemably entwined these are. But if we think about the actual normative values that each side was willing to endorse, we begin to see how to represent the practical disagreements between "moralists" and "egoists" in a way that is faithful to the original debate. Surprisingly, we can find enough common ground between the two positions to actually point to a solution to the Question; at the very least, we can get our correct bearings.

At the start, it might not seem as if there is much common ground to be found. Those defending "morality" would, at the practical level, espouse basic values which are conventionally considered "moral", such as honesty, forthrightness, and, in general, fair-dealing. Of course, those defending "egoism" would *espouse* the same values, at least publicly, but really would not value these traits beyond whatever their instrumental value they have for getting them what they want. What the egoists value most is the satisfaction of their own preferences and desires, typically understood as "getting what they want", whatever or how much it may happen to be. They also value those traits that make this happen, presumably some sort of brute power or sublime cleverness that allows them to get away with whatever is possible. As these positions were originally understood, they were diametrically opposed strategies of how to live. Despite this opposition, we can quickly see that there is also common ground, things on which both sides can agree, as soon as we frame their debate in terms of the Question: each side champions certain values that it thinks lead a person to live the Good Life. As Plato has Socrates ask Cleinias, "Do not all men desire happiness? ... What human being is there who does not desire happiness? There is no one, said Cleinias, who does not" (*Euthydemus*, 278e). So, both sides can agree that they are arguing over the best way to live happily, they agree that happiness or eudaimonia is the goal. And they both think the other's position leads in the wrong direction. They agree that one of them lives wisely and well and the other not so wisely nor well, that one values what is truly of value and the other has been fooled or duped into valuing something that is not genuinely valuable. They agree that one actually lives a Good Life and the other does not. They can even agree that people can be deeply, intransigently wrong about whether or not they are living the Good Life, since each thinks the other is in this predicament. What they disagree about is who is who: who is wise and who foolish, who really is living well and who is the dupe. Despite their differences, in fundamental ways their positions are symmetrical.

Granted, the agreement is at a fairly formal level, even though, for example, it commits both sides to thinking that one side is composed of fools who cannot see their own foolishness. When we move to a substantial or normative level of morality, where issues become concrete and particular, there is likely to be disagreement when "moral" issues arise. For example, both sides will disagree about whether it is ever conducive to the Good Life to surreptitiously betray a loyalty, or cheat, to get what one wants.

But one would think there must be some substantial elements of the Good Life on which both sides can agree. And there are. (The earlier agreements were dialectical, not substantive in nature.) Both sides can agree that, other things being equal, it is better (or at least not worse) to have food, clothing, and shelter than to lack them. And it is by looking with an eye toward further agreement that we will move the debate along. We can, for example, imagine both sides agreeing that people cannot live the Good Life if they hate themselves or, perhaps less severely, think horribly or very badly about themselves. Whatever the Good Life might be, everyone can agree that it does not involve self-hate or self-loathing; we do not have to take a positive stand on what the Good Life is to agree on this. One might even think that even though this is a substantial, normative issue, it is conceptual in nature; that is, it is knowable a priori that self-hatred is conceptually incompatible with the Good Life. It is not easy to see how one might prove such a claim, but any argument to the contrary seems to automatically be a *reductio ad absurdum*.

Close to this agreed rejection of self-hatred is an agreement that people cannot live as good a life as possible if they do not respect themselves. Both sides, one would think, would agree with the idea that people who go around behaving in ways that are self-disrespecting cannot be living the Good Life: egoists think that moralists are weak and self-disrespecting whenever they choose morality over self-interest; moralists think that egoists are shameless and lack self-respect. Perhaps the impossibility of living the Good Life without self-respect is not as obviously a conceptual truth as the claim about self-hatred in the preceding paragraph, but to affirm the idea that people who lack self-respect or are regularly engaging in self-disrespecting behavior can nevertheless live the Good Life is, at least prima facie, bizarre and absurd.[41]

There are really two claims at issue here. The first is the idea that self-respect is necessary to the Good Life, at least insofar as we cannot imagine a person who lacks self-respect living a Good Life; and the second is that people can be wrong about whether or not they have self-respect.[42] Perhaps the best argument for the first claim is that both sides think that *they*, not the other, are living the Good Life, and both sides also think they have self-respect. If we recall the case of the characters who thought of themselves as something like "egoists", like Thrasymachus, Callicles, Machiavelli's Prince, Hume's Sensible Knave, Nietzsche's *Übermensch*, and so on, it seems plausible to see them as having a grand and probably immodest sense of self-respect. We can call these folks "the Foscos", after the rotund, foppish, and devilishly cunning king of obfuscation, Count Fosco, the arch-villain of what is thought to be the first mystery novel, Wilkie Collins' *The Woman in White* (1860). As noted above, the Foscos of the world tend to see themselves as better than the common run of folk, who to them are little more than cattle, to be used

41. This does seem to beg the question against the person who wants only to live a pleasant, unreflective life and cares only a little, if at all, about self-respect. At this point in the debate, however, such a conception of the Good Life is not on the table. Anyone can be put in a situation in which they must choose between shameless pleasure and preserving self-respect. For some, there might be situations in which the pleasant is chosen over the self-respecting: consider some degrading pleasure or perhaps the pleasure the willingly servile person takes in serving well or by "fitting in" to the servile position to which he or she "belongs". But the relevant parties to this debate, like Socrates and Thrasymachus, would agree that it is absurd to think that the Good Life is consistent with placing no value on self-respect; to put the point in starker terms, both will agree that self-disrespecting shamelessness and debasing self-degradation are inconsistent with the Good Life (even if they disagree about the extensions of what is "shameful" and "debasing"). Subjectivism per se is addressed below.

42. These can be seen as premises in an argument concluding that people can be wrong about whether or not they are living the Good Life, but both sides have already agreed on this kind of fallibility for other reasons: namely, that they each think the other is wrong about this.

and manipulated with impunity. They have an air of superiority, and tend to be arrogant and condescending in their dealings with others. They do not enter the debate with the moralists thinking they lack self-respect or knowledge of what is truly valuable in the world.[43]

While Count Fosco is a quintessential example of this type, lesser forms of immorality more commonly found in day-to-day interactions with others, and even forms of immorality that pride themselves on their "moral rectitude" (e.g., soldiers fighting in the name of God), can be adumbrated together. As will be discussed at length in chapter 2, Foscos, of whatever stripe, fail by being inappropriately partial to themselves and what they care about. To cheat or immorally hurt others to help one's family is not really different than doing it to help one's self. Even more minor forms of immorality, such as being rude to a salesperson or not giving up one's seat to an elderly person on the bus, can also be seen as showing an inappropriate partiality to one's own cares and concerns, irrespective of how one's behavior affects others. As Aristotle notes, one swallow may not make a summer, but we can nevertheless insist that a swallow is a swallow. And a single circling vulture generally means there is something rotten down below. The Foscos are supposed to represent both the *petit* and the *grand mal* forms of immorality.

On the other side of the debate, we have people like Socrates, Confucius, and Sir Thomas More, or, more recently, Eleanor Roosevelt, Nelson Mandela, and the present Dalai Lama. It seems fitting to call this group "the Hartrights" after the agent of Fosco's undoing, William Hartright, the hero of the *Woman in White*.[44] It

---

43. My understanding of arrogance and the self-deceit involved in immorality has been greatly informed by Dillon 2004; also Tiberius and Walker 1998.

44. Note, these are not the "hapless dupes" that the Foscos of the world typically rail against. But, just as it would be wrong to hold up some thug or act of petty selfishness as our paragon of immorality, it is wrong to say that the sheepish dupes of the herd are going to be the

is surely not right to think that these luminary figures are the only people who exemplify the Good Life from this point of view. We can also imagine people whom history has never recorded, living both morally and quite well, even excellently, in some small village, without formal education or modern amenities. We need not at this point characterize these unsung examples beyond saying that they are honest, forthright, and fair-dealing: they live more or less successful lives built on what they have achieved by their own honest efforts and are people of principle who would rather lose than cheat and care more about personal integrity than social honor or fame; they value what they think is "the good" and "the right" over what is easy, convenient, or expedient for themselves. We may think of the Hartrights of the world as having self-respect, though it has a different foundation for them than it does for the Foscos. The Hartrights do not think they are inherently better than other people; they are apt to think that they are no better or worse, no more or less important than anyone else. They therefore see no automatic or intrinsic reason to sacrifice their self-interest for the sake of others. Their reputations make them out to be open-minded and reasonable. They are not moralists in the sense described above, nor are they unpleasant, dogmatic, stringent, or sanctimonious. They seem not, for example, to qualify for what Susan Wolf calls "moral sainthood."[45] They are more likely to err on the side of modesty than arrogance, though they certainly do possess the wherewithal to speak truth to power. But we should not think that their modesty hinders their

best spokespeople for morality. Of course, the Hartrights need not, themselves, be perfect or flawless human beings, just those who excel in their way, as opposed to the Foscos who excel in the opposite way. In general, most moral people are not heroes or saints and most immoral people are not villains. My thanks to Julia Annas for conversation on this point.
45. Wolf 1982.

self-respect; rather their self-respect simply does not depend on besting others or being better than anyone else.

So, both the Foscos and the Hartrights think they have self-respect and that self-respect is necessary for living a good life. Of course, too, both sides think the other side's conception of *self-respect* is mistaken. "People with self-respect", we might imagine Fosco saying, "do not give up having what they want in the name of being fair to others if they can have it without cost or penalty; this is just the sort of mewling weakness which people who truly respect themselves do not exhibit." And the Hartrights claim that those whose self-respect rests on a shameless foundation of a false superiority are fooling themselves into thinking they have self-respect when what they have actually amounts to arrogant puffery; people of self-respect do not stoop to cheat.[46] Both sides agree that dupes and fools wrongly think they are self-respecting; this is, in part, what it is to be a dupe or a fool.[47]

Before we proceed, we can identify one last area of bipartisan agreement: both the Foscos and the Hartrights would agree up front that the psychologies of people who live the Good Life are not riddled with self-deception.[48] If people are completely, even radically wrong about who they are, they cannot be living the Good

---

46. As a contemporary example, the Hartrights might point to Lance Armstrong as perfectly illustrating the way in which people can have a fraudulent sense of self-respect. They would even insist that Armstrong's self-respect would be fraudulent even in those possible worlds at which he never gets caught. The idea that people can be wrong about having self-respect is discussed in more detail in §1.6.

47. Fools need not be stupid, but most have a blind spot for their foolishness. As Plato puts it:

[T]he trouble with ignorance is precisely that if a person lacks virtue and knowledge, he's perfectly satisfied with the way he is. If a person isn't aware of a lack, he can't desire the thing which he isn't aware of lacking. (*Symposium*, 204a)

48. My understanding of self-deception is taken from Robert Audi's, which says that self-deception occurs when a person has a reason to believe something is false but a desire

Life. Examples include the main character in the movie *Don Juan De Marco*, who falsely believes he is Don Juan, history's great lover and gallant; the many people over time who genuinely but falsely believed they are Jesus Christ or the Messiah; or anyone who harbors self-deceptions of such magnitude that their self-conceptions are deeply infected with error. It seems reasonable to think that, regardless of how happy they may think they are, or how good a life they think they are living, their self-delusion prevents them from genuinely living the Good Life. There is an important appearance/reality distinction between deceiving oneself into believing one lives a Good Life and actually living a Good Life.[49]

Still, one might wish to adopt a more subjective conception of *happiness*, in which believing one is happy is strong evidence for, or is in fact sufficient for, being happy. Consider, for example, those who take "happiness" to name a feeling or a mood, such that a "happy life" is a life filled with pleasure or with one's (informed) preferences satisfied. Undoubtedly, a life spent in a subjectively satisfied mood could be said to be a "happy" life in one sense. But imagine that you could take a pill, right now, that would you make you feel as happy as it is possible to feel every day for the rest of your life; after you take it you will always have the feeling of subjective satisfaction that is supposed to be constitutive of happiness. Perpetually happy feelings might sound desirable. But then you realize you'll be in this

---

to believe it is true, and so they give the reason to think it false little or no credence; see his 1997 as well as his 1985. I have also greatly profited from Butler 1900a. For the relation of self-deception to self-respect with regard to arrogance, see Dillon 2004.

49. There is a last point of agreement we might want to consider, even if it fails to be useful in the end: the Foscos and the Hartrights will agree that the best life possible for a human will be pleasant: the Foscos seem far more likely to be hedonists than the Hartrights; the Hartrights of course having nothing against pleasure itself, but will tend to agree with the Aristotelian idea that pleasure is a happy byproduct of living well, and not the goal one should seek. These issues are addressed at length in §3.2.

same good, positive, happy mood *no matter what happens.* Even if a tragedy befalls you, if a loved one dies, or life on half of our planet is monstrously destroyed in a war or some other disaster, you will feel no worse nor better than on the day you have your greatest success or you fall in love. Does the pill still sound so desirable? Most would say no, as they did to Nozick's infamous experience machine: common sense says that feelings of satisfaction are themselves not the goal but that these feelings, when valuable, are so because they are supposed to be responsive to conditions in the world.[50] And while the common refusal to take the pill is far from a knock-down argument against subjectivism, it does show that, for most people, feeling "happy" in this subjective sense is not what is really of the most importance to us.

Of course, whether it is good or desirable to feel happy all the time is a contentious issue, especially since a subjectivist view of happiness is assumed by many of those who study *happiness* from the viewpoints of psychology and anthropology.[51] However, taking the debate between the Foscos and the Hartrights to be up and running, at least since Socrates argued with Thrasymachus, both sides do assume that people can be wrong about how happy they are: otherwise they would be unable to accuse those they disagree with of being wrong about what happiness is.[52]

Returning to the incompatibility of happiness and self-deception, it is probably the case that every human who has ever lived has engaged in at least a small amount of self-deception, and as such

---

50. Nozick 1974. See also the discussion of "living in a fool's paradise" in Lynch 2005.
51. For data on the subjective experience of happiness, see the World Database of Happiness website http://worlddatabaseofhappiness.eur.nl. For a fuller treatment of the failures of subjectivism, see Badhwar forthcoming.
52. While Daniel Haybron agrees with this general thought, thoroughly dismantling what he calls "the personal authority" view of happiness, he nevertheless adopts a psychological

we should not conclude that any tiny amount of self-deception is incompatible with living the Good Life. Indeed, there may be cases in which small amounts of self-deception are salutary to living the Good Life: self-deception is, after all, a psychological defense mechanism that can have adaptive value; problems only arise when it runs amok. The concern is with large-scale self-deceptions. The self-deceptive "Good Life" is simply not as choice-worthy as the authentically Good Life. Mutatis mutandis, it is better to be truly wise than to be a fool who is self-deceived into thinking he or she is wise; it is foolish to think there is no important difference here. The reasonable inference is that the typically inverse relations between self-deception and happiness are matters of proportion and that, absent special pleading, the degree to which people indulge in self-deception is, more or less, the degree to which their good lives are in some way hampered or harmed. One might idealize and say that the best possible life will be fully self-actualized and free of self-deception. Perfect self-knowledge is probably not actually

conception of *happiness* in which mood plays the central role. The thought experiment about the pill which puts one in a perpetually happy mood demonstrates the problem with such thinking; see Haybron 2008 and the more detailed discussion of these issues below in §3.2. Other accounts of subjectivism, e.g. that of Valerie Tiberius (2008), can accommodate the idea that we may be wrong about how happy we are, but are still open to the criticism that they understand wisdom as compatible with immorality as it is with morality. This runs deeply counter to ordinary thinking: we typically think that wise people know what is truly valuable, yet both the Foscos and the Hartrights think it is good to be wise and that wisdom is on their side. So, either the Foscos or the Hartrights are wrong; both cannot be right about who is wise. Importantly, the point is not that "happiness" does not or cannot name something subjective, but rather that this is not the sense of "happiness" we are concerned with when we talk about "living the Good Life" or attempting to answer the Question. See my 2010 for a review of Tiberius' book.

To reiterate a point made about metaethics regarding the Euthyphro contrast, I take it that ruling out subjectivism in this way does not beg any questions in favor of moral realism. Being an "objectivist" about the Good Life in the weak sense employed above should be compatible with expressivism or constructivism or any metaethical theory that can account for substantial moral error. For further discussion of the sorts of error which can be accommodated by nonrealistic theories, see Timmons 1999, chap. 3, and footnote 43 of §2.5.

possible for a member of our species, but we can approximate this ideal; and, presumably, the further away from it we are, the more our self-deception detracts from our living the Good Life. Foscos and Hartrights will both agree.[53]

The Foscos will agree because they do not see themselves as being self-deceived: they think they know what is valuable in the world and are ready to do what it takes to get it. They think that most people who willingly engage in clearly immoral behavior, as they do, are aware of what they are doing and think they are living as well as anyone can. It is the Hartrights who make "unnecessary sacrifices" while deceiving themselves that into thinking they are living as well as possible. The Foscos think the Hartrights have been duped by weak, conventional mediocrity. Those who consider themselves *Übermenschen*, or who like Machiavelli see themselves as exemplars of realpolitik, think they have seen through the veils of self-deception to the truth.

The Hartrights are also friends of the appearance/reality distinction, and the truth in general, though they are typically more modest about their claims to knowledge of it. Socrates is perhaps their model of modesty. Still, the Socratic tradition arguably takes as its very starting point the precept *Know Thyself*. So, the Hartrights will also think that people whose lives are riddled with self-deception are not going to be living the Good Life.

So, we have four important, substantial points of agreement between the Foscos and the Hartrights. The first is that, since they cannot both be right in thinking that they are living good lives, both have to agree that people can be wrong in thinking they are living

---

53. Contemporary debates about self-deception commonly to point out that people who are honest with themselves about themselves are more likely to be depressed than those who engage in some "healthy" forms of self-deception. For a full and empirically informed rebuttal of these ideas, see Badhwar 2008.

the Good Life. The second is that people who lack self-respect are not living the Good Life. The third is that both sides think that people can be wrong about whether they have self-respect. And finally, both sides agree that a great deal of self-deception on an individual's part is incompatible with living a Good Life. Given all this, how is the debate to proceed? Up until now, since the allure of getting what one wants whenever possible is not too difficult to see, the Foscos have typically put the burden of proof on the Hartrights to show why not getting what one wants, as morality sometimes demands, is better than getting what one wants with impunity.

If things are to change, and if the Hartrights are going to win the debate, there are two ways to go. The first is to locate some harm done to the Foscos that keeps them from living the Good Life. Or, we can locate benefits that accrue to people who forego immoral behavior, such that, overall, the benefits that accrue through acting morally outweigh any "sacrifices" this may entail. (Remember, as noted in the Introduction, simply showing the Foscos that their position is irrational will not be sufficient, as they might well prefer to be irrational if it gets them what they want over being rational when this implies doing with less.)

We will engage the first strategy in the remainder of this chapter through two arguments that show how immorality harms those who engage in it. The second strategy is the subject matter of chapter 3. As for the two arguments to directly follow, both bear some resemblance to the Platonic hypothesis that immorality is harmful to the "harmony of the soul": the conclusion to be defended is that perpetrating immorality is harmful to a person's self-respect. Since all agree that self-respect is necessary for the Good Life, showing that immorality harms a person's self-respect will demonstrate the harm of immorality to a person's life.

It is worth noting at the outset that the Foscos' defense of their position typically uses very different strategies than the arguments to come. Typically, people who reject "morality" do so based on normative values they assume everyone shares: worldly and material success, pleasure, power, social honor, and perhaps even fame. They then defend their position by noting that conventionally moral people are not as good at getting these as they are. If the Hartrights respond by saying, for example, "I don't want what I can obtain only by taking unfair advantage of other people, so in these cases I'd rather not have the reward or the honor at all", the Foscos will regard this as foolish, as just the sort of response one would expect of people who really do want the reward but lack the courage or strength to do what is necessary to get it. In essence, the Foscos' rejoinder is a question-begging, ad hominem attack. It is not based on shared premises about what the Good Life is but on assumptions about what is most valuable in life that will be rejected or at least disputed by the Hartrights from the start.[54] The two arguments comprising §1.5 and 1.6 are not like this, but rather are based on the four shared assumptions discussed above. Thus, they are dialectically stronger than the Foscos' arguments. And since

---

54. Aristotle begs just the sort of normative questions which the Foscos would when he writes:

> And those who have done many terrible deeds and are hated for their wickedness even shrink from life and destroy themselves. And wicked men seek for people with whom to spend their days, and shun themselves; for they remember many a grievous deed, and anticipate others like them, when they are by themselves, but when they are with others they forget. And having nothing lovable in them they have no feeling of love to themselves. Therefore also such men do not rejoice or grieve with themselves; for their soul is rent by faction, and one element in it by reason of its wickedness grieves when it abstains from certain acts, while the other part is pleased, and one draws them this way and the other that, as if they were pulling them in pieces.

> Obviously, Fosco would simply reply that he does not feel this way, even if some people who are called "wicked" do end up as Aristotle suggests. See Aristotle 1998, 1166b22–24.

they can be resisted only by giving up on one of the assumptions that was already agreed upon, the burden of proof thereby falls on the side that backs out of the original agreement. This will be the Foscos. So, for the first time since the start of the debate, the burden of proof will shift to those who defend immorality. This does not mean that traditional moralists have the upper hand; we have already seen how morality has been reconstructed from the ground up, so to speak, in a way contrary to impartial, traditional morality. Nevertheless, there is a vindication of justice and virtue over the egoism traditionally espoused by the Foscos. If this reconstruction and vindication is not the "holy grail" of moral philosophy, it may be as close as we will get.

A final word about the scope of the arguments to come. The conclusion—that immorality is self-disrespecting—is not intended to be perfectly generalized to entail that all immorality is self-disrespecting. This might be the case, but it need not be for the arguments to serve their purpose. (There may very well be some forms of immorality that are not self-disrespecting in the relevant sense.) All that is really needed to turn the tables on the Foscos and put them on the defensive is that certain paradigmatic forms of immorality, like acts constituting manipulation, oppression, coercion, betrayal, disloyalty, treachery, and so on, are necessarily disrespectful to their victims, and therefore, as we shall see, ipso facto harmful to those who perpetrate them. Establishing this conclusion alone will suffice.

1.5 THE ARGUMENT FROM ONTOLOGY

Here's a lesson that can be taught to a child: when people act badly, when they cheat or are immoral, they do so from a place of weakness.[55] For if the people were strong, there would be no need to cheat, no need for immoral behavior.[56] But immorality is not merely a sign of weakness: it encourages the person who takes it up to think that "getting what one wants" through cheating is no different than what one gets without cheating. Defenders of immorality must fool themselves into thinking there is no difference between winning "fair and square" and "winning" by cheating. Immorality looks like an easy way to get what one wants, but in an important sense it never really delivers. Its rewards are like the college diploma of a student who was a career cheater. In one sense it is a "real" diploma, since it was officially issued by the college, but in another, more important sense it is a fake: the acquisition of learning and knowledge it is supposed to represent was not, in fact, obtained. The underlying weakness and dupery will always be there at the root, and no amount of self-deception or the deception of others will change this. (Imagine the cheater, who, years later, has repressed the memories of having cheated.) The self-deception spoils what it infects: the cheater's

---

55. The argument in this section is taken from my 2008c. See also my 2008b. It is structurally similar to an argument against egoism in Nagel 1970 and to others in Korsgaard 1996, though, as noted in the Introduction, these latter arguments are based on showing immorality to be irrational and not self-defeating.

　　Insofar as the conclusion to follow is that immorality is harmful to those who engage with it, it is interestingly similar to an argument by David Brink, with whom I share much in the way of setup. Still, Brink's solution requires (what seems to me to be) an implausible theory of personal identity and our relations to people, modeled on a combination of Parfit-style "fisson" arguments and Aristotle's theory of friends as "other selves". See Brink 1990. Russell 2012 finds himself in a predicament similar to Brink's; see my forthcoming review. Also in the spirit of this book, Neera Badhwar (1993) has argued, by way of those who rescued Jews from Nazis, that some forms of morality (altruism) can be in a person's self-interest, and thus morality and self-interest are not necessarily at odds with each other. Finally, there is great similarity here to an argument by Jean Hampton (1993a), to the effect that selflessness is both immoral and harmful to those who live that way.

56. "... who is there, or whoever was there, of avarice so consuming and appetites so unbridled, that, even willing to commit any crime to achieve his end, and even though absolutely secure of impunity, yet would not a hundred times rather attain the same object by innocent than by guilty means?" (Cicero 1914).

putative success is not in fact genuine (cf. footnote 46 regarding Lance Armstrong in §1.4). A better sort of life is one in which goals are attained without cheating the way through: there is no real success with cheating, only an inverted comma sense of "success", only a superficial simulacrum of the real thing.

Unfortunately, if this lesson is not learned in childhood, a more sophisticated approach is needed to appreciate it. In this case, changing minds is much harder than teaching them. Immorality pursued is like a narcotic; at first it delivers pleasure, but ultimately it degrades its users. Living the Good Life, the truly moral life, on the other hand is like starting to exercise when one is out of shape: it may be unpleasant at the beginning, and its ultimate benefits can really be appreciated only by those who are in shape.[57] By making honest efforts, one learns to handle real failure and to experience authentic success. If one's lessons are well-learned, then, barring great misfortune, successes will become more frequent, and one's less-frequent failures will be more easily borne. This is the only possible foundation for a truly Good Life. And there is no way to fake it.

Perhaps the single most important benefit of the arguments to come is that they allow us to see the importance of the relationship between "respect for others" and "respect for self". The natural reading here, as noted above, is to understand "respect" in these two uses as univocal. Respect is respect, whatever the best theory of respect says it is, and it involves a particular set of judgments, attitudes, and

---

57. From the Hindu tradition, B.K.S. Iyengar (1966) makes a similar point:

> Both the good and pleasant present themselves to men and prompt them to action. The [sage] prefers the good to the pleasant…[and] feels joy in what he is. He knows how to stop and, therefore, lives in peace. At first he prefers that which is bitter as poison, but he perseveres…knowing well that in the end it will become as sweet as nectar. Others hankering for the union of their senses with the objects of their desires, prefer that which at first seems sweet as nectar, but do not know that in the end it will be bitter as poison.

responses. Presumably, when we respect something properly, we see it for what it is, for having the value it does, and we treat it with the honor and/or deference that our judgments tell us is due to it. This need only be roughly correct for the moment (much more will be said on the issue in chapter 2), as the present point is just that there would be something incoherent or inconsistent about respecting one thing for having some attributes and disrespecting another despite its having the same attributes as the first. When it comes to respect, we ought to treat equals as equals, and like cases alike; something has gone awry if we do not. This has all the markings of a normative principle of thought.

(Careful readers may balk. There is indeed some inferential slippage in the previous passage between "is" and "ought", a supposed fallacy to which Hume taught us to be sensitive. Notwithstanding his concerns: if this *is* equal to that, then they *ought* to be treated as equals. Why? Because it makes no sense to deny it; the denial is incoherent. Is this an exception to the rule that one may not infer an "ought" from an "is"? Maybe, but there seems to be no way around it.)

So, when we make judgments about whether or not to treat something with respect, we ought to apply our standards consistently: if cases are to be treated differently, this ought to be based on a difference between the cases. The same is true for self-respect and respect for others. If some people treat themselves with respect and others disrespectfully, when at bottom there is no relevant consideration that could ground this difference, then the first group of people are making a mistake in treating themselves with more respect than they treat the others. The question then becomes what the proper basis for respect is or what sets the standard for respect and self-respect.

Of course, the literature on respect is quite deep. One basic distinction in the grounds of respect that has gained some currency is the difference between what Stephen Darwall has called "appraisal respect" and "recognition respect".[58] Appraisal respect is based on the actions, achievements, intellect, or character of a person. As such, how much appraisal respect is given will depend on the particular characteristics of the person, with not everyone deserving the same amounts. Recognition respect is given based on the type of thing being recognized: a particular token belongs to a type, and by virtue of being a token of that type deserves to be recognized and treated as what it is—that is, a token of that type. For example, if we are walking in the woods and see a bear, we recognize it for what it is and give it the respect it deserves as such. If it were a dog and not a bear, we would treat it as a dog. For human beings, recognition respect is intended to establish a baseline level of respect for the *humanity* which we each instantiate, or for being the individual human beings or people or agents that we are. If appraisal respect is based on ways in which we may be different, recognition respect is based on what makes us all, despite our individuality, the same. Recognition respect determines the least common denominator among us, and this yields a standard of treatment which grants to each of us no less respect than what peers owe each other: to fail to do so would be to treat people as being other than what they are, with less respect than they deserve. Since human beings are more than

58. See Darwall 1977. For an earlier use of the distinction, see Telfer 1968.

The ancient Greeks did not have the concept of recognition respect. But see Russell 2005, where he argues that Aristotelian notions of pride (among other character traits) can only form the basis of a person's self-respect in such a way that prevents vicious people from truly possessing self-respect. If Russell is right, then this would be the basis of an argument against vicious people living the Good Life. My sense, however, is that Fosco would see much of Russell's (and Aristotle's) argumentation as question-begging, since both seem to claim that vicious people cannot have the "courage of their convictions" as virtuous people can and in this regard Fosco is no coward. Cf. note 54.

mere tools or instruments, and are not mere things, it is wrong to treat us as if we are. To treat humans as tools or things is to treat them without the recognition respect that they deserve.

The Foscos seem to have no problem, in principle, with according appraisal respect when they see that it is due. They typically think that people deserve respect for what they are able to do or get, how powerful or clever they are, and how good they are at making happen what they want to happen. The Foscos tend to see other people as something more like cattle than humans, or perhaps like pawns or pieces of various weight on a chessboard (excluding the king), and as a result do not recognize others as the human beings they are. And it is their lack of respect for others that justifies to them their manipulations of others; when people are manipulated into getting "the short end of the stick", they are getting what they deserve. As P. T. Barnum reputedly said, "There's a sucker born every minute" and W. C. Fields followed with, "Never give a sucker an even break". The Foscos' byword is "I'll let you have my way." Using others or unwittingly manipulating them into positions that will allow the manipulators to get what they want is okay by the lights of the Foscos: in such cases, they see everyone, dupes and dupers alike, as "getting what they deserve".

Presumably, the Foscos feel the same way about self-respect. A person's self-respect, according to them, is going to be based on these same standards of appraisal. In this way, they can respect themselves and feel good about doing so, given their successes in getting what they want.

The rub comes with regard to recognition respect. If the Foscos accept the existence of recognition respect, then they would have to acknowledge that they do not act toward others in accordance with it, and this would imply that if they grant recognition respect to themselves (recognition self-respect), they are failing to treat like cases alike. On the other hand, if they deny the existence of recognition respect, then they have to deny that people are not merely instruments, which implies that they deny part of what makes them be who they are as individuals and makes them be more than mere instruments. Either way, their self-respect will be at least in part founded on a fraudulent basis, since they act in a way that is actually self-disrespecting when they fail to recognize others as being deserving of respect. This self-disrespect is the harm of immorality, and it is to be remembered now that the Foscos agreed up front that people who act in self-disrespecting ways are failing to live the Good Life, whether they acknowledge it or not. They are only fooling themselves into thinking they are living the Good Life, when in fact they have turned themselves into the very self-deceived, self-disrespecting dupes they typically scorn, having sold themselves a false bill of goods. Making out these claims in detail will comprise the rest of this section and the next.

In addition to what was earlier agreed upon by both parties to the debate, a further presumption of the argument needs to be explained. This is the idea that who we are, our personal identities, are constituted by some traits that we uniquely have, such as having some particular parents or configuration of DNA, and other traits which we share with others, like being a human being, a male or a female, and so on. If we understand an "essential property" as one without which an item would cease to exist, then our personal identities are constituted by essential properties, some of which are unique to us and some of which we share with others.[59] The argument to come works on the idea that when people act immorally towards others, this implies a disrespectful attitude

59. Kripke 1972.

toward those properties that make the victims who they are as individuals; the immorality that is perpetrated implies that none of those properties count as a sufficient reason for perpetrators to refrain from treating victims immorally. But some of the essential properties of the victim are also essential properties of the perpetrator, implying that when perpetrators act with a lack of respect for those properties (by not treating them as a sufficient reason for refraining from the immorality), they ipso facto act with a lack of respect for those properties as they partly constitute the perpetrator's own identity. Insofar as this is true, the perpetrator's actions are self-disrespecting.

From the immoral person's point of view, were he or she to think it out in the first person, the basic line of thought would be something like this: insofar as I'm not acting from weakness of will, that I am freely and willingly choosing to do what I do, then my performing an immoral act is proof that there is nothing which I see in my victim that is sufficient to get me to refrain from the act. Insofar as this is true, I am disrespecting my victim in a fundamental way. But, however different in some particulars I may be than my victim, there are nevertheless fundamental ways in which I am essentially no different than my victim. So my act, ipso facto, also demonstrates a fundamental self-disrespect. Just as I can betray a victim without that person ever finding out, I now see that I can betray myself in just the same way.

What could these essential properties be that are capable of being the least common denominators that ground recognition respect? Three obvious candidates are rationality, agency, and humanity. Kantians might favor rationality, claiming that this feature is what makes people worthy of being treated as more than mere tools. Our rationality, Kantians would say, gives us dignity, raises us above the level of "having a price", makes us more or better or at least different than mere animals, and merits our recognition and respect.[60] Davidsonians favor agency as that which we must assume of others to allow us to interpret their actions and to understand them at all.[61] Either rationality or agency might suffice, though neither may do so straightforwardly, since we typically think that babies or those whose rational faculties are impaired are nevertheless entitled to be treated as more than mere tools or instruments despite their lack of either of these traits. Perhaps talk of potential rationality or potential agency might save the day, but such moves are not necessary if we recognize that being a human being, being a member of Homo sapiens, will suffice.[62]

First, note that being a *human being* captures the most salient range of items that deserve moral consideration. At least conventionally, we typically think that all people merit moral consideration, and we talk politically and legally about "human rights" as being basic and inalienable and "crimes against humanity" as being the worst sort of evil. (We don't talk about "the rights of rationality" or "crimes against rationality" or "crimes against agency.") Our humanity is absolutely central to us and is by itself sufficient to make us unfit to be property or to be treated as mere instruments or tools. Children and those who are mentally incapacitated are thereby included without having to appeal to potentiality. (Contra Donagan, the appeal to humanity does not imply that potential human beings, such as fertilized ova, deserve the same consideration as actual human beings.[63]) We are all of a single biological species; there is an

---

60. Korsgaard 1996.
61. This thought is developed in a metaethical context by Wheeler 2014.
62. The defense of the claim that biology, humanity, or human nature is at the bottom of recognition respect and morality is far from complete. A full defense would go far beyond the present remit. The arguments given below still work if either rationality or agency is what is really at the bottom of morality, or if there are any properties that make all the relevant moral agents essentially be of a single kind or class.
63. Donagan 1977.

extended sense of "family" which covers us all. There is also a sense in which we have strong modal intuitions about not being able to exist as the individuals we actually are without being members of the species to which we actually belong. Even if we grant that fairy tales about sentient or talking animals are not logically impossible, it is metaphysically impossible that I (or you) could have been an alligator or an aardvark. If we follow Kripke on this, we will agree that our origins are essential to us, and this applies as much to our species membership as it does to our particular parentage.[64] Our shared humanity ontologically binds us all together as equals; at bottom our biology makes us be *of a kind*. Importantly, the human condition shapes human morality.[65] There are worries already expressed about how traditional impartial, dehumanized morality alienates us from our happiness and keeps there from being a unity between moral reasons and the values by which we live.[66] It is less familiar to notice how being human shapes our actual moral lives.

---

64. Kripke 1972.

65. More will be said about the relationship of humanity to morality in §3.1. For now, a common-sense realism about human nature and biological species in general is assumed. While I do think *eidos*, or form, is central to the essence of a species, I of course deny those aspects of Arisotelian essentialism and teleology which imply either non-evolving, eternal morphologies or (as on some early modern interpretations) entelechies in the future pulling with backwards causation the present toward them.

    Studying human nature is the epitome of trying to step out of our own skins; at some level, the endeavor is doomed to be incomplete. So, the demand for an account of human nature that gives precise necessary and sufficient conditions for being *a human being*, which uniquely picks out all and only human beings, is unjustified. Fundamentally, the natural kinds of biology will never be as precise as those of chemistry are; biological kinds are naturally vague. While it sounds funny to the contemporary ear, life is plastic: it rises from the muck in a messy way. In any case, the very schematic account of human nature given in the text should be modestly undeniable: we are creatures who are born helpless, feel pain, have appetites, passions, etc. For criticisms of human nature, see Hull 1986 and Buller 2005. For views similar to my own, see Grene 1976 and Walsh 2008 for work on teleology; Walsh 2006 and Devitt 2008 on essentialism; and Tooby and Cosmides 1990, Cosmides and Tooby 1997, and Brown 2012 on human nature.

66. Stocker 1976; Williams 1973, 1981, chap. 1, and 1985, chap. 10.

Perhaps one way into the issue is to consider a concept touched on above, that of what is *humane*. We all can fairly easily tell the difference between humane and inhumane treatment, and all, even the Foscos, will acknowledge that morality points us in the direction of the humane and that this moral concept is clearly tied to the human condition, though it is hard to see how to derive it from pure rationality or agency. If natural selection had left us in a different state, what would count as moral treatment would change with it.

It is difficult to discuss this without entering into the realm of science fiction, for we are forced to consider how different morality might be for sentient creatures different than Homo sapiens. There is no reason at all to think that Human, Vulcan, and Klingon flourishing will be identical. It is not too difficult to imagine, for example, some sentient non-human creatures flourishing through servility. Some sentient species may be more predatory or more fearful or more sympathetic than others, and there is no reason to think that such differences will make no difference to the morality of these creatures. If, for example, we were born with a thick exoskeleton, such that bodily injury was very, very uncommon and death almost always occurred as a result of disease or old age, and our fears were consistent with this, then, if such creatures had the virtue of courage at all, it would not be human courage. If we were capable of photosynthesizing sunlight into biological energy, such that we did not need to eat, or if we did not reproduce sexually, then our relations to our appetites and passions would alter radically and so would what counts as "temperance". As humans, we are famously social, but if we were all less social and more like the proverbial "lone wolf", cooperating far less than we actually do, then what would count as "fairness" and "desert" would change accordingly. And our practical rationality is tied to what is possible for creatures such as us, as are our obligations: if there is any truth to the idea that "ought implies can", and what we can do is limited by human nature, then so too are our obligations. And more to the point, our shared human nature makes us all into a single class of "moral agent", flawed and imperfect as we are, though still more than mere instruments, and this alone has implications for how we ought to treat each other.

This is not to beg any questions about animal rights or environmental ethics; the claim is not that only members of Homo sapiens merit moral consideration. Rather, it is simply that all humans do merit such consideration, and that at a basic ontological, metaphysical level, all Homo sapiens are of a kind, and as such are, at bottom, equals, peers, and to that extent identical.[67] All humans have something in common with each other, and what we have in common is also essential to each of our own particular identities, such that we could not be who we are as individuals were we not human beings.

So far, so good: the only claim at this point is that our status as human beings has implications for morality and what counts as the Good Life for creatures such as us; this is all metaphysics and does not entail anything normative. The sort of behavior which the Foscos defend and the Hartrights condemn implies a failure of recognition respect: one person intentionally harms another for the sake of self-interest, where nothing about the victim is taken as sufficient reason by the perpetrator to refrain from causing the harm. What is left is the following line of inference, wherein it may be

---

67. The sort of identity referred to here may be thought of as "partial identity". On such a notion, a black cube and a white cube are identical with respect to their shape even though they are not identical with respect to their color. Another way of parsing the thought is to note that different particulars may all instantiate the same property. I take no stand here on the metaphysics of properties with regard to nominalism or taking them as universals. All that is required is a desiderata for any theory of properties: namely, accounting for the explanandum that, for example, two white things have something in common and to that degree are the same. For more on the idea of partial identity, see Baxter 2001.

understood that the "disrespect" referred to is a failure of recognition respect:

(1) If Xavier disrespects Yves, this implies that Xavier does not take anything about Yves as a sufficient reason for refraining from the disrespect.

(2) This implies that when Xavier disrespects Yves, Xavier disrespects what makes Yves be the person he is.

(3) What makes Yves be the person he is are his essential properties.

(4) Therefore, when Xavier disrespects Yves, Xavier disrespects Yves' essential properties.

(5) If Xavier has in common with Yves any essential properties, then Xavier's disrespect of Yves implies that Xavier is ipso facto acting disrespectfully toward those aspects or essential properties of himself that he has in common with Yves.

(6) Yves and Xavier each essentially have in common the property of being a human being.

(7) Therefore, by (1)–(6), when Xavier disrespects Yves, Xavier is disrespecting himself.

A couple of remarks can forestall misunderstanding the argument. (More objections will be treated §1.7.) First, the properties referred to as being "essential to a person" are those which are essential to personal identity. Without embracing any particular theory of personal identity, and barring the possibility of disembodied souls, we may nevertheless note that having mass is an essential property of a person and yet not essential to a person's identity in the way that being human or being a member of a particular family are essential. So, the essential properties referred to above are the properties which are essential to personal identity, whatever our best theory of that turns out to be. Second, as noted, the harms under consideration are intentional, and we may assume that there is no such thing as cheating, lying, or "stabbing a 'friend' in the back" by accident. The recognition disrespect that such intentional behavior implies need not, however, be intentional. If a student cheats on an exam, there is a real sense in which the teacher and the other students in the class have been disrespected by the cheater, whether anyone realizes this or not. Of course, recognition disrespect may be intentional, but it need not be. So, in the argument, when Xavier disrespects Yves, the assumption is that while Xavier's immoral behavior must be intentional, the disrespect done to Yves need not be; Xavier need not explicitly intend to disrespect Yves to nevertheless disrespect Yves. And (almost) needless to say, if the argument is sound, Xavier's self-disrespect is also not intentional.

Also, these are matters of degree, such that small disrespect toward others implies only a small disrespect to the self. It seems reasonable to think that the self-disrespect involved in acting immorally is proportional to the amount of disrespect done to the victim. Of course, these small self-disrespectful acts may have a cumulative effect, as the addition of single grains of sand can eventually become a heap. Similarly (as one might think), one horribly large act of immorality, a premeditated murder perpetrated for "the thrill of it", for instance, reflects a thoroughly corrupted character and a proportionally large amount of disrespect for the humanity of the victim. The self-disrespect toward the murderer's own humanity is similarly proportional. Again, "one swallow does not make a summer", but at least often, one circling vulture implies something rotten lying below it.

Another misunderstanding to be avoided is the thought that the argument above intends to show that the primary harm done in an immoral act is to its perpetrator. While both sides have agreed that self-disrespect is harmful, at least insofar as it interferes with a person living a Good Life, the argument should not lead us to conclude that the harm to the perpetrator is the most important harm that is involved in immorality or the most important reason to avoid immorality. What we are looking for is a reason to avoid immorality that may move the Foscos to refrain from it, and we have already seen that they are moved by considerations of self-respect. Nevertheless, the harm of disrespect is one thing, the harm of the immoral act itself is another, and, while the former is shared between the victim and the perpetrator, the latter harm all accrues to the victim. When people are murdered, they are certainly disrespected by the act, but this disrespect is not, in normal cases, the worst thing that happens to them. Nevertheless, if the argument is sound, then the murderer's humanity, an essential property of the murderer, is disrespected by the murder just as much as the victim's humanity is disrespected, for there is no qualitative difference between them.

Given all this, the argument is fairly straightforward. Taking a toy example, imagine two siblings, one of whom tries to insult the other by saying, "Your parents have the stupidest children I've ever met." In such a case, the first has said something that is self-disrespecting, whether intentionally or not. The property that the siblings share, each essentially having the same parents, implies that the disrespect intended for the sibling that was spoken to reflexively implies disrespect for the sibling who spoke. A real-life example is the virulent white supremacist Craig Cobb undergoing DNA testing and finding out that he is in fact 14 percent of Sub-Saharan African descent; his racist invective had been self-condemning and self-disrespecting all along. Mutatis mutandis, the same is true for all perpetrators and victims of immorality. Since the perpetrator is fundamentally no different than the victim—both are human—then the disrespect done to the victim's humanity is ipso facto disrespect done to the perpetrator's humanity. And if the perpetrator is disrespecting his or her own humanity, then this counts as self-disrespect, given that the perpetrator's humanity is essential to the perpetrator. The harm of being immoral is that it keeps one from seeing the value of human life, and if one is human, then one is kept from seeing the value of one's own life.

Of course, there are ways for the Foscos to object, and at least some of these will be considered below. But before this, there is a different, though related, argument for the same conclusion: intentionally engaging in immoral behavior is self-disrespecting.

1.6 THE ARGUMENT FROM EPISTEMOLOGY

While the argument of the previous section was based on metaphysical considerations about identity and shared properties, the present argument is epistemological.[68] It begins, as above, with the idea of treating like cases alike. The sketch of the argument starts by first seeing that one's knowledge of the world is based on making fair judgments about it and that the same applies to self-knowledge: one's judgments about oneself will not yield self-knowledge if they are not accurate, and they are not accurate if they are not fair. This idea is then taken in conjunction with another: that self-respect requires self-knowledge. From here, the conclusion can be reached that people lack self-respect if they are not making fair judgments about who they are, since self-respect requires respecting the self and this requires self-knowledge. Since immorality involves people making unfair judgments about themselves, immorality keeps people from having self-respect. Once again, we see that one cannot both

---

68. The argument of this section was first developed in my 2011.

be immoral and maintain self-respect. Since both sides have agreed that self-respect is necessary for the Good Life, once again immorality is shown to keep one from living it.

While more apt for a treatise discussing Kant's First Critique, the principle introduced above of "treating like cases alike" goes far beyond being a constraint on moral thought. There is a sense in which concept application, or the judgment that a particular item falls under a concept's extension, or is a "this" as opposed to a "that", requires fundamentally that like cases be treated alike.[69] It is deeply related to the concept of *reliability*, which is of course central to contemporary epistemology. The idea that we should treat like cases alike can be understood as a particular form of supervenience, an asymmetrical and weak form, obtaining between the "facts of the case" and the judgments we make about them, such that differences in judgment must be based on a difference between the facts of the cases; otherwise, cases are treated similarly (judgment being a form of treatment).[70] Treating like cases alike is similar to consistency in thought, except that one may be biased for arbitrary reasons about a single case even when there are no other similar cases: in singular cases, there may be actual bias but only possible inconsistency in thought. The principle is also related to Kantian universalizability, insofar as both prescind from letting particular, arbitrary facts of a case determine its outcome. It is weaker than universalizability, however, in that individuals may treat like cases alike and yet one person may treat them differently than another: universalizability is supposed to be a stronger constraint that guarantees uniformity

---

69. John Rawls, in his earliest presentation of the idea of justice as fairness, writes, "One can view this principle [what would come to be his "first principle of justice"] as containing the principle that similar cases be judged similarly, or if distinctions are made in the handling of cases, there must be some relevant difference between them (a principle which follows from the concept of a judgment of any kind)." From his 1957, 654.

70. This sense of "supervenience" dates back at least to Hare 1952.

across everyone's judgments. Perhaps the best understanding of the principle can be found in the Rawlsian explication of "justice" as "the elimination of arbitrary distinctions" between cases.[71] In this sense, we can do justice to even singular, exceptional cases. Now, this is not a sufficient condition for justice, since we can easily imagine cases being treated alike and all equally unjustly. But for our purposes, it is enough to notice that treating like cases alike is a necessary condition for justice, given that it requires that judgments be based only on the relevant facts of the case, without arbitrary, invidious distinctions being made between cases.

Insofar as we are discussing justice in these terms, it is a purely epistemological sense of "justice"; it is the link between "judgment" and "justification". Making just or fair judgments of cases yields knowledge; making unjust or unfair judgments does not. (This should be acceptable to both Fosco and Hartright; more on justice in §3.5.) As noted, treating like cases alike can be seen as a regulative principle of all thought, or at least all judging: one might be said to not be in the business of judging if one regularly treats identical cases differently. While judging in accordance with "treating like cases alike" is not sufficient for gaining knowledge through one's judgments, it is necessary.

The same holds when considering self-knowledge. As noted, there are ways in which we are each unique in the world and different from all else, and other ways in which we are not different at all. So, if we are to have knowledge about ourselves as well as knowledge about our place in the world or how we fit into it, we must be sensitive to both the ways in which we are different and the ways in which we are the same. In order for me to know who I am, I must know what makes me different from other things and

71. Rawls 1957, 653.

I must know what I share with them. In particular, given the social relations which every human being has relied upon (we are all born of women, babies cannot survive without adult help, etc.), we must understand ourselves in part by how we are related to others. Thus, if we are to have knowledge about ourselves, we must judge fairly who we are in relation to others. A human being's self-knowledge requires knowledge of other human beings.

So, in order to know ourselves, we must make fair judgments about ourselves, and importantly about how we are related to others. Knowledge of others will require that we treat like cases alike. But knowledge of ourselves will also require that we treat like cases alike. If we are in certain respects no different than others, self-knowledge requires that we acknowledge this, that we step back from ourselves to make unbiased judgments about ourselves vis-à-vis when these similarities become pertinent to the judgment. Bias in judgments, inflating the value of the self or discounting the value of others (or the contrary, in cases of self-abnegation), such that one fails to treat like cases alike as a result of the bias, will not bring about self-knowledge but rather a false and biased view of the self which constitutes self-deception and not self-knowledge.[72]

So, a necessary (though not sufficient) condition for self-knowledge, as opposed to self-deception, is that one make just and fair judgments about the self as compared to others. The next step in the argument is to see how self-respect requires self-knowledge. The reader may remember that both the Foscos and Hartrights agreed that people can be wrong about whether or not they respect themselves, and this was justified by each pointing at the other and claiming that the other lacks self-respect even if they do not know it. Crucially, one can lack self-respect as a result of not respecting

---

72. See again, Badhwar 2008.

who one truly is but rather respecting a false conception of oneself, which is itself the result of a lack of self-knowledge.

Now, some might doubt if people really can be wrong about whether or not they have self-respect, and seeing why this doubt is misplaced will be helpful. In general, it might be thought that the so-called "reactive attitudes", including respect, are subjectively constituted in such a way that we cannot be mistaken about them when we adopt them towards one person or another. For example, resentment has famously been taken to be the paradigm reactive attitude, and it seems hard to understand how we could be in error about our own resentful feelings toward someone.[73] Nevertheless, resentment can be founded on error and we can make a distinction between this error-laden, "fraudulent" resentment and what we might call "authentic resentment."

Imagine that Xavier intentionally disrespects or harms us; yet we mistakenly think that it is Yves who has done so. In such a case, we would direct our resentful behavior toward Yves without seeing our mistake. We can distinguish what we might call "de dicto resentment" from "de re resentment."[74] De dicto resentment is the resentment aimed at "the person who disrespected us", or the person who actually fits the description of "the person(s) who disrespected us". De dicto resentment is the sort of attitude we experience when we are harmed or we get evidence of being disrespected when we do not know who the culprit is. De re resentment is the resentment which we direct toward the person whom *we think* fits the description "the person who disrespected us", the particular person who would actually feel our resentment should we choose to express it.

While, of course, there are times when these two forms of resentment are directed toward the same person, what is relevant for us is

73. Strawson 1962.
74. I thank Matthew Noah Smith for suggesting the "de re/de dicto" terminology to help make this distinction.

that the de dicto and de re senses of our reactive attitudes can come apart: if Xavier intentionally harms us and we think it is Yves who has done so, then we will, on the one hand, de re resent Yves, since he is the recipient of our actual resentful behavior, the actual person toward whom we direct our feelings. On the other hand, we de dicto resent Xavier for, in fact, he fits the definite description "the person who disrespected us", as he is the guilty party. Given such a distinction, we can call "authentic resentment" the sort of resentment we have when the de dicto and de re objects of our resentment are identical (resentment without error, if you will). If the two come apart, we can call it "fraudulent resentment".

There is no reason to think that this de re/de dicto distinction cannot be made with other reactive attitudes, including respect and, a special case of this, self-respect. We can take an attitude of self-respect to the people we actually are, and we can also take an attitude of self-respect toward the people who we wish we were but are not. The person who is actually the object of our de re self-respect is, of course, the self. And we can de dicto respect ourselves under a certain description of who we think we are. But if we are deceived about ourselves and respect ourselves based on false and self-deceitful beliefs, then our self-respect is error-laden. If we stake our claim to self-respect on false beliefs about ourselves, then the de re object of our respect, our actual self, is not identical to the person who would fit the de dicto description under which we (falsely) think we are respecting ourselves.

The upshot of this discussion is that we can be wrong about whether or not we have self-respect, insofar as our self-respect can be either authentic self-respect or fraudulent, self-deceived self-respect. And the difference between having one kind of self-respect or the other hangs on whether we have self-knowledge about the bases of our putative self-respect. If we have knowledge of who we actually are, based on making fair judgments of ourselves especially as we compare to others, then our self-respect will be authentic. But if we have deceived ourselves about who we are, then we are merely fraudulently respecting who we wish we were and not who we actually are. So, self-knowledge is a necessary condition for having authentic self-respect.

Before moving on, we should recall that neither the Foscos nor the Hartrights should balk at any of this up front, given that we have assumed that each thinks they know themselves while thinking the other is self-deceitful: the Foscos arrogantly think they know themselves while thinking the Hartrights fools or dupes, whether the latter see it or not, and the Hartrights will modestly think they know themselves while thinking the Foscos have foolishly bought into a set of supposedly self-aggrandizing values which in fact do not lead to happiness, whether they can see it or not.

So, making fair or just judgments about oneself is a necessary condition for self-knowledge, and having self-knowledge is necessary for having self-respect. Hypothetical syllogism allows us to conclude that making fair or just judgments about oneself is necessary for having self-respect. The only question that remains is whether it is the Foscos or the Hartrights who have authentic self-respect. Both think it is themselves and both cannot be right. And when we consider recognition self-respect, based as it is on the undeniable ways in which we are all alike, the answer becomes clear.

All humans share many essential properties and, taken in conjunction with the idea of treating like cases alike, this entails recognizing that recognition respect functions as a baseline standard for interpersonal behavior. Taken together they entail that, insofar as each of us is the same as everyone else, we ought not to judge or treat ourselves according to a different standard than we judge or treat others. If we each think our own lives are more than merely instrumentally valuable, then we ought not to treat others as if their lives are merely instrumentally valuable, since in this regard we are essentially identical. This provides us with a bottom-line standard of respectful self-regarding and other-regarding behavior, based on everyone being more than instrumentally valuable. If people demand the respect that is owed to a human being who is, as such, more than a mere tool or instrument, and then go on to fail to treat others as being deserving of the same sort of respect, this shows them to be in denial about those aspects of themselves that they share with others.

This behavior is characteristic of immorality: as noted above, perpetrators of immorality find in their victims no sufficient reason to refrain from committing the harm. Perpetrators of immorality take their own lives as ends in themselves and take their victims as the means by which these ends are obtained. So, immorality keeps its perpetrators from seeing themselves and their position in the world truly and accurately as compared to other human beings. Perpetrating immorality is proof that like cases are not being treated alike by the perpetrator. Immorality induces self-deception by making it seem to immoral people that they are justified in their own immorality, justified in thinking of themselves as somehow better than those of whom they have taken unfair advantage. Insofar as immorality engenders self-deception, it prevents the self-knowledge that we have already seen is necessary for authentic self-respect, that is, respect founded upon fair and just self-assessments. And we agreed long ago that self-respect is necessary for the Good Life.

Therefore, immorality is bad for you.

1.7 OBJECTIONS AND CONCLUSION

The four most obvious ways for the Foscos to object are by (i) insisting on there being something special about them which justifies their treating themselves differently than others, (ii) denying that anyone's life has more than a merely instrumental value, (iii) claiming that we ended up with a very different conception of *self-respect* than we started with and that it is not clear why self-respect understood in this way is necessary for happiness, or (iv) reneging on the agreement that self-respect is necessary for a person to live the Good Life or be as happy as possible. However, before turning to the Foscos' replies, there are two objections from directions friendly to morality which deserve our attention.[75]

The first objection is that the central insight of these arguments, namely, that immorality is inimical to happiness, is consistent with the social conception of *morality*, contrary to the diagnosis of the initial problem offered above. One might, the objection goes, retain the social conception of *morality* and reframe the arguments to show that immorality is harmful to well-being and, therefore, to happiness.

In response, this is a welcome way of framing the issues. That the arguments can retain their cogency across theoretical divides is an indication that they are forcing our attention toward real yet neglected relations between how we value ourselves and how we value others that have not heretofore been properly appreciated. In the most general, though perhaps not the most insightful terms, this is an accurate way of explicating the point: let's assume for the moment that we are beginning with a standard nonmoralized approach to *well-being* (see § 1.2 above). On such a view, a person's life can have a high quality of welfare and either be moral or immoral. If so, then the conclusions of the reframed arguments from above lead to the conclusion that, contrary to the starting point, well-being and immorality are not consistent. This is still a significant result, and it does seem to preserve thinking about morality in social terms. Why not hold onto the social conception of *morality*?

75. I thank anonymous reviewers for bringing these two objections to my attention.

The answer is consistent with our diagnosis of the problem. The original problem arose due to thinking of morality as a social matter: it is failing to see the self-regarding aspects of morality which caused us to see it as being ineluctably set against self-interest. Plato's unsatisfactory answer to the problem from *Republic*, cast in terms of the way that immorality causes "psychic disharmony", shows correctly that the way to respond to Glaucon's challenge is to attend to how immorality negatively affects its perpetrator's eudaimonia. The answer is only unsatisfactory because the ancients did not have the psychological concepts needed to properly unpack the metaphor of "psychic harmony". We now have a worked out conception of *self-respect* that makes it clear that, since respect is respect, self-regarding self-respect must not be fundamentally different than other-regarding respect for others. Were we to have always acknowledged that how we treat others is not independent of how we treat ourselves, we would never have thought of morality in purely social terms in the first place. Perhaps the social conception of *morality* can be preserved by adding Ptolemic epicycles to our moral theories, but this does not change the fact that it is what caused the problem in the first place. (A different sort of argument against the social conception of *morality* is given in §2.3 below.)

There are also the dialectical advantages to abandoning the social conception: we do not beg the question against the immoralists and egoists who have plagued the defenses of morality. As long as we adopt a social conception of *morality*, our opponents are not even in the game and any defenses of morality will have to be "modest", that is, not based on premises that everyone adopts.[76] Even such modest arguments are not easy to give of course, but in the end they are preaching to the choir. The only chance of reaching morality's

76. Again, see Hills 2010.

dialectical opponents comes from abandoning the social conception of *morality*. The best place to begin is not with the question of "how ought I to treat others?", or "what do we owe each other?", but "how ought I to live?" when understood in a perfectly general way.

Another objection is that morality may actually demand more from us than we can garner from taking self-respect and respect to require the sort of parity between people that has been suggested. Many prominent moral doctrines demand a humbler set of traits. Thus, Jesus preached for us to take a seat at the lowest place, and that the meek shall inherit the earth; that when we are struck on one cheek, we should turn the other to be struck again as well. Buddhists teach humility and Gandhi transcended the traditions of Hinduism by demanding that even the Brahmins on his ashram take their turns cleaning the toilets. As noted above, Susan Wolf's picture of "moral saints" suggests something similar.[77] Each counsels a form of servility as a path to righteousness even though this seems to require a sacrifice to one's self-respect.

Of course, such demanding moralities may be questioned in their own right, and the meanings of the examples and parables are open to multiple interpretations. One is that they are assuming a (natural?) human tendency toward arrogance and are recommending practices to counteract those tendencies. Another is that the protreptic nature of exhortation tends toward hyperbole; perhaps the intention is to point very clearly in one direction, knowing that no one would or even could fully go the entire distance. Or finally, perhaps, there really is a deeper truth that defies philosophical comprehension. In any case, if morality demands a servile lack of self-respect, then even more work will be needed to justify it. Most will insist that morality must not systematically ruin the lives and

---

77. See her 1982.

happiness of those who are willing to practice it religiously. It seems right to insist that morality be humanely livable.

But turning away from worries brought on by flights of moral nobility, we can turn to how the Foscos would reply to the above arguments. The first response (i) would be for the Foscos to insist on being special in a way that justifies what they do to others. Let us grant that they are special in some way, perhaps they are unusually clever or insightful about what motivates people, and this allows them to get away with what they do. The problem however is that, even if they are in some way special, to act while under the impression that they are justified by their "specialness" leaves them in denial about the ways in which they are not special at all. Special human beings are nonetheless human beings. The arguments above hang on the fact that both perpetrators and victims of immorality are equally, undeniably human and this is all they need. There are no properties, no such *je ne sais quoi*, that make some people more "special" in the required sense, and even if there were, they would not negate the shared humanity essential to all human beings. Being "special" does not negate the fact that "non-special" human beings are not merely tools or instruments and therefore deserve not to be treated as such.

A different take on (i) is to appeal to haecceities.[78] An haecceity is a purely metaphysical property which serves to distinguish one object from all others, a pure sort of "thisness" which individual items have that serves to distinguish them from any other possible item, even one which is, in every other way, qualitatively identical to it. The history of the concept of *haecceities* is itself troubled, since they were devised in the Middle Ages to solve philosophical problems concerning identity. Still, let's grant their existence

---

78. I thank Pekka Vayrynen and Todd Jones for bringing this idea to my attention.

for the sake of the argument. Perhaps the Foscos could claim that there is something about their haecceities that makes them "special" in a way that justifies their behavior. The suggestion is, nevertheless, problematic. The first problem is that it seems to confuse *being unique* with *being special*. If there are such things as haecceities, then it is metaphysically guaranteed that everything is unique. But being unique does not make something special, especially if everything is "equally unique", as haecceities tell us is the case. An haecceity is a bare property, which only serves to distinguish one thing from something else which is otherwise qualitatively identical to it. If the Foscos were sufficiently different than everyone else, such that these differences could justify their behavior, then there would be no need to appeal to haecceities in the first place. Given this lack of difference, an appeal to an haecceity could only serve to establish that the Foscos are unique individuals, but this alone justifies nothing since, as noted, everyone is equally unique. And certainly, an haecceity would not be able to somehow "override" the considerations adduced in the preceding paragraph: no matter how different one person is from everyone else, this difference does not negate the similarities which nevertheless obtain between them.

The problem with (ii) denying that the life of a human being has more than instrumental value is that it leaves us with the question of what humans are supposed to be instrumentally valuable for, without any hope of having an answer. All instrumental value is value for the sake of something else, and the idea we are considering is that there is only instrumental value in the world. If the Foscos say everyone's lives have merely instrumental value, it is reasonable to ask to whom or what it is they are valuable. They cannot say that they are instrumentally valuable to themselves, for that gives the "self" a value other than what is merely instrumental, namely a value which is an end in itself, and this is exactly the sort of value which the objection denies. And why would anyone accede to the position of a tool for the sake of something else, which is itself merely a tool for the sake of something else, which is itself…? How could someone accept such a position and maintain his or her self-respect and dignity? It cannot be done. At the very least, this seems revisionary of the sort of self-respect with which the Foscos began.

Perhaps they could adopt a more Humean picture in which having any sort of value is the result of being valued in that way, attempting to secure for themselves a sort of value which no one else possesses. There are valuers who value things either instrumentally or for their own sakes, and at least some valuers value themselves for their own sakes. If this sort of valuing is the only way that value comes into the world, then perhaps the Foscos' happiness is the only thing which they value for its own sake. Thus, they might think they are making no mistake in valuing themselves differently than everyone else. The worry about such a view is how it severs the qualities of what is being valued from the judgment that it has value, since this leaves no constraint on valuing that evaluations respect even the weakest notion that value supervenes on the properties of what is being valued: that if two things are to be judged differently, this must be based on a relevant difference between them. Were the Foscos to try to adopt such a view, they would then have nothing to say in response to the demand for reasons for thinking that they are the only things in the world to be valued for their own sake. They might insist they have self-respect but would have to acknowledge that their self-respect has no foundation or ground whatsoever; their "self-respect" would be baseless.

Response (iii) is the thought that the Foscos might accuse the argument of a "bait and switch." True, they may admit, that at the start of the argument, the necessity of self-respect for happiness was assumed by all parties, but that by the end of the argument, there was a very particular conception of *self-respect* that was employed and that it is not clear why this sort of self-respect is necessary for happiness. Indeed, we can imagine the Foscos insisting that they are happy to "recognize" the humanity that they share with others, but insist that this does not imply that anyone deserves to be treated with anything other than instrumental value. What gives someone genuine self-respect or makes someone worthy of being treated with more than instrumental value, Fosco might say, is living such that one insists that one's self-interest never be held hostage to anything: self-respecting people do not "self-sacrifice." Wisdom, on this view, is seeing that the fulfillment of one's self-interest is what gives a person's life more than instrumental value, and that sacrificing self-interest in the name of morality is treating oneself as an instrument of morality and is what makes one's life have only instrumental value. Rather, wisdom is being willing to do whatever it takes to get what one wants.

The first response to this idea is to point out how wonderfully convenient it is for the Foscos to see things in just this self-justifying way! They assume a particular set of normative values, a particular view of how to live the Good Life, then call it "wisdom", and then use that to justify to themselves their own behavior. Of course, their motives for believing these ideas about wisdom are suspect: if self-deception is more likely to occur when one has a desire to believe what is most convenient, then the Foscos are likely to be deceiving themselves (see §1.4 above).

Even if this point about self-deception is correct, however, it is still possible that the Foscos believe the truth about wisdom for the wrong reasons, and perhaps wisdom does in fact counsel us to do whatever it takes to fulfill our self-interest. What reason is there to deny this? Well, one would be that wisdom is (perhaps analytically?) not self-undermining. If so, then it suffices as a response to this objection to point out that the Foscos have adopted a self-undermining view of wisdom. For, were it to be received by all as "the truth about wisdom", it would be much more difficult for anyone to achieve what they want in life, and this is a self-undermining conception of *wisdom*. If everyone adopted this view, we would immediately be back in a Hobbesian war of "all upon all", trusting no one and figuring everything's value through a cost/benefit analysis. Could such a superficial and self-undermining view of *wisdom* ground a genuine form of self-respect? Could wisdom really be such that everyone is worse off if they live according to its dictates?

Without adopting any particular theory of wisdom, there is good reason to rule such a view of it out. The value of human life cannot be *solely* measured in terms of our ability to achieve our personal self-interest. At the very least, part of what gives our lives the value they have is that human beings are creatures who are able to make choices about how to live. Were human beings to lack this ability, we might very well be of merely instrumental value. (In fact, this is probably false, but it may be granted for the sake of argument.) The Foscos would have to acknowledge this: the human ability to make of our lives what we can is what gives us more than instrumental value. So, a necessary condition of a life's having more than instrumental value is independent of our pursuit of our self-interest; a necessary part of what makes human life valuable is our (limited) ability to make of our own lives what we will. No genuine sense of human self-respect can ignore this. To think that self-respect may *only* be attained by being good at getting away with immoral behavior is to live in denial of a necessary constituent of what makes human life be of more than of mere instrumental value in the first place. The Foscos cannot deny that this is part of what makes their lives be more than instrumentally valuable, and yet they cannot insist that they alone have this ability. So, they must recognize that genuine self-respect cannot be based solely on how well one pursues self-interest and that what they owe to themselves in this regard is identical to what they owe everyone else. In the end, the objection fails.

Still, the Foscos might insist, "Why should it matter to my happiness that I value myself in a way that accords with the truth about the value I possess?" The answer here is that it may not matter as long as one is willing to acknowledge that one is willingly duping oneself into believing that one is more valuable than one truly is. Perhaps it is not so bad to dupe oneself into believing that one is better than one is. But remember that this was the very reason that the Foscos condemned the Hartrights in the beginning: the accusation was that moral people were duping themselves into believing they had self-respect and were happy when, in fact, this is not the case. The Foscos can find no succor from embracing self-deception, given that their argument against their opponents is based on a condemnation of this exact same form of self-deception.

Another possibility related to (iii) is to think that the only sort of self-respect that makes sense is appraisal self-respect. Upon reflection, however, such a scheme is untenable. We accord appraisal respect based on character and/or achievements, which implies that what we are appraising must be more than mere instruments that can only do what they do and cannot be or do otherwise. Of course, we can appraise instruments for how well they operate or what they can accomplish, but this does not bring with it any sort of respect. Appraisal respect only makes sense against a background of recognition respect.

Response (iv) was reneging on the agreement that self-respect is necessary for the Good Life and accepting that people can be happy without self-respect. The problem here is that this leaves the Foscos in a position similar to what was found in the conclusion of

the previous paragraph. Remember their argument against morality in the first place was that it leaves those who accept it without
self-respect, as mere sheep or cattle. If the Foscos try to accept this
conclusion to save their own practices, they lose whatever advantage they had over defenders of morality in the first place. And they
would have nothing to say in response to people who do have genuine self-respect and who claim that this makes their life go better, as
the Foscos acknowledged at the start. Perhaps there is some room
to maneuver here, but arguing that self-respect does not add to the
quality of a person's life, and that happiness is consistent with lacking self-respect, is going to be a tough sell, to say the least.

The final option for Fosco at this point is to argue that fraudulent
self-respect is as good as authentic self-respect at making us happy,
that one can live just as well with the fraud as without. First, we may
note once again that the Foscos thought it was the dupery of the
Hartrights that kept them from having self-respect and happiness,
and now they are reversing themselves with regard to the negative
effects of dupery on happiness. Second, there is another reversal
of the Foscos' position, which began with the idea that they pos-
sessed realpolitik and that the Hartrights are the dupes, upon whom
a fraud is being perpetrated: the Foscos must now acknowledge that
their putative realpolitik was actually shot through with error. But
most important is to consider whether or not a person can live as
happily with fraudulent self-respect as they can with the authentic
variety. Perhaps if one values only hedonistic pleasure, this might
be so. Let's assume it for the sake of argument. The question then
becomes whether or not the pleasures of immorality outweigh the
harms to one's self-respect being based on false beliefs about oneself.
The Foscos may insist that the fraud is hedonically invisible, neither
pleasurable nor painful, and so the fraudulent self-respect may seem
as pleasurable to them as other people's authentic self-respect may

seem to them. But, even if true, how could they possibly know such a thing?

In fact, they cannot. Recall the discussion at the start of §1.5 about lessons that children can learn, as well as the comments from later in the same section about the difference between wise people and fools who thinks themselves wise. There does seem to be a difference in the quality of pleasure that is involved in, for example, truly and fairly winning a competition by giving the best performance and "winning" by cheating. This is what justifies the scare quotes: "winning" by cheating is not really winning. If one always cheats, one can never know how the difference feels. And it would be odd to hear of someone who could find no reason to choose winning as a result of skill over "winning" by cheating: we would think that person had never truly won something or had never taken pleasure at winning an open competition where one does not need to break the rules and take some unfair advantage just to make it look like one is better than others. (Recall the quote from Cicero in footnote 56 at the start of §1.5.) Clearly, it is better to actually be the best than to merely look like the best. Self-deception would be the only reason to deny this. Cheaters, by definition, claim special advantage for themselves and therefore do not actually win anything; they only look like they do. If they could win, there would be no reason to cheat. The difference between winning fair and square and "winning" by cheating is the same as the difference between authentic and fraudulent self-respect. Living the Good Life is not the same as looking like one is living the Good Life. If Lance Armstrong never got caught, he would nevertheless be the fraud we all now know him to be.

Maybe Fosco could pull off a dialectical defense of a position in which cheating *is* as good as truly winning, but this is not a promising prospect. Even on purely hedonistic grounds, it seems better to win fairly than to use a cheating technique to fool everyone into thinking that one won fairly. If one is going to take pleasure in beating others in a competition, it seems straightforwardly more pleasurable to "beat them at their own game" (which we can assume to be fair) than to cheat them and not give them a fair chance. It bespeaks craven insecurity to think of oneself as being capable of only a simulacrum of victory, or even to preferring the simulacrum of winning—that is, "winning"—to actually winning. It is certainly not unreasonable to think it is better to be authentically second than fraudulently first. At the start, it was Fosco accusing Hartright of bad faith. Now, however, it is clear where the bad faith lies: the "Good Life" of a cheater is as much a fraud as is the "self-respect" of the immoral person.

Perhaps, however, the Foscos would say that the pleasures of "winning" by cheating do not depend on the pleasures of winning at all, rather that the pleasures of "winning" have to do with having the reputation of "being a winner" and its attendant rewards. What is important, Fosco might say, is not whether or not one is a winner but whether or not everyone thinks one is a winner. The problem is that making this move requires thinking that there is no important difference between being a fraud and not being a fraud, and if this is the case then it is hard to see how to hold onto the distinction between being a dupe and not being a dupe, which is essential to the Foscos' argument the against the Hartrights. Rejecting the appearance/reality distinction is not really an option for those who claim to speak the truth.

The Hartrights have no such troubles. The tables have turned.

Chapter 2

Becoming Good

2.1 THE PARADOX OF HAPPINESS

One way to look back on the arguments of the first chapter is by seeing the tension between self and other that sometimes ends in immorality as arising from the tension between partiality and impartiality. The traditional view is that "other" and "impartiality" align with morality, while "self" and "partiality" incline toward immorality.[1] One lesson from the first chapter is that any dichotomous view of morality and self-interest keeps people from living as well as they can. It is possible, however, to see the tension between partiality and impartiality as a tension *within* moral decision-making, in which all relevant considerations have moral salience, regardless of how things ought to play out in the case. In some moral situations, impartiality is of paramount importance and partiality ought to play no role in deliberations, particularly where justice is concerned. But in other moral situations, thinking impartiality or considering what "morality" demands is ruinous: Bernard Williams' famous example

---

1. Even in discussions of morality which are friendly to partiality, the emphasis is often on showing that a particular form of partiality is morally acceptable, as if the fallback default moral position is impartiality; the impartial justifies the partial; the universal must make concessions to humanity; morality must make concessions to the self. For example, see many of the essays in Feltham and Cottingham 2010.

is a man whose wife and a stranger are both drowning at the same time and he cannot save both. In such a case, to even think about "morality", or what to do from a deliberatively impartial point of view, or about doing "the right thing", is to have "one thought too many".[2] Sometimes one ought to think impartially, other times not, and in general, there is no formula that can settle the matter across all moral circumstances.

One nice feature of seeing the relation between partiality and impartiality as being within morality is that it allows us to capture what goes wrong both with egoists, who are improperly partial to themselves, and also with those often well-meaning people who are improperly partial to others. We can be improperly partial to others in a variety of ways. The impropriety of nepotism in the distribution of public offices is one. So are various forms of preferential treatment of groups found in, for example, racism or sexism, where people favor others who are arbitrarily like them over everyone else and may falsely think they do so with complete rectitude. (It may be helpful to remember Rawls' idea that justice is the elimination of arbitrary difference, discussed at the start of §1.6.) Members of many religions have often been improperly partial to their respective fellow-travelers, and examples abound in the history of war of jingoism gone awry. A very different kind of improper partiality can be seen when servile people willingly treat others better than they treat themselves.

People who do a poor job of balancing partiality and impartiality often end up behaving in self-disrespecting ways, whether they realize that this is happening or not: immorality, more often than not, involves a disrespect for humanity (or for rationality or agency), and this can cause the immoral agent to engage in self-disrespecting behavior by virtue of that agent's essentially being human (or rational or an

2. Williams 1981, 17–18.

agent). And while the lesson is quite general, it is of vital importance in the debate over the answer to the Question, "How ought I to live?".

The lesson of the first chapter is that being immoral harms one's happiness by inherently working against one's self-respect, without which one may not be happy. Many unsatisfactory objections to this were discussed. In the end, Fosco's most cogent reply might go something like this: "I've always agreed with Glaucon's suggestion that morality is a necessary evil, and I used to think that immorality practiced with impunity had no cost at all. Now, I admit that I must accept the arguments that have been given and concede that the cost of being immoral is paid in the coin of self-respect, and I accept that the loss of self-respect negatively affects my happiness. Still, giving up the rewards of immorality is more of a sacrifice to my happiness than what I lose through the self-disrespect that is the cost of immorality. So, even if immorality is detrimental to my happiness, it is less so than being moral. Therefore, all things considered, it is still best for me to be immoral."[3]

Responding to this worry is the first (but not only) goal of this chapter. One way to approach this response is to discuss the paradox of happiness, which infects the Foscos' conception of *happiness*:

> *You can't be as happy as you can be,*
> *if your goal is to be as happy as you can be.*

This, essentially, is the paradox of happiness.[4] Strictly speaking, it is not a paradox if by paradox we mean the acceptance of a logical contradiction, such as we find in the liar paradox. It is more of a practical paradox, similar to a Catch-22 situation: one may not φ

3. I thank Joel Kupperman for discussion on this point.
4. For an overview, see Eggleston 2013.

unless one first ψs, and one may not ψ unless one first φs. In the words of Joseph Heller's *Catch-22*:

> There was only one catch and that was Catch-22, which specified that a concern for one's safety in the face of dangers that were real and immediate was the process of a rational mind. Orr was crazy and could be grounded. All he had to do was ask; and as soon as he did, he would no longer be crazy and would have to fly more missions. Orr would be crazy to fly more missions and sane if he didn't, but if he were sane he had to fly them. If he flew them he was crazy and didn't have to; but if he didn't want to he was sane and had to. (1995, 56-57)

As a simple case: one may not get a job without experience and one may not get experience without a job. True, this sort of situation can be described as "paradoxical", but they are typically not impossible to manage: in general, people without experience get jobs all the time and often acquire experience prior to getting a job. Bureaucratic stringency aside, often there are ways to "work around" such practical paradoxes, even if "straight solutions" are not possible; very often, taking a different approach to the paradox reveals a way to avoid it in the first place. If Heller's Orr was so desperate to avoid flying, he could have tried to demonstrate his insanity in another way, or he could have simply gone AWOL. "Solving" these paradoxes are practical problems because they concern the successful formation and pursuit of goals to aim for, purposes which may or may not be consistently adopted. We want to avoid setting goals which are impossible to attain or which, more generally, are self-defeating. We do not want to doom ourselves to failure.

So we ask the Question again with an explicit concern for self-defeat: "How ought I to live?" We answered it first by noting that living as well as possible is living the "happy life", and in chapter 1 we learned some other, fairly skeletal, lessons about happiness. What we do not yet have, however, is anything approaching a positive or substantial account of what happiness is; at this stage of the dialectic, "happiness" is still little more than a name for the goal. The problem is that certain ways of filling out what "happiness" means engage the paradox of happiness. If one understands "happiness" in those ways, then it will be impossible to be as happy as possible. Conceptions of *happiness* are self-defeating if aiming at them prevents one from becoming as happy as one can be. An easy example is that if I think happiness for me involves being servile, then this prevents me from truly being as happy as I can be: presumably, happiness and self-derogation are mutually exclusive, and if so, a conception of *happiness* that requires me to be servile actually undermines my happiness. To fine-tune the first goal of this chapter: it is to argue that thinking that *happiness* requires the relentless pursuit of self-interested happiness is similarly self-undermining.

The relevant implication is that immoral people, like the Foscos, have bought into a self-undermining conception of *happiness*. They may think it better to sacrifice self-respect for the sake of pleasure, wealth, or being honored, but if so, they are misguided; as we shall see, it is actually more conducive to happiness to adopt an evaluative framework that does not require sacrifices to self-respect and which values goodness and virtue above pleasure, wealth, and honor.

2.2 THE MOST IMPORTANT THING IN THE WORLD

By setting their personal happiness as their ultimate, overriding goal, the Foscos run straight into the paradox of happiness. Why? Henry

Sidgwick proposes one answer. Sidgwick called his take on the paradox of happiness, "The Fundamental Paradox of Egoistic Hedonism":

> A man who maintains throughout an epicurean mood, keeping his main conscious aim perpetually fixed on his own pleasure, does not catch the full spirit of the chase; his eagerness never gets just the sharpness of edge which imparts to the pleasure its highest zest. Here comes into view what we may call the fundamental paradox of Hedonism, that the impulse toward pleasure, if too predominant, defeats its own aim.[5]

Following Sidgwick, we can begin our exploration of what happiness is with a hedonistic theory of personal happiness. On this view, the happiest life is one in which we experience the most pleasure, and if this view is married to an egoism saying that *my* pleasure/happiness is always the goal, then aiming at my own pleasure will at times interfere with my attainment of pleasure. In Sidgwick's words, "the impulse toward pleasure, if too predominant, defeats its own aim".

Sidgwick acknowledges that he adapted these ideas from Joseph Butler, who presented the first, and perhaps ultimately most persuasive, argument against the idea that we fundamentally always act out of self-interest, or what he called "self-love". This idea, that all human action is in fact self-interested action (whether we realize it or not), is often called "psychological egoism" and, in arguing against it, Butler crucially distinguishes between being motivated by self-love or my own happiness or "what's best for me", and being motivated by the external things that make us happy. "Happiness or satisfaction", Butler says, "consists only in the enjoyment of those objects which are by nature suited to our several particular appetites,

5. Sidgwick 1907, 48.

passions, and affections".[6] He claims that if we are always motivated by "what's best for me", as opposed to being motivated by what's best for those things which make us happy, then we will do a poor job in attaining and caring for those things that make us happy. He thinks that if we attend to our happiness too zealously, we will not pay proper attention to those external things that make us happy. In Butler's words, if we are too moved by self-love, we are apt to end up feeling "useless solicitude and anxiety, in a degree and manner which may prevent obtaining the means and materials of enjoyment [that make us happy]".[7] In the same way that caring too much about winning can take our minds away from the game, making it less likely that we will win, overweening concern with our own happiness makes it less likely that we will become happy. For Butler, the paradox of happiness arises out of the single-minded way in which those consumed by self-love are motivated by their own happiness. In order to attain the most happiness, they must distract themselves from thoughts of it.

But there is a problem with explaining the paradox of happiness as an inability to stay focused on happiness while doing one's best to become happy: Fosco may readily respond, "Well, okay, while I'm working my next confidence game, I'll ignore my own happiness and focus on doing things as well as I possibly can. I'll delay thoughts of gratification until the job is done. I agree that if I think too much about the rewards of my labors I'm more likely to make a mistake and get caught. So, when I find myself thinking too much about my happiness, I'll push those thoughts aside and focus on doing well what I need to do to get what I want; if athletes can do this, so can I. But I do not fool myself into thinking that my

6. Butler 1900b, Sermon XI, §9.
7. Butler 1900b, Sermon XI, §9.

overriding motivation is something other than my happiness. I am no dupe. If I learn that my mark has no money, I will give up the game, since further pursuit will not contribute to my happiness. So, I still do not have a reason to aim, overall, at anything other than my own 'happiness'." This response appears to be adequate. So, the possibility that the Foscos are taking the best path to their happiness is still open.

So we will have to look for other ways to explain the paradox that do not hang on the issue of distraction. Are there other ways in which making our own happiness our first priority can keep us from being as happy as we can be? The answer is yes. There are a number of interrelated ways in which an overweening concern for one's happiness is self-defeating. Before we explore them, the first thing we need to do to take another look at Butler's distinction between our happiness and what makes us happy. One way to take his point here is to claim that people will end up happier if they make the external things that make them happy their first priority, instead of making their own happiness their first priority. If one knows, say with certainty, that bringing P, Q and R fully into one's life will make one as happy as possible, and that is one's goal, then one should form intentions that promote bringing P, Q and R into one's life. Having done so, one no longer needs or has reason to be motivated by happiness per se. If we take good care of the things that make us happy, then our happiness will take care of itself.

This is not, however, an argument for thinking that P, Q and R are thereby more important to a person than happiness, since one might continue to value them in purely instrumental way. And even if P, Q and R do have noninstrumental value, they still might be less valuable all told than one's own happiness. They will only become more important to someone than that person's happiness if they have a value greater to that person than happiness does. Fosco-style egoists will deny this is possible, since they insist that nothing is more important to them than their happiness. So, they will refuse to take the step of valuing anything more than they value themselves. Given the paradox, this implies that they must settle for less happiness than is possible. They needlessly defeat themselves.

Foscos must hold fast to the notion that their happiness always trumps concern for those things that instrumentally make them happy, that regardless of the value those things may have, the happiness of the Foscos always has more all told. Indeed, if they stop believing this, they must acknowledge the possibility that their beliefs about what truly has value in the world are alienated from their egocentric behavior. In this latter case, again, it is the immoralist, not the moralist, who is a "house divided against itself". Why can't the Foscos insist that their happiness is of the highest value? Why will their refusal to subordinate their happiness to whatever it is that makes them happy undermine their happiness? The answer is that if we make our happiness the most important thing in the world, then those things which make us happy can never have more than instrumental value to us and this is to ignore much of the value in the world. If we may innocuously assume that the happiest life is found by bringing what has most value in the world into it as much as possible, then the Foscos are selling themselves short.

We have already seen in chapter 1 that thinking that one is the only thing in the world that has more than instrumental value is self-deceptive. (This was the argument for why a rejection of recognition respect led to an inability to value oneself properly.) Things with noninstrumental value are better and deserve better, than things with merely instrumental value. So, let's say P, Q, and R have instrumental value, but are also valuable for other reasons. They have value in themselves, intrinsic value, or are necessary constituents of what has intrinsic value, and are therefore more valuable than things which are merely of instrumental value. If our goal is to bring what is best into our lives so that we can be as happy as possible, then we should prefer things that have more than instrumental value to those which have only instrumental value. So, if P, Q, and R have both instrumental and noninstrumental value, and we refuse to recognize their noninstrumental value, recognizing only their instrumental value, we will not be valuing them fully, as they deserve to be valued, and will not be treating them as they deserve to be treated. Thus, part of their value is unappreciated, they will not be enjoyed to their greatest extent.[8]

This is still not an argument for taking P, Q, and R to be of more value than our happiness. As noted, we should only do this if P, Q, and R are in fact more valuable than our happiness, on top of (or independent of) their value in making us happy. The Foscos may try to acknowledge the noninstrumental value of P, Q, and R, yet still insist that nothing is more important than their own happiness. But as soon as they acknowledge that things in the world can have value apart from their instrumental value to the Foscos' happiness, they can no longer simply continue acting as if nothing is more important than their happiness: this would amount to implausibly thinking that things other than themselves have noninstrumental value, as their happiness is noninstrumentally valuable, while also insisting that nothing could have more noninstrumental value than their own happiness. Acknowledging this latter claim is false requires a denial of their way of life, but thinking it is true is absurd. If it is

<hr/>

8. In chapter 1, we gave the Foscos self-interested reasons to be moral, but this did not imply that self-interest was the only, much less the best, reason that exists for being moral; self-interested reasons were simply what would appeal to the Foscos and get them into the game. A similar point can be made here: mentioning the enjoyment of these these non-instrumentally valuable things is only to induce the Foscos to get in the game. Clearly the greatest value of something with non-instrumental value is *not* its ability to be enjoyed.

false, then they must acknowledge that how they live is inconsistent with what they recognize to be of value in the world. But if it is true that everyone's happiness has noninstrumental value, then the Foscos would have to claim that the value of their individual happiness outweighs or trumps all the rest of the noninstrumental value in the world combined, regardless of quality and quantity; they have to insist that, when all is said and done, they are the most important thing in the world. And this does seem absurd.

Imagine meeting a person who honestly thinks that his or her happiness is always more important than any other consideration or combination of considerations. What possible reason could that person give to justify such a belief? (Imagine thinking that your happiness turns out to be the most important, valuable thing in the world. What a wonderful coincidence *for you!*) But, of course, nothing could possibly substantiate the claim, for a number of reasons. Many were discussed in the first chapter, about the way all of us share the common denominator of being human beings, making no one of us fundamentally better or more valuable than any other of us. And this can be seen in the basic decency of not treating others as if they are mere tools or instruments but rather as having the proper noninstrumental value of a human being that is shared by all human beings. There is simply no property a human being could have, an "I know not what" or some *je ne sais quoi*, which would make that individual intrinsically better or more valuable than everyone else, or would make others less valuable than they in fact are. There is simply no possible justification for a person to think that his or her happiness is the most important thing in the world. And thinking it is self-defeating; it keeps one from appreciating what is truly valuable in the world.

Only when the Foscos, and egoists generally, acknowledge this can they begin to value things, themselves included, as they deserve to be valued, as they ought to be valued, which ultimately requires abandoning egoism or the idea that we ought to always be motivated by our own happiness. This is not an argument that happiness must be self-effacing or that we must alienate ourselves from our efforts to be happy in order to attain happiness.[9] It is merely an argument for appreciating our happiness for what it is, intrinsically and in relation to everything else, and for not being anything more than it in fact is.

By always aiming at one's own happiness, one ends up treating one's individual happiness as if it were more important, more valuable, than anything else in the world. This is simply not true, and none of us can act as if it were true without making a significant mistake. The argument for this does not rest on any sort of realism about what is good or what has value.[10] Even for subjectivists or relativists, who say that there are no objectively mind-independent facts about what is valuable, it still does not make sense to think and act as if one's own individual happiness is the most important thing in the world: assuming neither subjectivists nor relativists are solipsists, they will have to acknowledge that nothing can stop others from valuing their own lives and happiness just as subjectivists and relativists value theirs, and that these are relevant facts to be taken into account when properly deliberating about what ought to be done. (Subjectivists and relativists presumably do not wish to deliberate about what to do, simply being in denial of facts which are inconvenient to them.) And given this, again, it is absurd to think

9. On this view, happiness is not "self-effacing" in a manner analogous to the way consequentialism seems to counsel us to abandon consequentialism when doing so will lead to better consequences. For the claims that virtue theory or eudaimonism is self-effacing in roughly this way, see Hurka 2001. These issues come up again in §2.4 and §3.7. For a full rebuttal, see Annas 2008.
10. As acknowledged, I am a moral realist, but do not want to assume realism in the discussion here. The intention is to make the normative ideas compatible with a variety of metaethical theories. For more on my view of moral realism, see my 2001.

that the value of one's own life could outweigh or trump the value of everything else in the world.

One might still worry that this assumes some sort of objective truth about value. If we are subjectivists or relativists or some other nonrealists, then we may think people cannot be *wrong* in thinking of themselves as the most important thing in the world, since there are no correct or true answers to questions about what does or does not have value in the world. Many philosophers will be tempted to advert to a famous line of thought developed by David Hume. In the section of his *Treatise* entitled, "Of the Influencing Motives of the Will", he famously wrote, "'Tis not contrary to reason to prefer the destruction of the whole world to the scratching of my finger".[11] Hume here is defending the idea that only passions or desires can move us to act; "reason alone can never be a motive to any action of the will". "Reason", wrote Hume, "is and ought only to be the slave of the passions". Not only can reason not move one to act; Hume concludes that reason "can never oppose passion"; reason is "incapable of preventing volition". We must care about something one way or another in order to act. Our desires determine the ends of our actions as well as motivate them, while reason cannot do either. So, one might conclude that if all one cares about is oneself and one's personal happiness, then it is not contrary to reason or to the facts to think and act as if one's own happiness were the most important thing in the world.

Now, let us agree with Hume, if only for the sake of argument, that reason and belief by themselves cannot move us and that it is impossible for reason to "oppose" passion. Even if we agree that reason cannot be a psychological force or motivation contrary to the force of passion, we can see that reason can still point out

---

11. Hume 1978, bk. II, pt. III, § III.

THE MOST IMPORTANT THING IN THE WORLD

mistakes in thought or belief concerning what we are passionate about, and may "oppose" a passion founded on this kind of mistake. Hume, of course, knew this: he precedes the sentence about finger scratching with the following caveat, "Where a passion is neither founded on false suppositions, nor chuses means insufficient for the end, the understanding can neither justify nor condemn it". It may be helpful to put the quotes together and round them out with what follows:

> Where a passion is neither founded on false suppositions, nor chuses means insufficient for the end, the understanding can neither justify nor condemn it. 'Tis not contrary to reason to prefer the destruction of the whole world to the scratching of my finger. 'Tis not contrary to reason for me to chuse my total ruin, to prevent the least uneasiness of an *Indian* or a person wholly unknown to me. 'Tis as little contrary to reason to prefer even my own acknowledg'd lesser good to my greater, and have a more ardent affection for the former than the latter.

If a passion is based on false belief or improperly engages instrumental reason by choosing poor means to attain passion's end, reason can "oppose" or "condemn" the passion. Still, our passions themselves are unreasoned. One might simply have a bare "existential commitment" to the value of having unscratched fingers (or to the value of counting blades of grass).[12] The question one longs to ask Hume is how anyone could possibly be more passionate about avoiding a scratched finger than the destruction of the world, or come to prefer a lesser good to a greater one without

---

12. Allan Gibbard 1990, 155 says, "[W]e seem to distinguish between accepting something as a demand of rationality and making an idiosyncratic existential commitment to it".

making any false factual suppositions or mistakes in thought or belief. Common sense, one would think, surely insists that it is a mistake to value the less valuable over the more valuable, that it is only "not contrary to reason" to prefer the world's destruction to the scratching of a finger if it is also judged that, between the scratch and the destruction, the latter is bizarrely considered the lesser of the two evils. The value of the unscratched finger is placed above the value of the world. And we must wonder how any sane person could come to such a conclusion without making some "false suppositions". Must not there be some beliefs or suppositions about *the value of an unscratched finger* when compared to *the value of the world* (which contains the finger in the first place!) in order to prefer the world's destruction to getting scratched? If so, what are these suppositions and how could we possibly think none are false or mistaken if they yield such a preference?

Perhaps Hume did not mean to be taken literally and was only trying to dramatically make a point. Or, although he doesn't say so, perhaps he did assume that this overriding passion for an unscratched finger would have to be based on a false belief. Still, it is the example he chose and there is no obvious reason not to take him at his word, which seems to read as a claim that the understanding can neither justify nor condemn a preference for having an unscratched finger over the destruction of the world. Perhaps the preference is an existential commitment. But it is difficult to imagine a world in which no mistakes are made about what has value and in which one can prefer the monumental destruction of the world over the trivial scratching of a finger.[13] The schema of

---

13. As Christine Korsgaard points out in her 1986, 12n7, Hume (1978, 120) may have the resources to account for the problem in his discussion of the ways in which passions can influence the belief: "A coward, whose fears are easily awakened, readily assents to every

evaluation required to yield such a preference is bound to depend on some falsehood or mistake or illusion; and the burden of proof that it does not lies squarely on whoever skeptically disagrees. The destruction of the world entails the destruction of the finger, so maintaining the preference is self-defeating. Claiming that there is nothing practically irrational about self-defeating preferences is a *reductio ad absurdum par excellence*. If one prefers the destruction of the world to getting a scratch on the finger, then either one has some false beliefs about what is of value in the world, or one is irrational or insane. In any case, the only conclusion to draw is that our subjective passions ought to be subordinated to how valuable things in the world are: passions, as powerful as they may be, cannot make it rational to take something trivial as being more important or valuable than something cataclysmic.[14] (At some level, this seems analytic given the meanings of "trivial" and "cataclysmic".) If this conclusion is sound, then reason is *not* the slave of the passions: it is in fact "contrary to reason" to let things of lesser value be treated as if they have greater value than those things which are of greater value.

(This does not beg the question against Hume, but it does not defeat him either; it does point to the ways in which his skepticism is at odds with good common sense and bears a greater argumentative burden than he acknowledges.)

Just as it is hard to comprehend valuing world destruction over finger scratching, it is hard to understand how the Foscos can think and act as if their personal happiness is the most important thing in

account of danger he meets with". There may be a way to construe the coward's beliefs about what is dangerous as irrational and not merely false, though Hume does not develop the thought in this direction.

14. Ruth Chang draws a similar but less exaggerated distinction between "nominals" and "notables" in a discussion of ways in which values can appear incomparable or incommensurable when they really are neither of these. See Chang 1998.

the world. Even if one is truly the cleverest, funniest, kindest, and generally most wonderful person in the world (or the strongest, most powerful, and ruthless person in the world), this still could not justify believing that one's happiness is the most important thing in the world.

Thinking of our own happiness, or the happiness of those about whom we are partial, as more important than anything else in the world requires acting as if we are more important than everything else in the world put together. Thus, if we are *not* willing to sacrifice everything in the world for the sake of our own happiness, then we have to acknowledge that we have recognized that some thing, or some combination of things, is more important than our own happiness. This is the thin edge of the wedge that leads to the leveraged downfall of Fosco-style egoism and improper partiality.

Once we have realized that our happiness is not the most important thing in the world, we have begun a re-evaluation of egocentric values, and we may thereby learn to put ourselves in our proper place in the world. Doing so will force us to come to grips with how important our happiness truly is. Again, we do not need to conclude that our happiness is not important or that we ought never to act out of self-interest. Indeed, as noted above and discussed in the next section, morality requires us to take special care of ourselves. Still, we can now see how living as if our own happiness is always our ultimate goal can only be the result of a misapprehension or misevaluation of what is of value in the world and of how important our happiness is relative to everything else. It would be self-defeating of us to deny it, since the denial involves being wrong about the value of our happiness. Rather, we will be happiest when we value our happiness for what it is, as opposed to deceiving ourselves into believing it is something more or less than it is.

The paradox of happiness arises in part when people make the mistake of thinking that their happiness is the ultimate, final end of all their actions, which entails not understanding the comparative value human beings have relative to each other. But this is not the only mistake that generates the paradox of happiness. The first mistake, as discussed by Butler, is conflating *happiness* with *what makes one happy*. The second is overvaluing one's happiness when compared to other things of value in the world. And the third is conflating the reasons for thinking something is valuable with the reasons for pursuing it: Foscos see their own happiness as their goal and value or disvalue all other things in the world only insofar as they contribute to or hinder their happiness. Things are good or have value if they make the Foscos happy, and the only reason to pursue those things is to bring about happiness. We can agree that things can have instrumental value because they make a person happy. But we will say more than that if we assert that we will be made happy if we bring things into our lives because they have a value that is independent of this instrumental value. We can think that P, Q, and R are good or have the value they do because they make us happy, or we can think that having them makes us happy because they are good or valuable in themselves, that their value does not depend on whether or not they make us happy. In this latter case, we are (in fact) instrumentally made happy by P, Q, and R, in that they cause us to be happy, but what we value about them need not depend on this instrumental ability. Rather, we can value them because of something distinct from their happiness-producing ability; we can be made happy because we have brought these independently good and valuable things into our lives. In this way, they do not cause us to be happy as much as they actually, constitutively become *part* of our happiness. We can value P, Q, and R as means to the end of our own happiness, but we can also value them as ends in themselves, as valuable independently of how they may contribute to our happiness.

In spotting the Foscos' mistakes and limitations, we can find a way to carry out a normative reconciliation of self and other that avoids Sidgwick's Fundamental Dualism of Practical Reason, as discussed in chapter 1. The trick is to value only what is truly of value, what is truly good, and only to the proper degree.[15] We can agree that our own individual lives have value, that our individual happiness is important, but the trick is to value ourselves and our happiness appropriately, as being neither more nor less important than it deserves.

To put this in terms of partiality and impartiality, improper partiality is due to improper evaluation. When we value things improperly, we end up making mistakes. But when we value what is of value properly, or correctly and truly, and act accordingly, then we will do as well in our lives as we can. We will see the option of being unfairly partial to ourselves for the sham it is: if we know that X is more important than our individual happiness and yet act as if this were false, then our "happiness" will not reflect our values. By our own lights, our "happiness" will be fraudulent because it comes at the expense of something we recognize as being more important than our happiness. If we are honest with ourselves, then we will recognize that we only stand a chance of becoming happy if we value our lives appropriately, relative to the other things that are of value in the world. This weak form of *objectivity*, which rules out only mistakes and self-deception, and requires a clear-eyed, unprejudiced view of the contents of the world, is all that the argument needs to move

---

15. This is, of course, not an original thought. See Aristotle 1998, 1140a, 24–26. For modern examples, see Murdoch 1971; Foot 2001; Hursthouse 1999; and Adams 1999, chap. 3, as well as his 2006; and Annas 2011.

forward. (More on objectivity in §2.5.) Given the Foscos' commitments to realpolitick, to seeing beyond the convenient appearances to the underlying truth, there is even good reason for them to agree to the correctness and value of valuing things correctly.

The egoists and Foscos of the world think that their happiness is the most important thing in the world. But this puts blinders on them, keeping them from seeing much of the value in the world and all the value that is independent of what instrumentally brings them happiness. Only by seeing that we are not the most important thing in the world will we begin to see things aright. Being improperly and immorally partial to ourselves, or our families, or our communities, or to anything gives us false beliefs and expectations about how to live well and be happy. This is not, by itself, to set up a particular alternate set of values in opposition to the Foscos in a question-begging way, but only to spot a self-defeating error in their ways of thinking, valuing, and being in the world.

Falsely granting or unjustifiably withholding value is the result of inappropriate partiality, and this lack of correspondence (or coherence?) between what we think has value and what truly does have value in the world works in a subtle but persistent way against happiness. To understand "the Good Life" in improperly partial ways is to undermine one's "self". But it is not only egoists and Foscos who do this. As we saw in chapter 1, though cashed out in slightly different terms, an analogous problem plagues traditional "moralists" like Kant and Sidgwick, since both think that living as well as possible, living as one ought to live, requires a strict and alienating impartiality that bifurcates practical rationality and turns people into "houses divided against themselves". This impartiality is as improper as the Foscos' partiality, albeit less destructive. The Foscos and the moralists alike find a schism in practical rationality between the egocentric consideration of the self and the appropriate consideration of others, between what makes us "happy" and what "morality" demands. As noted above, the Foscos side with pure self-interest, and Kant and Sidgwick side with pure "morality", and this is an unnecessary dilemma.

What is preferable is a picture of practical rationality that does not require us to choose between sacrificing our self-respect (or what is otherwise of value in the world) for the sake of what makes us happy, and sacrificing our happiness for the sake of self-respect. The key lies in fitting our conceptions of our happiness and the Good Life *into* our conception of what is truly good or of value in the world. This is neither self-effacement nor sublimation, but commensuration. We are justified in acknowledging to ourselves and to others the value of our individual lives and the respect this properly demands. No one is inherently better than anyone else. And sometimes circumstances demand that we acknowledge that something is more important than we are, and this, by our own lights, demands that in certain circumstances we do something which in ordinary circumstances would be out of the question. We cannot do better or end up happier than to give due weight to the value of our own lives in relation to the value of the rest of the world. We only harm our ability to be happy when we deny these truths. We ought to be partial toward ourselves to the proper degree, and no more. If we understand that "a happy human life" results from living in the best possible way and if we value other things in the world to the degree they deserve, and no more, then we avoid schisms in practical reason and paradoxes in our concept of *happiness*. If we always act for the sake of what is good while paying proper attention to the good of our own lives, then we may not be as happy as is humanly possible, but we will be as happy as it is possible for us to be, given the context of our lives, such as we find them.

Michael Stocker has an excellent discussion of the way in which egoism cannot properly account for the value of things in the world, and he then shows how this same problem affects traditionally moralistic theories about how to live.[16] By his lights, the problem begins with the thought that egoists cannot give a proper account of "love, friendship, affection, fellow feeling, and community". Focusing on love, Stocker writes:

> [I]t is essential to the very concept of love that one care for the beloved, that one be prepared to act for the sake of the beloved. More strongly, one must care for the beloved and act for that person's sake as a final goal; the beloved, or the beloved's welfare or interest, must be a final goal of one's concern and action.
>
> To the extent that my consideration for you—or even my trying to make you happy—comes from my desire to lead an untroubled life, a life personally pleasing for me, I do not act for your sake. In short, to the extent that I act in various ways toward you with the final goal of getting pleasure—or, more generally, good—for myself, I do not act for your sake. (1976, 456)

Fosco-style egoists cannot take someone else's interests to be more important than their own. They cannot willingly forego their own interests for the sake of something which is taken by them to be more important or better, for ex hypothesi, their own good is their highest value. If egoism is correct, then even our "love" for our beloved should always be functionally dependent on our own interests.[17] If egoism is correct, then one ought not to love the beloved for his or her own sake, but rather one ought to love the beloved

16. Stocker 1976.
17. The phrase "functionally dependent" is from Slote 1964.

for one's own sake, for the instrumental value the beloved brings to one's own life. And as a picture of human love, this is shamelessly bleak. Undoubtedly, there are egoists who think that they genuinely love others but, if they are genuinely egoists, this is simply false. And the degree to which they genuinely do love others, the degree to which their beloved's interests are a final end for them, they are not being true to their egoistic principles. The same holds true for anyone who is inappropriately partial to anything.

Stocker argues that the problem for egoists is that they cannot reconcile their reasons for acting with their values. This establishes a schizophrenia in their thought and, as noted, a similar problem exists for traditional moralists. Here, we can bring Williams back into the discussion: moralists end up with a similar schism in their thinking because they espouse impartial thought as the means to discerning the right thing to do, when it is impossible to think this way without sometimes having "one thought too many".

2.3 TAKING CARE OF YOURSELF

Giving up on egoism (or other forms of inappropriate partiality) does not, however, require that we ignore our self-interest or the interests of whatever it is that we care about. (Below, references to forms of proper and improper partiality beyond the self are often left out but are not to be forgotten.) What is required is that we put ourselves and our happiness in proper perspective. It is reasonable for us to take ourselves as central to our own lives.[18] Most of the time, no one can know competent adults as well as they know themselves. And so other people are only rarely in a better position than

18. Cottingham 1991, 1998, 2010.

we are to paternalistically say what is good for us and what is not.[19] (The situation is obviously different for children; exceptions for adults may arise between some longtime spouses or between therapists and patients.[20]) And so most of us rightly take it for granted that we are more responsible for our own actions than we can be for anyone else's, and vice versa. And given this, it is reasonable that we look out for ourselves with special care, acknowledging that others will do the same for themselves.[21]

If the "Argument from Epistemology", given in §1.7, is sound, then justice demands that we treat ourselves fairly, on the pain of self-disrespect. The question is whether or not being fair to ourselves allows, or even requires, us to take good care of ourselves. And the quick and obvious answer is that it does, for a putative moral theory which holds that we are not justified in taking care of ourselves whenever possible would fail on that point alone. Of course, we still have to figure out what counts as "taking good care of oneself" and this is, as we have seen, a large part of the game. But we have learned that it certainly does not mean "doing what is in one's self-interest, no matter what". A slightly less tautologous and perhaps more persuasive answer is that we frequently feel justified in our day-to-day lives in behaving partially toward the people we love, relative to strangers, and the best argument to justify this particular form of partiality is that to deny it is tantamount to a denial of love, which yields a morality that is inhumane and unlivable.

If we are sometimes justified in being partial toward those we love, then it is odd to say, as the more stringent moralities do, that

19. Mill 1992, chap. 4.
20. Thanks to Andrew Schroeder for this thought.
21. There is a structural similarity here to what Samuel Scheffler has called "agent centered prerogatives", though the present thesis remains anti-consequentialist for reasons discussed in §1.2, and which will come up again in three paragraphs.

treating ourselves as well as we treat them is not justified. Even the Bible entreats us to "Love thy neighbor as thyself", not to "Love thyself as thy neighbor". As the cliché goes, coined in a quote from Falk in §1.3, "Charity begins at home". So, just as there are times when we ought to be partial to those we love, there will be times when we ought to be partial to ourselves. Happily, people who are not living in extremely difficult circumstances can easily find ways to indulge loved ones in a manner that is completely partial but comes nowhere near to impropriety. (We may buy birthday gifts for our children and not the children of our neighbors, for example, and this lacks impartiality yet seems wholly proper.[22]) Similarly, those of us who are not too unfortunately placed should not find it hard to indulge ourselves with propriety. Those who are living in dire straits have unfortunately less opportunity to be partial to themselves or those they love, though of course have no less right to be.

Naturally, the questions become more difficult and pressing when circumstances are more difficult and pressing. There is likely no general answer to the question, "When ought we to be partial to ourselves?" Herbert Freeman Jr., the Hurricane Katrina survivor discussed above in §1.3, decided that in his situation he would not treat himself as an exception, would not be partial to the filial piety he felt toward his deceased mother (though we must acknowledge that feeling threatened by a soldier carrying an automatic weapon almost surely influenced his decision). His was, perhaps, a tough call. We can easily imagine situations in which we should be willing to "make sacrifices" to our self-interest because we think partiality to ourselves would be no better than, or is, a form of cheating. (More on such sacrifices in a moment.) On the other hand, we can imagine—and this is the point—situations similar to Freeman's in

---

22. Thanks to Sam Wheeler for the example.

which his failing to insist on being treated as an exception would be wrong, in which a person ought to indulge his or her filial piety (or self-interest) and in which no one else concerned would be similarly justified.[23] We should acknowledge that there are times when one ought not act in accordance with the rules which purport to apply to everyone.

Falk's case of the dutiful daughter, also discussed in §1.3, is one in which we think she ought to be partial toward herself, by putting her interests over the interests of her oppressive parent, despite the common "rules" about filial piety (and, contra consequentialism, this is true even if putting her parent's interests above her own would produce the best overall outcome). If we can say that Freeman might have been right to stay with his mother, it is clearer that the dutiful daughter ought to leave her onerous parent. The dutiful daughter is a good example of justified partiality toward oneself, even more so an example wherein the partiality does not seem to contravene morality in the least; if it did, it would make no sense to say that she *ought* to leave.[24] Rather, we think that since morality, understood as schematically as possible, requires us to "do the right thing" and that "the right thing" in this case is for the daughter to refuse to be servile to an unjustifiably demanding parent, we conclude that morality requires the daughter to act against the interests of her parent, against the strictures of "filial piety", and in her own self-interest.

<hr/>

23. This is not to suggest that it is impossible for others to be similarly justified or to say that similarly exceptional cases should not be treated similarly. It is merely to point out that exceptional cases exist and that they cannot be specified in general terms that would allow them to be articulated as part of a moral rule or principle. There are always similar hypothetical cases and similar possible worlds. The important practical point is that, at the actual world, a person, being unique as each person is, can find him- or herself in a situation in which no other actual person would be justified in doing what he or she is justified in doing.
24. See as well the cases discussed in Hampton 1993a, also cited in §1.3.

One might object, noting that treating oneself as an "exception to the rules" or as an exceptional case to which normal rules do not apply is not the same as "being partial" to oneself, that "being partial" to oneself requires "breaking the rules". But when the husband, without thinking twice, saves his drowning wife over a stranger, so that he certainly does not have "one thought too many", we do not in any way take him to be breaking "the rules". (Let's even stipulate that the stranger would have been easier to save than the wife, but that this fact did not enter into the husband's thoughts.) The "rules", whatever they may be, cannot be such that they prevent a person from doing the right thing: the reason we have rules in the first place is to help us do the right thing; rules make no sense if they are set up in a way that defeats the ends they are meant to promote. (This would, again, be self-defeatingly paradoxical.) Of course, there are plenty of ways to be partial to oneself which do "break the rules", but these will represent immoral choices, and the reasons to not indulge in them have already been discussed. What is important is that "the rules" of morality actually do require us to act with proper partiality toward ourselves (or our loved ones) in certain circumstances and do not require us always, in every circumstance, to think or act impartially. A fortiori, sometimes one ought not to consider things from an impartial point of view lest one have "one thought too many".

So, there will be times when we ought to be partial toward ourselves, when morality fortunately tells us to do what is in our personal best interest. The difficult cases to understand are those in which morality seems to require us to act against our best interest, in ways that seem contrary to the idea of "taking good care of oneself". Indeed, these are probably the cases the Foscos would seize upon to rationalize immoral behavior: those in which it seems more rational to be immoral than moral, given the seeming sacrifices morality requires.

It is crucial to understand correctly the uses of "seem" in the previous two sentences. If we realize that some things in the world are more important than we are (because they concern issues or numbers of people that may swamp our self-interest or because we have chosen to make them so important to us for our own personal reasons), then, when taking care of these things requires us to put them before our self-interest, to make a "sacrifice" that we would otherwise not make, we should nevertheless be willing to make it. Morality can *seem* to require us to act in ways that constitute personal sacrifice. If, however, we say that morality represents a justified defense or promotion of what is truly of value in the world and that a person living the Good Life can be fully committed to what is truly valuable, then what may *seem* to others like a "sacrifice" may in fact be an expression of that person's highest, most deeply felt values. There is a sense in which we cannot sacrifice what is most important to us when we act on our most deeply held values: when virtuous people do not cheat in order to win a prize, they do not think of "not having the prize" as a sacrifice, on the contrary, they would rather not have it than to "win" it falsely by cheating. In this sense, however it may seem, morality actually never requires us to make a sacrifice. And when we have to choose the lesser of two evils, morality always requires us to make the smallest possible sacrifice.

These ideas rest on an important reconceptualization of what a *sacrifice* is.[25] While it may seem that the things we take to be more valuable than ourselves require us to make sacrifices, in an important sense, they never do. Whenever we have to choose between attending to our own good or to some other valuable

25. The account of *sacrifices* that follows is similar to what can be found in Badhwar 1993 and Rosati 2009.

thing in the world, and the choices are mutually exclusive and exhaustive, we are in a situation in which, colloquially, we must "choose the lesser of two evils". When we choose the least bad option, we may feel that what we chose was the best option but still a regrettable one, notwithstanding its choice-worthiness. And when we have to choose between two genuine evils, we should readily admit that the lesser of two evils is still a regrettable evil; it is harder for us to appreciate its choice-worthiness since it would never be choice-worthy ceteris paribus.[26] The easiest way to appreciate this is to consider the counterfactual result: how things would have turned out had we chosen the other horn of the dilemma, the "greater of the two evils". During a famine, one ought to feed one's children, even if this means going hungry oneself. Of course, there are situations and there are situations, and if the only way to save one's children is to eat, then one ought to eat.[27] But if food is merely scarce, one ought to go hungry so that one's children do not. In this case, my going hungry is a lesser evil than my children going hungry. If one is concerned with living as well as possible given the circumstances that one happens to find oneself in, then living as well as possible may require one to go hungry.[28]

---

26. But see Brandt 1972 and Hare 1972, who both seem to think that if one does what one ought to do, one can thereby never have a reason or cause for regret, or have justified bad feelings about it, even in cases of choosing the lesser of two evils. This, in effect, denies the phenomenon of having "dirty hands" on the grounds that one has done "the right thing". For discussion of "dirty hands", see Stocker 1990.

27. This sort of priority is captured in the instructions we receive on airplanes to put our own oxygen mask on first, before a child's. Thanks to Ginny Faber for this example.

28. Compare with Badhwar 1993: "the premise is that if a person *identifies* with values she regards as more important—if these values are embodied in her central dispositions of thought, emotion, and action—*then* her greatest interests will be identical with these values".

Now, in what sense is going hungry in this circumstance a "sacrifice"? One will of course experience the discomfort of hunger, and so one sacrifices the satisfaction of feeling sated. But there is a more important sense in which to think of one's hunger as a regrettable sacrifice is to abandon the values one has chosen to live by, namely the value that one's children are more important to oneself than one's own "Dear Self". Of course, it is unfortunate that one may not have enough food for the whole family, but such conditions are sometimes beyond a person's control. Given the choice of going hungry or having one's children go hungry, one ought to choose to go hungry. Given that one values one's children more than oneself, the option to be sated while one's children starve is worse, the greater of the two evils. Indeed, in a sense, given who one is and the values one has accepted, to feed oneself first may not even be a "live option".[29] If that is the case, given one's values, then giving one's food to one's children is starkly *not* making a sacrifice, given that one has no other choice. Of course, if one had the choice, one would choose that there be enough food to go around.[30] But since, ex hypothesi, eating is not a live option, one willingly, voluntarily, gives the food to one's children. In these horrid circumstances, this is not just "what one ought to do", not just the best option, it is the only option. Thinking of it as a "sacrifice" requires singling out the value of taking care of oneself and isolating it from all of one's other values. If we assume only this narrow, purely selfish,

29. I take the term "live option" from James 1896, 327–47. Also in the background are Frankfurt's "volitional necessities" from his 2004.
30. From Plato 1994, 469b:

> Polus: Would you prefer then suffering wrong to doing it?
> Socrates: I should *prefer* neither for my own part...

and egocentric point of view, then giving food to our children is a sacrifice. If our point of view is that of our lives as a whole, which includes being a loving parent, however, there is no true sacrifice, since eating while one's children starve is not a live option.

Of course, famine and starvation make the story dramatic. Civil disobedients or whistle-blowers who choose to do the right thing and end up in jail can be equally dramatic. Even more night-marishly far-fetched, we can imagine the evil genius who forces us to choose between saving our child and the murder of millions of people. But we do not need such dramatic examples to see the point. Instead of having to choose who will live and who will die, we might just as easily imagine having to choose between going on a cruise and saving for our children's education. Perhaps choosing the cruise is a live option, especially so if we have always dreamed about taking a cruise and remain strongly tempted. So, if we choose to not go on the cruise, we may in one sense be making a sacrifice. But it is only a "sacrifice" if we isolate the value of the cruise from the full set of values that together only justify the choice to not go on the cruise. Yes, it might be pleasant, in the short run, to go on the cruise. But foregoing a short-term pleasure out of respect for our most deeply held values, such as the value of our child's education, values built up over the course of a lifetime, is only a sacrifice on an uninformed or incomplete point of view. If we stand back and consider our life as a whole, there really is no choice at all.[31] Ultimately, we are not making a sacrifice when we are being true to our most deeply held values.

---

31. "[Reflective human beings] want to be able to stand back from the motives and reasons and values that influence their choices, and submit to them only if they are acceptable", Nagel 1986, 127.

Perhaps the point here trades on the parent-child relationship. What about when one's values lead one to sacrifice one's own material good for the sake of a stranger? Again, we should compare acting on all of one's values and making the "sacrifice" against sacrificing one's values as a whole for the sake of the some material good. There is a sense in which whatever is chosen, something is "sacrificed". But morality does not demand that we be unfair to ourselves and our values; indeed, it requires us to take good care of ourselves and disallows our being unfair to ourselves. So, we should go ahead and choose the lesser evil, which in this case is foregoing the material good for the sake of the stranger.

The moral of the story at this point is that if you are moral and true to yourself, and if you act on what you truly value, then to the greatest possible extent, you will make no sacrifices.

So, we should take good care of ourselves while recognizing that we are not the most important thing in the world. We now know that morality prescribes that we endeavor to take as good care of what we value most as is possible, given the lives that we happen to be living. This is not to say that the philosophical literature is in agreement on this score. As noted, plenty of moral philosophy and religion demands that we be moral saints and always sacrifice ourselves and our interests for the sake of others, even strangers.[32] If we adopt "the social conception of *morality*", described in chapter 1, in which morality exists only to act as a check on our self-interest, then naturally we will view morality as being incompatible with being good to and taking care of ourselves. And we should not be surprised to find that some, like the Foscos, who accept this conception of *morality*, reject living morally due to all the "sacrifices" it requires of us. At

---

32. See, for example, Wolf 1982 and Finlay 2008.

this point, hopefully, these conclusions can easily be seen as a *reductio ad absurdum* of the social or impartial conception of *morality*. If someone or something tells us that our own concerns should have no more importance to us than the concerns of strangers, and that strangers are similarly supposed to view our concerns as being just as important as their own, then we all end up being as responsible for everyone else as we are for ourselves. This is morality deformed.

Given how the paradox of happiness shows us how and why we must give up thinking of our own happiness as the most important thing in the world, and given the rejection of the self-alienating social conception of *morality*, it seems to make more sense to say, along with common sense, that morality tells us to value what is objectively good in the world, and this entails valuing ourselves appropriately. Where only adults are involved and there are no pre-existing relations between them, in most cases they will be justified in taking care of themselves before taking care of others. Any humane morality will tell us to treat ourselves kindly and to even indulge ourselves occasionally, even regularly, especially when this can be harmlessly done at no real cost to anyone else. (We should also, of course, avoid indulgently spoiling ourselves or our loved ones.) The minimal claim is that morality, when correctly conceived and even at its most properly stringent, will nevertheless always require us to be at the very least fair and just to ourselves, and not only fair and just to everyone else. And being fair and just to ourselves requires us occasionally to be partial toward ourselves.

Another way to make this same point is to see, once again, morality as the study of how best to live: it requires us to tend to ourselves and to those close to us, to care for ourselves, our loved ones, and what we find that has value in the world, as best we can, given the circumstances in which we find ourselves.

2.4 BEYOND THE PARADOX OF HAPPINESS

Contra Sidgwick, the problem of the paradox of happiness is not caused by misplaced attention. It is rather that adopting certain conceptions of *happiness* force us into a position in which our self-interest or our drive to be happy alienates us from those things in life which are unprejudicially valuable and are the only things capable of making us truly happy.

As suggested, there is a way through the paradox. It involves adopting the proper attitude toward our happiness, relative to the attitude we take toward what is objectively valuable and makes us truly happy. We have already touched on some of the ways in which we must value ourselves and our happiness appropriately vis-à-vis other things of value in the world. But there is more to be said about the process by which we may come to the point where we are properly valuing ourselves and others, or which processes will lead us to get it right. We can, in fact, take one step further with Sidgwick. For, even if he misdiagnosed the problem which brings on the paradox as one of distracted attention, he did see the practical way through it.

According to Sidgwick, there is a recognizable though inchoately understood process which, when identified and understood, will allow us to transcend the paradox. He writes, in regard to his Fundamental Paradox, the following:

For it is an experience only too common among men, in whatever pursuit they may be engaged, that they let the original object and goal of their efforts pass out of view, and come to regard the means to this end as the ends in themselves: so that they at last even sacrifice the original end to the attainment of what is only secondarily and derivatively desirable. (1907, 137)[33]

It will be important to take a closer look at the mechanism by which something that is only originally valued as a means to an end can become something which is valued as an end in itself.

The distinction between means and ends is basic, and the phenomenon Sidgwick describes is easily recognizable; indeed something similar was discussed above regarding the ways in which objects may have both instrumental and noninstrumental value. We begin with a pursuit of end E and choose M as our means to E. Upon becoming more and more involved with M, we may learn to see its value in a new way, and after re-evaluating M, we may take it to be more important, of more value, than E. At this point, we pursue M for its own sake, not for its instrumental value as a means to E. A student might, for example, begin the study of an art, activity, or discipline purely to fulfill a degree requirement. And becoming familiar with the discipline, the student may continue on in it because he or she finds it intrinsically interesting, independent of the role it plays in fulfilling requirements.

---

33. This is not to suggest that Sidgwick is the only or the first philosopher to develop the line of thought that is to follow. It is arguably found in the Stoic theory of appropriation (*oikeiosis*). As Cicero puts it:

> A man's first affiliation is towards those things that are in accordance with nature. But as soon as he has acquired understanding... and has seen the regularity and, so to speak, the harmony of conduct, he comes to value this far higher than all those objects of his initial affection; and he draws the rational conclusion that this constitutes the highest human good which is worthy of praise and desirable for its own sake. (1914, III, 17)

The translation is from Long and Sedley, 1987, 360; for discussion, see Annas 1993, Becker 1998, and Gill 2004.

So, what is involved in this re-evaluation? The situation is more or less complicated, depending on whether or not M has any other reason to exist other than E. If M is a hammer and E is carpentry or building, then there is not much more to hammers than that they are used to pound in nails or pull them out when necessary. One may come to appreciate the utility of the hammer in new ways, appreciate the good design in, say, the curve of the claw which pulls out nails, but absent very special pleading (a strong sentimental attachment to a particular hammer?), one will never find a reason to subordinate the importance of building to the importance of the hammer, since the latter exists wholly for the sake of the former.

If, however, M exists for reasons that have nothing to do with E, the situation is more complex. In such a case, M may have ends of its own, independent of M's ability to bring about E. To have a better sense of the complexity here, let us contrast an impoverished case with a more complex one. Say two people, Xena and Yvonne, have the same E and choose the same M, where M is also (instrumentally, intrinsically, and/or constitutively) valuable for reasons that have nothing to do with E. Xena, we may imagine, masters the use of M for the purpose of attaining E by investigating all the different ways that M can produce E. Xena never considers M independent of its ability to bring about E, never considers M's other values or ends at all. But since Xena can get M to reliably bring about E without having to consider these other ends of M, Xena sees no need to do more. Contrast this to Yvonne, who learns to make M bring about E, but who also considers M independent of its instrumental ability to bring about E; Yvonne learns about M's other ends and values and how these are brought about. She may do this out of pure curiosity or an enthusiasm to become better at making M bring about E. Either way, Yvonne learns about M in ways that Xena does not and cannot appreciate without learning the same lessons. Yvonne's understanding about M will be more complete and objective than Xena's since it is based on the consideration of M as it is, in itself, independent of E. This knowledge may not necessarily make Yvonne better at making M bring about E, but very often it will. This is because Yvonne will be better than Xena at taking care of M, based on the knowledge that Yvonne has about M that Xena lacks. Xena's care for M may well be lopsided given her ignorance of other aspects of M that Yvonne appreciates. Xena's care of M will be geared toward its ability to bring about E, while Yvonne's care will be more wholesome for M itself. And since Yvonne can take better care of M as a whole than Xena can, Yvonne will more reliably make M bring about E than Xena.

What can happen next, depending on the ways in which M is valuable, is that Yvonne may learn to appreciate M's value as much or even more than E. How this might happen psychologically will depend on how Yvonne learns about M's value, though happily there seems to be no reason to think that the details of this learning process would affect how we conceptualize the experience of re-evaluation mentioned by Sidgwick. The fact is that many people, though perhaps not people like Xena, have had the experience of learning to appreciate the value of something independently of what it can do for them. And while the value of M, independent of its ability to bring about E, might be dwarfed by the value of E, it need not be. Let's assume that E is a final end of Yvonne, and a means to it is M. After spending some time employing M for the sake of E, she learns enough about M to decide that the ends of M, or M considered as an end in itself, are more important or valuable than E itself is. Of course, this does not imply that E has lost any of its value, but it does imply that if Yvonne sincerely thinks that M is more valuable than E, then Yvonne will choose (weakness of will aside) to act for the sake of M's ends before acting for the sake of E. This need not entail that Yvonne cease to use M for the sake of E, but merely that if a forced choice between them arose, Yvonne would reliably choose M. Of course, since Xena lacks Yvonne's knowledge of M's value, Xena will think "sacrificing" E for the sake of M is foolishness itself. In this, Xena may be totally wrong.

So, the experience described by Sidgwick is familiar, and establishes a lack of parity between people like Xena and those like Yvonne. People like Yvonne have an understanding of M that people like Xena cannot comprehend. Nevertheless, there will be those cunning egoists, like the Foscos, who realize that the way to get the best performance out of M in bringing about E will be to learn about M as fully as possible, including learning about M independent of its usefulness in bringing about E. They need not re-evaluate M or M's ends as being more important than E, but they may think that if they act *as if* M and M's ends were valuable in their own right, they can do better at getting E through M. We can treat things *as if* they were ends in themselves, even though we really do not value them as such; this is one way to do the right thing for the wrong reasons. To behave in this "as if" manner is to be manipulative, in the pejorative sense of the term: we might learn that treating some M duplicitously, as if it were valued in and for itself when it is truly not, is the best way to get the most instrumental value out of it. If people set out to "use" others for their own ends, they may act as if they care about these other people for their own sake, treating them as if they were valued as ends in themselves without really so valuing them. People can, and those like Fosco will, treat means as if they are ends and yet ultimately use or discard them as mere means when this is most convenient.

As noted, we can start out treating something as merely a means to an end and go on to see those means as more valuable than the original end. When this happens, what was once merely means *becomes* our end. And we can contrast this with the "as if" case we find with the Foscos. Let's call the former a "genuine re-evaluation" and the latter an "ersatz re-evaluation". While both the genuine and ersatz re-evaluations may appear indistinguishable throughout a variety of contexts and circumstances, they are in fact, at bottom, always psychologically distinguishable (even if not through mere introspection): the difference between them ultimately determines our motives when interacting with what we are treating as (if it were) valuable as an end in itself. If the re-evaluation is ersatz, then at bottom we do not really care about what we are in fact only using as a tool or an instrument, and this will become apparent whenever the "re-evaluated" M requires a "sacrifice" paid in the coin of E. If the re-evaluation is genuine, then we are ultimately motivated by the objective value of M in itself, and not merely by its usefulness in bringing about E.[34]

And at this point we are (finally!) in a position to fully see our way through the paradox of happiness. The paradox tells us that we cannot be as happy as we can be, if our goal is to be as happy as we can be. We begin with Butler's distinction between our happiness and what makes us happy. Originally, we are interested in what makes us happy because it makes us happy; that is, for only its instrumental value. As we then become invested in what makes us happy, we can begin to see past what it does for us and start to see it as it is in itself. This is a natural outgrowth of seeing the instrumental value in something: we will become most effective in extracting instrumental value from something if we understand the instrument itself as well as possible, which in certain cases will result in valuing it intrinsically, independent of its instrumental value, and sometimes as being ultimately of greater value than the end for which it was originally being used as an instrument. This is how to become as

---

34. Fosco might reply at this point that this is not a reason to favor genuine over ersatz re-evaluation. The response to this is to revert to the arguments about the harms of immorality explained in chapter 1.

happy as possible without aiming at becoming as happy as possible. The solution to the paradox follows from this.

Now, of course, we can be wrong about what will make us happy, but we need not be. And if we get it right, then that which makes us most happy is highly likely to also have noninstrumental value. This result in fact seems correct, for it makes little sense to think that bringing something of mere instrumental value into our lives is going to make us happy: our happiness is not some switch which only needs instrumental flipping by the right tool. It makes more sense to think that bringing what is objectively good, what is of value in itself, into our lives is what will make our lives go well and be part of, or contribute constitutively to, our happiness. So, if we have chosen well, and brought into our lives what in fact makes us happy, and we then begin to appreciate its intrinsic value, it begins to *partly constitute* our happiness instead of merely being instrumental to it. We will see the intrinsic value of what brings happiness into our lives and we may then begin to treat it as an end in itself.

At this point, we are taking happiness to be the goal of our lives, treating our own lives as ends in themselves, as having intrinsic value. We are also treating what makes us genuinely happy as intrinsically valuable, and treating it as an end in itself. But there still might be situations in which we have to choose between our happiness and what truly makes us happy. Since our motivational structures are divided, we are bound to sometimes be at war with ourselves. Seeing past the paradox, coming to terms with ourselves, requires us to reconcile these two values, since refusing to do so will split our motivation and may well keep us from taking good care of *either* final end. If we automatically determine that our happiness is more important than that which makes us happy, then we will not take as good care of what makes us happy as possible. In other words, if we always value our happiness over what makes us happy, we will end up undermining what makes us happy for the (putative) sake of our happiness (otherwise known as "burning down the house to roast the pig"). This will not be true, however, if we think that what makes us happy is more important than our happiness. Obviously, taking something else to be of more value than ourselves will only be correct when we find something that both makes us happy and which we think is truly as valuable or more valuable than our own happiness (as, for example, parents ought to think of their children).

Let's assume that we find something like this (as parents do). If we take care of it well, our happiness will, for the most part, take care of itself: barring great misfortune (a subject of §3.7), if we value what is unprejudicially valuable, happiness will follow. If we invest ourselves fully in what makes us happy, and if we have chosen well in this regard, then there is no further reason for us to be motivated by our own happiness per se on top of being already motivated by what we already take to be valuable. Again, this is not "self-effacing" since we are still valuing our happiness as part of "what is of value in the world" and valuing it with proper partiality. Our own happiness would only have an independent reason to enter into our deliberations if taking care of what we think makes us happy fails to do so, presumably because of some mistake we have made in figuring out what makes us happy. And at those times, we may find that what we thought would make us happy does not, because it does not have the value that we thought it did. (We fall in love thinking our beloved is a good person, when in fact he or she is a scoundrel.) A second re-evaluation may now be required. But apart from reconsidering possible past mistakes about what makes us happy, considering our own happiness, in itself, becomes otiose. That the issue of our own happiness may rear its head when we confront our mistakes in re-evaluation shows that *happiness*, on this view, is not self-effacing.

Insofar as caring about our happiness interferes with our caring about what makes us happy, caring about our happiness is self-defeating. Tending to what truly makes us happy is what will make us happy, though we must not be motivated to tend to it because of its instrumental value for our own happiness (this is ersatz re-evaluation): rather, we must *genuinely* be motivated to tend to it because it is itself of value, as an end in itself, and for no other reason. Doing less would be to take less good care of what makes us happy than is possible, which will to that degree interfere with our becoming as happy as possible.

Living as well and being as happy as we can be requires us to genuinely give up on a view of our happiness as the most valuable thing there is. Thus, our happiness should not be what pre-eminently motivates us, it should not be our goal, our "ruling principle", our "that for the sake of which" all our actions are engaged. This is not self-effacing, it is growing up. We must get past our selves, we must *outgrow* the view of our happiness which makes it the prime motivator of our lives. And at this point, merely acknowledging that one's happiness is objectively no more valuable to oneself than another person's happiness is to that other person will force a re-evaluation of automatically acting for the sake of one's happiness. With Falk's "dutiful daughter" in mind, even if one determines in a particular case that one's happiness does merit being treated partially, as the most important value present, there will be other times in which there will be no plausible rationale for being partial to oneself, for treating one's happiness as if it were of utmost import or the single most valuable end to pursue. Only by learning the lesson that we must value our happiness for what it is, neither more nor less, will we start seeing the things in the world, ourselves included, for what they truly are and are truly worth. Through this, one may see how acting as if one's happiness is the most important thing in the world reveals a foolishly self-defeating mistake in one's evaluation of the contents of the world.

Once we genuinely accept that our happiness is not the most important thing in the world, and attempt to put our own importance in the world in perspective to everything else that is also of value in the world, we are on the way to seeing ourselves as we really are, as opposed to who we merely wish we were. What we learn from the paradox is that the way out of it is to see correctly where and how we fit into the world: learning and fully accepting the fact that there are things in the world which are truly more important than ourselves. We overcome the paradox by outgrowing the underdeveloped values that led us to it.

2.5 DEVELOPMENTAL PRACTICAL RATIONALITY

We have now come to the point at which we can see how we become moral and live the Good Life as the result of our practical rationality going through a developmental process. What the Greeks called *phronesis* we translate as "practical rationality", or perhaps better "practical wisdom", by which we refer to the deliberative means employed to figure out what to do when faced with real-life, practical decisions. As odd as it might sound to a contemporary ear, practical rationality, phronesis, is a virtue insofar as acting rationally in practical contexts can be a well-developed character trait that aids and partly constitutes a well-lived life. Indeed, all the Greek schools of moral philosophy considered phronesis to be the most important virtue, and some even accepted the thesis that all the other virtues are reducible to it: courage is just wisdom in the face of what is fearsome, temperance is wisdom in the face of temptation, and justice is wisdom about how people ought to be treating to each other. Plutarch puts the point as follows:

(4) [a]s the knife, while being one thing, cuts different things on different occasions, and fire acts on different materials although its nature is one and the same. (5) Zeno of Citium also in a way seems to be drifting in this direction when he defines prudence [*prudentia, phronesis*] in matters requiring distribution as justice, in matters requiring choice as moderation [temperance], and in matters requiring endurance as courage. (6) In defence of this they take it to be science that Zeno is here calling prudence. (1987, 440e–441d)

As plausible as this "identity of virtues" thesis might be, we need not endorse a "unity of virtues" thesis at all to see the centrality of phronesis in the project of living as well as possible.[35] People can be better or worse at practical rationality, and those who are preternaturally better are called *phronimoi* (singular: *phronimos*). Phronimoi are good at understanding in a deep way the situations they find themselves in. They do not just experience their own emotions, moods, feelings, and affective attitudes, but also understand why they are feeling what they are feeling. They do not just react to people's behavior, but also understand the motives behind the behavior. They consider the political, conventional, and cultural features of their circumstances. They have a deep understanding of human psychology, and human nature in general, and are able to see through facades that people put up to cover those aspects of themselves that they wish to hide (perhaps from themselves as much as from everyone else).

---

35. See my 2014, for a rejection of this line of thinking and a defense of the idea that phronesis is necessary but insufficient for having the other virtues.

They are good at perspicaciously "figuring out" what is *really* going on, at diagnosing problems, and at seeing correctly what ought to be done to solve them. (Phronesis as expertise in solving the practical problems of human life is discussed in §3.10.) Practically wise people see things for what they are by evaluating them accurately, and this implies, crucially, that they value things, people included, correctly, or as they ought to be valued. This is, of course, not to say that anyone is infallible or perfect in their practical reasoning, any more than true courage requires being perfectly courageous. Being practically wise, like all virtues, is, in the end, an ideal that we may only approach with greater or lesser success.

No one is born practically wise, as a phronimos, nor can it be learned in an a priori fashion. Phronimoi must learn empirically how things in the world work. While practical rationality has received a great deal of attention in contemporary philosophy, the vast majority of it has concerned the substantial principles (*logos*) which lie behind it, or its scope or structure, or the logical form of its judgments or, in other words, the nature of the end state of what it is like to actually be practically rational. Our concern is what happens to a person on the way to becoming rational about practical matters, how this happens, and what is learned along the way.[36]

36. Of course, these thoughts about practical rationality are not the first contemporary treatment of the idea that it undergoes a developmental process. See, for example, the account in term of "maieutic ends" in David Schmidtz's 1996. See too, Wong 2006. Discussions of development are more common in ancient theories of virtue, where the idea is prevalent. Aristotle spends a great deal of time discussing how we learn to be virtuous; see 1985, 1103a ff.; see also Cicero 1914, bk. III, chap. v, which features the Stoic theory of appropriation or *oikeiosis*, mentioned above. For other virtue-based contemporary discussions, see Hursthouse 1999; Foot 2001; Swanton 2003; Russell 2009; and Annas 2011.

The issue of the development of morality has been of more common interest to psychologists, including Piaget 1932 and Kohlberg 1973. For more recent work on the seeds of morality found in babies, see Bloom 2004 or Vaish, Carpenter, and Tomasello 2010.

Before we proceed, it is worthwhile to pause to note how revolutionary the thesis that "practical rationality is a virtue" might seem to contemporary moral philosophers.[37] The two most prominent theories of practical rationality today derive from Hume and Kant. Hume, or a broadened Humean view, limited the scope of practical rationality to (a broadened view of) instrumental rationality, such that the question of which final ends to adopt are not within its bailiwick.[38] Kant, on the other hand, understood practical rationality to concern the motives from which we act, be they respect for the moral law, or duty, or the like, and, notably, the actual consequences of the action were not part of the equation. It is not hard to see how both of these pictures are incomplete: while having proper motives and a well-developed instrumental rationality are both certainly essential elements of practical rationality, a self-reflectively practical attitude toward our own lives obviously requires us to figure out what the goals or ends of our lives ought to be and neither traditional theory has anything to say about this. Our discussion, however, has been based on the questions "how ought I to live?" and "what sort of person should I be?", and it seems hard to imagine more practical questions. In any case, most today find the conception of *practical rationality* as a moral virtue quite surprising, despite how commonplace it was for the Greeks.[39]

This older conception of *practical rationality* or *practical wisdom* is far more basic and fundamental to our lives than modern

---

37. See also Bloomfield 2012; for other references to work on this conception of *practical rationality*, see footnote 27 §1.2.
38. For the broadened Humean view, see Williams 1981.
39. One reason for this is because "prudentia" is the Latin translation of "phronesis", and the former was translated as "prudence" in English, which became attached to the idea of *forethought* and the ability to sacrifice a small good now for a larger good later. Eventually, prudence became so unhinged from morality that Sidgwick opposed the two, seeing prudence as the employment of practical rationality for the sake of egoistic self-interest.

theories take it to be. True, when fully developed, practical wisdom involves the sorts of perspicacious insights gestured toward three paragraphs back. But, on this view, practical rationality is ultimately, to use Rosalind Hursthouse's term, "mundane".[40] When construction workers build, they engage their practical rationality, and when medical doctors diagnose and treat patients, they do so too. We need practical rationality to diagnose and solve all the practical problems of life, and it operates on the same basic principles (*logos*) whether we use it in applied physics, ethics, or carpentry. Figuring out what sort of person to be, which character traits to develop and which to discourage, requires *building* one's character. We talk about the reasons for action having *weight*, and we try to temper our character to become *resilient* to the vicissitudes of life: building, weight, and resilience are all taken from physical, practical life. As noted, in §3.10 there is a more extended discussion of the contents of *phronesis* given this conception of it. For now, our concerns are more schematic: what happens to people as they develop practical wisdom.

We have discussed the transformation that takes place when one becomes interested in something because of its instrumental value, and, by learning about it, may come to see its intrinsic value. The process was called a "re-evaluation of values". One evaluates one's own values in order to bring them into accord with what one learns regarding what is of value in the world. A common-sense line of thought here is that when this happens, or when one becomes able to develop a disposition to do this, one moves from childhood into adulthood; one becomes responsible for one's values. At this point, people are able to question the values and practices they learned from their childhood experiences (or from their parents or their

---

40. Hursthouse 2006.

communities) to determine whether or not they are really the values they wish to live by. Of course, not everyone asks these questions, either consciously or unconsciously. But there is a point in our cognitive development when we become *able* to evaluate our values, and at that point, whether or not we engage this ability, we become responsible for the values that we have.[41]

This seems to be a reasonable proposal, and if it is, then it shows us that there is a baseline developmental stage at which our values become our own. The present point, however, does not concern when or why people become responsible for themselves, their values, and their actions; rather, we want to see how our most deeply held values, the ones we aspire to live by – our moral values – need to develop if we are going to live as well as we can. (Here we are employing Frankena's and Falk's formalist conception of *morality*, as discussed in §1.3.) We find ourselves at the beginning of adulthood with a set of values inculcated within us as children, and we are now capable of questioning them and accepting or modulating them. If we juxtapose this process with the process by which we value something first for instrumental reasons and later for its intrinsic value, we can see that we are capable of taking our evaluative schemes as objects of scrutiny. We can stand back from our values to see if and to what degree they accurately represent what has value, what is good, in the world.[42] For example, we might have been brought up to think that our tribe is civilized and that all other tribes are barbaric, and

41. There is data demonstrating post-adolescent brain development and myelination in the prefrontal cortex, indicating that the brain continues to mature into a person's early twenties; see Sowell et al. 2001. Laurence Steinberg (2004) argues that adolescents are more likely to engage in risky behavior due to a lack of self-control than an inability to properly assess risk; this implies a lack of temperance more than prudence or courage. For more on temperance, risk assessment, and courage, see chapter 3. My thanks to Katherine Alfred for the reference to Sowell.
42. Again, Nagel 1986, 127.

thus we grew up feeling justified in taking whatever we wanted from them whenever we could; that, in general, "theirs" was ours for the taking as long as we could get away with it. But as we grow a little older, we may notice that other tribes seem to think the same thing about themselves vis-à-vis everyone else. And when we reflect on this, we may even recognize that had we been members of another tribe instead, we would still likely assume the exact same superiority. This reflection may cause us to question our actual tribe's superiority and to realize that it is mere prejudice, and that to take this superiority as a given is to treat an arbitrary distinction (that we happen to be members of this tribe, as opposed to another) as if it justifies our self-preferential behavior, when it does not. We may resolve to stop attributing value to items in the world for arbitrary or prejudiced reasons. If we succeed, we will have learned that what we pre-reflectively valued did not accord with what we now know is of value in the world, and we may alter our values and our behavior as a result.

Our evaluative schemes are supposed to accurately depict or represent what is of value in the world, and we know that some schemes are better than others: no one thinks that any particular set of values is as good as but no better than any other set of values. Some of us are better than others at correctly representing what has value as being valuable, such that things which are good are valued positively and things which are bad are not. One need not be a "realist" about values to accept this sort of picture: all one needs is a conception of *value* which admits the possibility that value judgments can be prejudiced and mistaken, and should therefore be open to (some substantial amount of) objective scrutiny: at the very least, we must all realize that the evaluative schemes of humans can be prejudiced by any number of factors and that we are more likely to value things appropriately if we rid ourselves of prejudice as much as possible; at least insofar as *prejudice* analytically implies *error*.

We must be able to recognize this possibility for moral error both in others and in ourselves. Notions of "objectivity" which are too weak to imply a realist's ontology may very well accommodate this aspect of everyday morality.[43] (Not being able to give a substantial account of moral error and moral progress would be a serious, perhaps fatal, strike against a metaethical theory.) The more objective we are, the more our judgments lack arbitrary bias, the less likely we are to make mistakes in behavior; the more objective we are, the more likely we are to value things as they ought to be valued. And if we value things as we ought to, and successfully behave according to these values, then we will approve of and act for the sake of what is good (of what has high positive value) and disapprove and work against what is not (what has high negative value). Insofar as we do this, we will live as well as we can.

So one important aspect of moral education involves the developmental process by which we move from egocentric and frequently prejudiced evaluative systems, to more objectively informed evaluative systems. We grow from thinking of something in terms of what its value is to us to what its value is in itself. We may think of this evolution as a "maturation of evaluation".

In terms of our moral genealogy, we humans enter the world very far from being self-sufficient, and our evaluative systems (such as they are) are entirely determined by our subjective needs. We

43. For this notion of "accommodation" and an excellent discussion of the degree to which nonrealists can explain moral error, see Timmons 1999, esp. chap. 3.

Objectivity is obviously a fit topic for a book of its own. Another way to understand it is by contrast to subjectivity, where this latter involves one or another form of infallibility. For example, if sentimental value is purely subjective, then if my memory of an object is correct, I can't be wrong when I judge it to be of sentimental value to me; the object takes on increased value *for me* due to the arbitrary reason that it reminds me of something in my past. The opposing sense of objectivity requires epistemic modesty on our part, that we acknowledge our prejudices and fallibility, as well as some amount of metaphysical "mind independence" on the part of the value, such that we can learn about our mistakes (cf. footnote 52 §1.4).

naturally see the fulfillment of our subjective needs as our end. We begin by thinking that our subjective ends have intrinsic value, and that items in the world have more or less instrumental value given how they promote or obstruct the fulfillment of these ends. (Of course, babies and children need not explicitly think in these terms for the terms to accurately describe how our evaluative systems begin and develop.) We start by taking the satisfaction of our ends as our happiness, as our final end, and the world as being filled with items that help or hinder the attainment of this end. Our subjective needs and our evaluative abilities push us into the world to learn about its contents, such that we may satisfy ourselves with some and avoid others. We learn, for example, that wishful thinking and fantasizing will not help us attain our goals. It behooves us to evaluate items in the world in as unbiased a way as possible. Being sensitive to what is in the world pays itself back: a clear-eyed view of the world will let us see what is truly helpful and truly harmful.

The only way to do this well is to put aside our subjective biases, our instrumental reasons, for the sake of our investigation. The drive to investigate places a premium on cognitive sensitivity.[44] And this sensitivity yields a picture of how items are, independent of their instrumental value to us and, as already discussed, we learn that there are other things in the world besides ourselves that are valuable as ends in themselves. At least some of these other things are people, and we learn that others have ends that are as important to them as our ends are to us. As our evaluative systems mature, we become capable of evaluating objects in the world more objectively, where this amounts to the degree to which we are sensitive to what is unprejudicially of value in the world, and not just sensitive to what is of instrumental value to ourselves.

44. Insofar as our emotions can serve these epistemic ends, they will become relevant as well. For the epistemic value of emotions, see Stocker and Hegeman 1996.

Two thought experiments might facilitate this sort of objective understanding of the world. The first is a Rawlsian thought experiment to help settle objectively general matters of value: we imagine ourselves behind a veil of ignorance, where we only know generic facts about what human beings are and are otherwise ignorant of the particular facts that make us the individuals we are. In such a way, we are drawn to see which of the evaluations we typically make are actually biased, or prejudiced, or arbitrary and which are not. The second thought experiment would help with deliberating objectively about what to do in a particular circumstance. Imagine fixing the positions of the people and things involved in the situation, their interrelationships, and values, but substituting strangers for all the actors, including oneself, while making all the substitutions be as relevantly similar to the actual case as possible. Assuming we care about the moral situations we actually find ourselves in, this would be to imagine the same situation but without having any vested interest in it. This makes us more objective. We can then ask ourselves, "If we weren't involved; if the current situation were only a hypothetical one, with people similar but not identical to us standing in our spots, what would we think about it?" This is not to imagine "standing in another's shoes", or to apply the Golden Rule, but rather to imagine what our reaction would be if we heard about a stranger who behaved as we are now thinking of behaving. One way to gain an objective purchase on the world is to stand back from it, to try to understand it in a way that is abstracted from our own personal ends.

But understanding things fully and objectively requires us to understand the ways in which we are related to these things with which we interact, for we are agents in the world. Often our presence alters the situation we are in, even if we are not actively at its center; the presence of bystanders matters. In order to judge things objectively, ourselves and others included, we have to see what difference we can and do make in the lives of others, intentionally or otherwise unwittingly, and this self-knowledge requires knowledge of others (e.g., as described in chapter 1). By trying to understand people objectively, as being both independent of us and yet affected by us, we learn the importance of seeing them as something more than how they fit into a plan to satisfy our needs.

Centrally, this maturation of evaluation, of our values, will require the use of sincere epistemic reflection on our evaluative practices at both the cognitive and emotional levels: empirical observation, judgment, and reaction may not be enough to teach us what we need to know since our goal involves conceiving of the items we are evaluating independently of our actual interactions with them. At this point in our development, a crucial insight must occur: in order to see the world for how it truly is, we must, as self-consciously and honestly as possible, systematically put aside our prejudices and biases. In fact, being a little harder on ourselves than we are on others can be a palliative habit to counteract a natural human tendency to be overly partial to ourselves.[45] Sincerity is necessary: merely pretending to put away one's biases is not the same as putting them away; this pretense is at play in the "ersatz re-evaluations" discussed above. If we only pretend to put away our biases, then the bias is still there and still operational in the judgments we actually form. The only way to see the world as it is, not as one wishes it were, is to stop thinking like the Foscos or others whose overweening partiality guarantees misevaluations of what is of value in the world.

It is important, however, to remember that aiming to make unbiased, objective evaluations does not mean derogating our own needs relative to the needs of others.[46] Our needs are still our

45. Butler 1900a.
46. Again, this is contra Wolf (1982) and other stringently impartial moralities.

own: they are at once our business more than anyone else's and no one's business as much as our own. In life, we must act, and our acts will inevitably be performed from the first-person-singular point of view. But after we have re-evaluated our values, our decision procedures about how to handle specific situations are now guided by the consideration of things from an objective point of view. From this point of view, we must live our own lives and take care of ourselves, but we must also realize that sometimes, especially when the straits are dire, we are not the "be all and end all" of the story: we are not the only important thing in the world, and there are times in which, by our own re-evaluated lights, things more important than us ought to take precedence over us. From a selfish or underdeveloped point of view, giving precedence to others may seem like a sacrifice. But from a mature point of view, we can see that it is not. By the light of our own re-evaluated values all told, we make no sacrifice. The only way to act in accordance with our best (re-)evaluations, is to place what is most valuable, all things considered, at the head of our priorities, to get our other values straight behind this, giving due partiality to ourselves and to what we care about, and then to act accordingly. Tragedy may ruin a life (to be discussed in §3.7), but when it does, it is because there was *no* option available that could have avoided the ruin or the harm to what is judged most valuable: this is why it is a tragedy. In such cases, there is no escape without harm to one's own Good Life.

Attaining the sort of objectivity just discussed will make us better at navigating through the world in a way that allows us to both respect our values and attain our personal ends as best we can in our real-life circumstances. It will also, naturally, sometimes cause us to modify our ends. Our ability to re-evaluate our values can yield an objective conception of the world and its contents, not based on or prejudiced by our partial and subjective needs or by an impartial "morality". If we naturally see the fulfillment of our own ends as a good, we will be pushed by our objectivity to see the fulfillment of the ends of others also as a good, even if in some legitimate sense their fulfillment is generally not as important to us as our own. Eventually, this maturation of evaluation yields a picture of the world in which we are able to place ourselves in proper perspective to everything else; and the more objective our evaluations are, the better we will be at correctly seeing our rightful place. This is moral maturity, a developmental stage with epistemic and practical ramifications.

2.6 IMMORALITY AS INCOMPLETE DEVELOPMENT

At this point, a brief review of the chapter may be helpful. We have investigated the paradox of happiness and seen that it is self-defeating to adopt a strategy for living that immorally and exclusively aims at our own happiness, without regard for anything else in the world beyond its instrumental value to the attainment of that end. We saw that we must, if only for purely self-interested reasons, abandon pure self-interest. (This also follows from the arguments in chapter 1, which concluded that immorality was harmful to happiness.) But we also learned that self-interest itself ought not to be completely abandoned: we should not stop taking good care of ourselves. Rather, we should always at least give ourselves our due. Once we combine the need to learn about how things are objectively with the knowledge that we are ultimately better off not being the sort of people who only act for their own sakes, we at once become sensitive to, alive to, other-regarding considerations and put ourselves in the only position from which happiness is a genuine possibility. Happiness founded upon a false, foolish conception of one's preeminence in the world is false, fraudulent "happiness". We start living well when we start valuing items in the world objectively.[47]

Living badly involves making mistakes about what is of value in the world, treating things that are not objectively valuable as if they are and/or treating things that are valuable as if they are not. Prejudiced judgment only contributes to the cruelty and unfairness of an already cruel and unfair world. When one corrects for bias and learns to see the value of things for what they truly are, it is a win-win situation for one and all.

In the process, we have come to see how important we really are and can build our self-respect firmly on this knowledge, which, as we have seen, is itself the only justifiable basis for self-respect anyway. Inappropriate prejudices toward ourselves, our families, our communities, cultures, and religions are all self-defeating in the end. Again, this is not a call for full impartiality, but rather for an evaluative framework which builds in some partiality toward ourselves, though always tempered by the value that things objectively have.

While ultimately an empirical claim, we should not be surprised to find out that recognizing and tempering the natural bias toward ourselves (and those closest to us) is part of growing up well. We must outgrow and give up our undeveloped, egocentric value systems. The degree to which we do not do so is the degree to which we harm our own happiness, not to mention the happiness of those who get the short end of the stick as a result of our undue partiality toward ourselves.

This gives an answer to the old question of why people act immorally. Famously, Socrates said the answer was ignorance, that people always act for the sake of what they think is good, that no one

---

47. The "start" in this sentence is important. I do not mean here to be giving an account of the nature of the Good Life. This account will be in terms of virtue, as discussed in chapter 3.

knowingly does the wrong thing.[48] Perhaps this is true in some sense, but Socrates' view seems false as it is straightforwardly construed: it implies that if immoral people just knew certain facts, about which we could simply inform them, they would automatically stop acting immorally. Unfortunately, it seems highly unlikely that all immorality can be chalked up to simple ignorance. A more modern answer is that people act immorally because they are irrational.[49] On the present view, this answer also fails because it does not account for those villains or other egoists whose behavior does not seem to be hampered by irrationality in the least. Certainly, the Sensible Knaves of the world are not hampered by instrumental irrationality insofar as their conniving is successful. If, contra most modern philosophy, one wishes to say that practical rationality is also involved in the selection of ends, then perhaps immoral people are guilty on these grounds, especially if *being practically rational* implies not making any mistakes. If, however, *practical rationality* is strictly procedural and does not, contra Kant, by itself imply any substantial theses about what is of value in the world, then it might well be very hard to find irrational flaws in the thinking of immoral people. In general, rationalists think that when people do not respond properly to reason, it is due to irrationality (or ignorance). Regardless of whether or not Kant is right about the possibility of deriving substantial moral principles from pure procedures, the obvious problem is that we typically do not hold people responsible for what they do if it is due to irrationality. Thus, if immoral behavior is caused by irrationality, and if people are not responsible for being irrational, then we cannot hold people responsible for their immoral behavior. Something's gone wrong.

48. *Meno* 77b-78b, *Protagoras* 358c, *Gorgias* 468c5-7. See Santas 1964 and Weiss 2006.
49. Two examples of this tradition are Korsgaard 1986 and van Roojen 2010.

Perhaps, however, we should stop trying to convict immoral people of ignorance or irrationality, and recognize that a better way to address them is as if we were addressing someone with a peculiarly stubborn or rebellious mindset, someone willing to "cut off their nose to spite their face", who clearly cannot see what is truly good for them, despite their protestations to the contrary. On the present view, people are immoral because they value the wrong things, because they make evaluative mistakes, though this does not imply that those mistakes can be attributed to simple ignorance or irrationality. Immorality is caused by a lack of development, not a lack of rationality. We can understand immoral people as being stuck at a certain level of maturational development and who have a hard time seeing, or are incapable of seeing, what is good for them.[50]

Perhaps the best way to explain immoral behavior is to point to the fact that *immoral people do not have good values*: they value some things excessively and other things not enough, and these misplaced values arise out of the prejudiced evaluations they make. The problem is in what immoral people find valuable, not one of an irrationality that infects how they deliberate and act given the values they have: if you believe you are the most important thing in the world and value yourself above all else, then it is not procedurally irrational to act like an egoist. So, there is good reason to think that the reason people are immoral is not because they are ignorant or irrational, but rather because they have not matured to the point where they can see the objective value of things in the world. They are developmentally stuck in a egocentric (or family-oriented or patriotic or religious) view of the world, in which an item's value is

---

50. The idea that immoral people have not matured fully from the moral point of view can be found in psychological work on moral development by Piaget 1932 and Kohlberg 1973.

determined solely by how it promotes or hinders what they want or care about. Even if they are "happy", in the sense that children can be happy, they are not as happy as fully mature adult human beings are capable of being.

There are two principal ways in which this process of development may fail. Immorality is the result of not learning certain developmental lessons, but we can distinguish between what we might call "self-righteous" immorality and "malicious" immorality. Self-righteous immorality is perpetrated in the name of morality and righteousness. Often, people who do terrible, immoral things think they are acting as morality demands; they think they have retained their rectitude when they have not. Racists, sexists, and religious fanatics all serve as good examples. Racists are unapologetically biased toward "their kind", thinking they are superior to everyone else, while sexists, typically men, think that they are superior to the members of the opposite gender. All religious wars fall into this category of self-righteous immorality. Self-righteously immoral people typically believe they are meting out justice, and of course they are horribly, dangerously mistaken.

"Malicious immorality" is usually harder to understand. The easy cases of malicious immorality are those in which people know they are doing wrong, but do it anyway because they think it is the only way to secure a benefit or to avoid a harm. Criminals, cheats, and liars often know their behavior is wrong, and perhaps even regret it, but they do it anyway, rationalizing to themselves a justification for what they do; others are simply in denial about it. Even those who do not engage in explicit self-justification may nevertheless tacitly accept their behavior by callously ignoring or not caring about the harm they do to others. Importantly, they need not explicitly think that their ends and reasons are more important than those of their victims. Their immoral tendencies may express themselves in a more piecemeal fashion and may be deployed only out of a sense of desperation. The self-deception they ipso facto engage in, at least insofar as they think they have self-respect, has already been discussed in chapter 1. They may lull themselves into complacency and self-deceit by habitually telling themselves that they are not the sort of person who would do something like *that*, hypocritically condemning it in others when encountered, yet neither would they be able to honestly deny any direct accusations. Sometimes acts of immorality are perpetrated for the sake of covering up past acts of immorality, and once the process begins to feed on itself, it is hard to stop.[51]

The harder cases of malicious immorality are those in which people do not commit immoral acts as a means to an end, but are rather those in which people commit moral acts simply because they are immoral.[52] The truly wicked, those who glorify the immoral harm they wreak, are thankfully few and far between. (We can hope that if we cross paths with them, we just slip on by.) There are many who have denied that such gleeful evil exists. As noted, Socrates thought that we necessarily act for the sake of what we think is good. Others who take the view that it is impossible to knowingly engage in evil for its own sake might think it is impossible to hold as a principle of practical rationality "evil be thou my good". And at some point, though it is far from clear when, we move from malicious immorality for which its perpetrators are responsible to irrational pathology for which people are not held morally responsible. There is of course such a thing as criminal insanity. The degrees to which these pathological conditions have both genetic and environmental

---

51. A good example of the sort of immorality described in this paragraph is the doctor Judah in Woody Allen's movie *Crimes and Misdemeanors*, who has his inconvenient mistress murdered when she threatens to reveal his illicit financial and sexual affairs.
52. Milo 1984 calls this sort of behavior "Satanic"; Benn 1985 calls it "malicious wickedness".

components (nature and nurture) makes their etiology all the more difficult to ascertain.

At the very least, it seems hard to deny that people can delight in evil, not seeing it as mere "necessary means", but intentionally perpetrating it for the sake of cruelty and malice. Just as these people cannot fully understand what it is like to be moral, moral people cannot fully understand delighting in evil. But most people have had at least a small taste of how teasing others, being mean, or pulling the wings off flies can be a pleasure, and those with a healthy sense of self-respect and self-esteem know the bad after-taste such behavior and pleasure leaves in one's mouth. (Almost everyone has been cruelly used at least once in their life.) It is not hard to see how easy it would be to slip from being maliciously evil and sane to being simply and wantonly insane. And this should be considered in comparison to the perhaps-impossible scenario in which one "slips" from being morally good and truly wise to being insane.

Chapter 3

Why It's Good to Be Good

3.1 HUMAN NATURE AND THE GOOD LIFE

Let's take stock. We began with the Question, or "How ought one to live?" and our first challenge was to figure out the relationship between morality and the Good Life. We found that self-respect is (i) necessary for morality, insofar as *respect* is a central moral concept, and that respect for others and respect for self are bound together such that one cannot properly respect oneself without properly respecting others; and (ii) that human beings cannot be happy, cannot live the Good Life, without self-respect.

We also learned from the paradox of happiness that if we focus on the Good Life as our goal, if this becomes our overriding priority, then we will not live as well or as happily as possible. Instead, what we must do is learn to appreciate what is objectively valuable in the world (in the sense of "objective" discussed in §2.5) and then bring as much of it into our lives as we can; only by so doing will we succeed in living as happily as we can.

So, what image of the Good Life emerges from these foundations? What sort of people are genuinely happy? Here is a sketch. The people who are happiest (almost) always know the right thing to do and how to do it well. They are people who are good at making decisions and enacting them: their snap judgments are reliable and their deliberations far more often than not yield sound conclusions and effective action.[1] By the time they are old, they have often earned a reputation for wisdom in their community; it is they to whom people will turn for advice on the matters of life. More particularly, their values accurately represent what is objectively valuable in the world, and the goals they pursue are based on this.[2] They may be farmers, midwives, businesspeople, artists, scientists, academics, truck drivers, or members of the clergy. Through native talent and hard work, whatever they do most, they do unusually well. Barring bad luck or misfortune beyond their control, they are likely to be very successful in both their relationships with others and their careers. Their persistence and honed powers of observation allow them, eventually, to spot exceptions and opportunities and to capitalize on them; sometimes, it may even seem as if they "make their own good luck".[3] When things go bad, they bounce back as well as is humanly possible. They know how and when to act boldly and fearlessly, but they are more likely to move judiciously than rashly, more likely to delay gratification than go for a quick thrill. They are slow to anger and do not hold grudges. They know when to give other the people the benefit of the doubt; when to agree to disagree. They are always humane and often merciful. Still, they are far from "pushovers" and have and stand by their principles. They do not care only about success, how they succeed matters; they would rather not win than cheat. They do not compromise what is important for the sake of pleasure or fun, though they enjoy life and know how to have as good a time as any when the right time comes. They are neither arrogant nor servile, neither bullies nor sycophants; they are

1. Kahneman 2011.
2. A naturalistic basis of a correspondence theory of truth for moral discourse can be found here.
3. See Plato 1952, 279d ff.

rightly thought of as people who are "self-possessed", people with "self-respect". They know themselves better than most; they are honest with themselves and others. They do what they say they are going to do; they are not hypocrites or promise breakers; their word is their bond. They are brave and fair, self-disciplined and wise. They are capable of excellence and as much as humanly possible live up to their potential.

Of course, this is just a sketch. And there are other pictures of what a good life might be. (Some options are discussed in §3.2.) But the suggestion to be defended here is that if one is the sort of person described above then, barring tragic misfortune, one will live as happily as a person can live. This is the Good Life. But this sketch needs fleshing out and, to do that, the way to start is by situating the properties of the Good Life within the human condition, within the lives of human beings. We are not concerned here with the good lives of angels or elephants or Vulcans, but with the Good Life for us.

A natural place to begin is with the idea of *naturalism*. "Naturalism" is, of course, a term of art in philosophy, and all its definitions are to some degree stipulative.[4] Nevertheless, we can get a grip on what it means by comparing it to some common antonyms, in particular "supernatural" and "non-natural", and by thinking about, at least superficially, the accepted method of studying natural, empirical phenomena, namely science.

By contrasting the natural with the supernatural, we can locate our concern in *life* and the question of how, as members of the species Homo sapiens, we ought to live it. This means shelving questions about God and an afterlife to focus on the here and now. The

---

4. For a fuller discussion of naturalism much in accord with what is intended here, see McPherson 2013.

argument for ignoring the supernatural is simple. Whether or not God exists, our goal, in the here and now, ought to be the same: to live well. If God created human beings, then it is presumably God's will that we live as well as human beings can live; and if God does not exist, we still have every reason to live well as human beings can.

Non-naturalism is harder to pin down than supernaturalism. Most non-naturalistic theories say that, while we are human beings, we are also peculiarly rational, where rationality is likened to pure logic and mathematics, which themselves resist being understood in wholly naturalistic terms. Most famously, Kant divided us in two, separating our empirical, phenomenal nature from our noumenal, or rational nature, when he told us that how we ought to behave is determined by rationality and involves sublimating our natural impulses. More commonly nowadays, philosophers concerned with morality resort to non-naturalism when they think it is impossible to give a naturalistic account of the subject.[5] Such recourse may be necessary, but it is clearly a "second-best" position, especially when we remember the problems born from dualism of this sort, as discussed in chapter 1, in this instance between the natural and non-natural: we should not willingly embrace a theory that alienates us from ourselves, unless there are no other options. This does, however, leave the naturalist with the burden of explaining how *reasons* are to be naturalized in a way that supports a unified account of practical rationality and the Good Life. Unfortunately, this book is not the proper venue to consider such metaethical questions; fortunately, these have begun to be addressed in other work.[6]

---

5. Shafer-Landau 2003; Enoch 2011.
6. Nussbaum 1988; Hursthouse 1999; Foot 2001; Bloomfield 2001 and 2012; Thomson 2003; Setiya 2007. There are, of course, other ways in which one might try to naturalize practical rationality, such as by attempting to reduce it to sentimentality or the expression of fitting

HUMAN NATURE AND THE GOOD LIFE

Even if such projects fail, and rationality cannot be fully naturalized, we can nevertheless insist that rationality must be naturalizable to at least the degree that the full account of Homo sapiens is
biological, and hence naturalizable, and rationality is a proper part
of that full account. (Even Kant had his "practical anthropology".)
So, once again, insofar as human beings are rational by nature, we
should, as much as possible, avoid theories of rationality which
imply dualism: our ability to be rational is so much a part of human
nature that trying to explain it non-naturally works against our
self-understanding as biological organisms. If there is an evolutionary just-so story here, it is that natural selection endowed us with
the capacities to form true beliefs about the world and deliberate
about what to do, so that we may, at minimum, survive and procreate; rationality facilitates these capacities. Indeed, rationality makes
us capable of much more than merely surviving and reproducing
since we are capable of flourishing: we may be weak and scratching out a life or strong and thriving. To pit rationality against our
natural selves so that rationality (whatever it is) must be added
to human nature from the outside (as it were), instead of emerg-
ing from within human nature, is a bitter pill, to be swallowed only
under duress.

Rejecting supernaturalism and non-naturalism and embracing naturalism as a starting point for morality puts the truth about
morality under the purview of empirical science, broadly construed.
We will only discern what the Good Life is for human beings by
observing and studying ourselves a posteriori. And since Mother
Nature outfitted us with the requisite self-reflective capacities, we
have been thinking about ourselves for a long, long time. There

attitudes or some sort of social construction. It is still an open question which naturalistic
theory is most satisfactory.

is no principled reason to think that these investigations cannot ultimately be systematized and become the bases of empirically informed theories about what makes for a good human life (for a caveat, see footnote 65 on human nature in §1.5). It is possible to gather data about morality, but many sorts of controlled experiments on it would be immoral or unethical, recalling Milgram, such that the manipulations they would require are prohibatory. And each of us is, to a degree, unique, and all have only a single chance to make any given decision: experiments in living cannot be repeated. But if the empirical toolbox for morality is impoverished relative to the other sciences, this only makes it harder to learn about morality; it certainly does not take moral knowledge out of the realm of empirical knowledge. (The epistemic challenge for morality is similar to trying to learn about physics through almost pure observation, without being able to perform many controlled experiments.)

Now, some might say that even after we put aside supernaturalism and non-naturalism we are still stuck with forms of dualism that are wholly located within human nature, primarily found in supposed tensions between reason and emotion. Indeed, many studies of morality undertaken from an empirical point of view begin with the idea that there are competing "systems" in the human mind: an older, more intuitive, sentimental, emotional system and a newer more deliberative, analytic, and rational system.[7] If Plato envisioned rationality as the reins on our emotional horses, Jonathan Haidt has more recently described rationality as the tail on an emotional dog or the rider on the back of an emotional elephant. Unfortunately, in all these images of the human mind there is a built-in dualism keeping one side dominant.

There is no reason to deny that our minds are constituted by different mental systems (a more antiquated word is for these is

7. Haidt 2001 and 2006; Greene 2007; Nichols 2004.

"faculties") which have evolved separately over time. The question is why we should simply accept the idea that our faculties are non-reconcilable, or that they have not evolved to act, do not best act, in concert, in a fully integrated and unified manner. However important a role we wish to give sentiment or emotion in human life, we should embrace the idea that certain emotions are appropriate or inappropriate in a given circumstance, and that our emotional reactions can thus be justified or unjustified.[8] And however important we wish to make rationality, we would be foolish to try to alienate our emotional responses from an account of what makes a human life go well. A flourishing life is not the product of a mind embattled with itself. So, again, if there is a perspective on morality and human happiness in which our emotional and rational processes are integrated, in the choices we make and in the development of our character, then such a view has a prima facie advantage over views that keep us divided.

And, in fact, such a view has been around for a long time. Virtue ethics dates back to the ancient Greeks. The etymology of "virtue" is through "virtus" in Latin, which translates "arête" in Greek, which itself translates as "excellence". The virtues of an animal or an object are the ways in which it is excellent; to be virtuous is to be excellent in a particular way for that type of thing. For creatures such as us, this implies having certain character traits, such that being virtuous on the whole or having those character traits leads, ceteris paribus, to an Excellent Life or, more modestly, to the Good Life. (The "ceteris paribus" clause will be explained in §3.7.) On the classical theory, the cardinal virtues for human beings are the character traits of courage, justice, temperance, and wisdom; "cardinal" is from the Latin "cardinalis", meaning "hinge",

---

8. On fittingness, see, for example, Jacobson 2011.

so that the cardinal virtues are the hinges upon which the Good Life swings.

Virtues have the virtue of being fully natural, which allows us to avoid the super- and non-natural; and because they require the integration of our rational and emotional faculties, virtuous people have, and act with, the sort of integrity just described. The virtues are also empirically accessible and have lately been the object of empirical study, in the fields of moral psychology and "positive psychology", so we are now modestly beginning to learn about them empirically. (Some of this work is discussed below.) The virtues are determinate yet flexible, action-guiding yet non-absolutist. Since they are sensitive to details and counterexamples found only in unique circumstances, they are not explicitly codifiable within fixed recursive procedures. Still, they can function as "rules of life" for human beings without inhibiting individual differences or requiring that there be a single Good Life for all humans.

So, how are we to understand the virtues – again: courage, justice, temperance, and wisdom – so that we can see how they lead us to the Good Life? The answer can be found by looking at how they figure into human nature. The overall view here is *teleological*, that is, one in which we look to the point, purpose, or goal of an item to explain what it is for that item to be as it ought to be. So, for example, the purpose of the heart is to pump blood and this explains why healthy hearts do what they do. A contemporary way of thinking about teleology is through the notion of *proper function* from the biological point of view.[9] If we are talking about the Good Life for a human being, then we are taking ourselves to be objects

---

9. See chapter 1 of *Moral Reality* for an extended discussion of "proper function". Of course, the word "teleology" has a notorious history, though recently it has regained empirical respectability. For our purposes, we may simply identify *teleology* with whatever is required to explain the use of "proper" in the concept of *proper function* in biology and its contrast

of an empirical investigation, the goal of which is to find out how all the parts of a human being function properly and in concert, as nature "designed" them to function, so that we may attain the "final end" natural to human beings. We attain our final end as the result of doing what we ought to do, thinking as we ought to think, saying what we ought to say, and, in general, being as we ought to be. (As noted in §1.5, if human nature cannot bear this explanatory burden, other options for carrying the normative load are rationality or agency per se.)

On one hand, our biological mechanisms, which include human psychology, are the product of natural selection, so that there is an analytic connection between what excellence is for Homo sapiens and how they live well. Virtue underpins this connection, as we can note that living virtuously—being brave, fair, temperate, and wise—makes us, on average, fittest to survive and procreate, and makes it most likely that our progeny will also thrive. On the other hand, our biological functions are linked to what makes our lives go well from the moral point of view: by developing the virtues, we will live as we ought to live, attaining the final end which is natural for creatures like us.

Even those friendly to the virtues may balk at the idea of trying to ground them in biology and evolutionary theory.[10] It is not

---

malfunction. Does teleology really require backwards causation or a substance like *élan vital* or some non-reducible, non-natural entities, something like *entelechies*? No. The truth about teleology will not require anything beyond what is required by the truth about biology, which is naturalized if anything is. Maybe biology reduces to chemistry and physics, maybe it does not; indeed it is questionable whether or not thermodynamics can be reduced to statistical mechanics. The present point is only that whatever scientists and philosophers end up saying about biological teleology, the same goes for virtue and morality. For the notion of reduction at play and discussion of thermodynamics, see Sklar 1995, chap. 9. For the irreducibility of biology, see Grene 1976 and Ayala 1976. For the recent ascent of teleology's respectability, see Walsh 2008. See also the Appendix to *Moral Reality.*

10. See Hurshouse 1999, Foot 2001, and Kraut 2007.

uncommon to think that there are too many violent and ugly parts of human nature for morality to fall back on evolution in this way. True, there are evolutionary explanations for harmful and immoral traits such as humanity's proclivities to violence, racism, and sexism but, on the present account, the best explanation for the continuing prevalence of these traits is that they are now merely vestigial: they effectively promoted survival and procreation in an earlier epoch when life was shorter, nastier, and even more brutish than it is now. But given environmental changes to human society, these once helpful traits no longer have adaptive value. To make this claim is not to embrace a Lockean conception of human nature over a Hobbesian one. It follows Aristotle, who says, "The virtues therefore are engendered in us neither by nature nor yet in violation of nature; nature gives us the capacity to receive them, and this capacity is brought to maturity by habit."[11] Nature does not determine us to live one way or another, though not all ways of living are equally conducive to flourishing. On a different note: if humans flourish by excelling in those character traits which we adapted for survival and procreation, this allows for the possibility of flourishing without reproducing. The appeal to evolution should not impede an account of virtue cashed out in terms of what makes for a flourishing life, and such an account should be capable of avoiding the sorts of worries often raised about naturalistic theories of virtue.

Returning to proper function, for temperance and courage, they are to manage, respectively, our appetites and fears in the manner to which creatures of our kind have adapted. (Each cardinal virtue will be discussed below.) As a different sort of example, though related to virtue, natural selection has left all but the pathological of us with the capacities to experience shame, guilt, and conscience: emotional

11. Aristotle 1934, 1103a24–5.

and cognitive *daimon*, warning us off of being bad. The capacity to experience these emotions and "pangs" of conscience may be well or poorly developed, like any muscle, and when not well developed, it interferes with our ability to be happy. To point to a single, central aspect of the entwinement of morality with human nature: we ought to be loving and affectionate with babies and small children, and ought not to either neglect or abuse them; not because we have a contract with them or because they are potential rational agents, but because they are human beings, because we have all been as helpless as they are now. How many of us are lucky enough to wish our childhoods were harsher than they were? Of course, a complete grounding of morality in human nature is another book entirely, one focused on metaethics. Nevertheless, this work need not be complete to see how developing and engaging the virtues is central to what makes the lives of human beings go as well as possible.[12]

So, what is the final end for a human being? The answer has already been given: happiness or the Good Life. The Greek word is *eudaimonia*, and perhaps the best translation of it is "flourishing". The goal of human life is to flourish in ways characteristic of Homo sapiens; this is what happiness is. Chapters 1 and 2 have already filled out some of the content of human happiness by appealing to ideas of self-knowledge and self-respect, and to the process by which we may re-evaluate our values so that they are informed by the way the world is and not by our prejudices.

Still, one might worry that the notion of a *single* final end for all human beings presents an overly constrained picture of happiness which does not make enough room for individuality; that it

---

12. See also § 1.5 above and Bloomfield 2012. Thanks to Valerie Tiberius for discussion on these points.

precludes the idea that each of us will only live happily by living lives tailored to our individual talents, needs, and environments.[13] How can it be that there is only one way to live happily? One way to understand the relation of happiness to individual human lives is by analogy to nutrition. Nutrition is in some ways "relativistic" or "contextual": what is good nutrition for a cow is not for a human; good nutrition for a baby human is different than what it is for an elderly human; good nutrition for Milo the wrestler will be different than that for a pregnant woman, and so on. (The relativism involved here need not imply anything nonfactual.) But notice that all humans require proteins, vitamins, fats, and carbohydrates in their diets to live. There are some universal requirements for good nutrition for human beings, for example, a prolonged Vitamin C deficiency causes scurvy. And roughly, good nutrition for an individual is a matter of having the proper amounts and ratios of calories in the forms of proteins, vitamins, and so on relative to that individual's constitution and state of health.

If we understand happiness and the Good Life in terms of the virtues, and our analogy is between the Good Life and good nutrition, then the virtues stand in the place of the universal components of good nutrition, namely, proteins, vitamins, etc. So, just as good nutrition involves properly relating the universal nutritional components to the individual's constitution and health, happiness involves properly relating the virtues to the individual's needs, talents, and environments.

Virtue theory alone will not tell an individual whether to be a farmer or a banker. But neither, one might think, should it. What virtue theory does say is that if we are virtuous, if we are wise, then

13. Kant argues that happiness cannot be the foundation of morality since there is no uniform way for people to be happy, Kant 1959, 415–16.

we will choose, as much as possible, avocations or professions, or lifestyles in general, that are good for us as individuals. Someone who is temperamentally suited to being a forest ranger, and who is wise, will not choose a career behind a desk. Wise extroverts will not choose lives of reclusive contemplation. Not only will virtuous people choose the right goals in life for them, but they will of course pursue these goals in the right ways, at the right times, by doing the right things. Still, the sort of relativity involved in nutrition can be seen here: the courage of a nurse might express itself very differently than the courage of a firefighter, but both need courage to do their job well.[14]

If one is placed in an environment in which, unfortunately, one is not able to make these lifestyle choices for oneself, if, say, war erupts and one must fight, one will still do best in one's circumstances by being as brave, wise, temperate, and fair as one can be. Being virtuous is not a guarantee of the happiest life possible *tout court*, for reasons that will emerge below, but it does guarantee that one will be *as happy as possible*, given one's individual circumstances and talents and needs. Filling out these claims, and pointing to other beneficial aspects of being virtuous and how these contribute to the Good Life, is the main point of the balance of this book.

3.2 PLEASURE, MOOD, AND SELF-FULFILLMENT

But before we do, we must pay attention to at least some alternatives to this picture of human happiness as being based on the virtues,

---

14. Annas 2011.

since understanding how they come up short will shed further light on the cogency of taking the Good Life to be the virtuous life.

The first alternative is the life of *pleasure*. Hedonism says that the best life is the life with the greatest amount of pleasure, calculated by also "subtracting" pain. The theory has, of course, a long history. Philosophically, it was systematically treated by the Greeks in the schools of Epicurus and the Cyreniacs, and it is still present today in increasingly sophisticated versions. Indeed, some contemporary philosophers, for example Fred Feldman, do not even think of pleasure or enjoyment in sensual terms, in the sense in which pleasure contributes to the Good Life, but instead take pleasure to be a propositional attitude (believing, desiring, hoping, and wishing being other propositional attitudes).[15] In this non-sensual conception of *pleasure* we can be pleased by a sensation, but the pleasure is not a sensation. So, to take pleasure in the taste or warmth of hot coffee on a cold winter day is to take a particular propositional attitude toward the drinking of hot coffee on a cold winter day or, perhaps, to take this attitude toward *the fact that* one is drinking hot coffee on a cold winter day. One reason to move away from sensual pleasure is to leave room for people who would rather live tranquil lives than lives filled with sensuality, since the latter may not be conducive to pleasures of tranquility. Thus, nonsensualist hedonism leads us to think about the Good Life in terms of how much it is enjoyed, propositionally, by people living it.[16]

On such views, living the Good Life is the result of the various attitudes we take toward the events which compose our lives, the best life being the life with the most "propositional pleasure". The main worry about hedonism, of both the sensualist and the

---

15. Feldman 2002.
16. I thank Ben Bradley for helpful discussions about hedonism.

propositionalist kinds, is that the locus of value is found in certain reactions which we have to the events in our lives, as opposed to finding value in those very events themselves. If I take pleasure in the fact that I have lived a decadent or a tranquil life, then it is not my decadence or my tranquility which is the ultimate bearer of value, but rather my reaction to them. Thus, a common criticism of hedonism is that it allows us to take pleasure in things that are shameful or base and that doing so does not amount to the Good Life.[17] Indeed, Feldman acknowledges the issue by building in a condition that the attitudes must be "desert adjusted": propositions must be "pleasure-worthy" for the pleasure we take in them to contribute to the Good Life. Such a maneuver does avoid the problem of shameful pleasures, but does not really get at the problem with hedonism.

If one can take the same pro-attitude toward both good things and bad things, making it necessary to apply a condition to rule out the value of the pro-attitude taken toward the bad things, it shows that the value of the attitude derives from the value of that to which the attitude is a response. The ultimate bearer of value is not the attitude: the very same reaction might be inapt if it were caused by something else. If we can take pleasure in what is bad, then pleasure per se cannot be good: any goodness that attaches to pleasure is derived from the goodness of the object of the pleasure. As such, hedonism fails to give us a proper account of the Good Life.

A different way of seeing the problem with focusing on reactions is by reflecting on the evolutionary nature of pain and pleasure. These were naturally selected as feedback mechanisms so the body could respond appropriately to the environment: pain is

---

17. It is interesting that hedonists rarely if ever discuss shame or shamelessness. In a recent search on the *Philosopher's Index*, there were over 500 articles on hedonism and 300 articles on shame, but there were zero hits for a search on "hedonism & shame" and only ten hits for "pleasure & shame".

supposed to register when something injurious or harmful is happening, while pleasure registers something beneficial or salutary. Unfortunately, both mechanisms can yield false positives: stretching exercises can be painful if we are out of shape or getting over an injury, even though they are beneficial to the body; on heroin, one feels pleasure, but heroin is bad for the body. Again, the locus of what is good or bad for a biological organism simply is not to be found in pleasures and pains. Even if there were no such false positives, hedonism is like confusing the position of the speedometer needle with the speed of the vehicle.

This not to deny that pleasure can make us feel happy. There are many valid meanings of the word "happy" and no reason to deny any of them. But we are interested in the "happiness" at play in living a "happy life" or the Good Life, and as such happy *feelings*, as responses or reactions to the events in one's life, are simply too shallow to do the required conceptual work. Just as it is not feelings of self-respect per se but rather having genuine self-respect that contributes to happiness, the value in a happy life is not to be found in happy feelings; the value is in what causes these feelings and that they are caused in the right way, for the right reasons, at the right times, and so on. Similar problems plague "desire-satisfaction" accounts of happiness: I may desire to count blades of grass or to pull the wings off flies, but satisfying such desires does not cause me to live well or make me happy in any but the most superficial sense.

Another view says that it is the quality of our moods or other affective states that determines how much happiness there is in our lives. Daniel Haybron has admirably defended such a view, and he begins his defense by comparing the seemingly high-quality lives of people living on a (more or less) untroubled island with the lives of people living on the mainland, who are more "mainstream" and

materially comfortable yet seem, intuitively, less happy.[18] He sets
out the issue on the first page of his book:

> Consider, then, two communities, A and B. A typical member of
> A, on a typical day, is in more or less the following condition: at
> ease, untroubled, slow to anger, quick to laugh, fulfilled, in an
> expansive and self-assured mood, curious and attentive, alert
> and in good spirits, and fully at home in her body, with a relaxed
> and confident posture. A denizen of B, by contrast, is liable to
> be: stressed, anxious, tense, irritable, worried, weary, distracted
> and self-absorbed, uneasy, awkward and insecure, spiritually
> deflated, pinched, and compressed.

Clearly, the poor citizens of B are not living well by anyone's
lights. But what do we want to say about the citizens of A? Are they
genuinely living happy lives? Well, ex hypothesi, they *feel* happy;
let's assume that they do typically walk around being in a happy
mood. But what if their positive moods or affect could be brought
on by something that does not merit this reaction. What if they were
achieved by taking a pill or through brainwashing? We might imagine an Orwellian society in which people all have the same desirable
moods as the citizens of A, yet are forced to live dreary, meaningless
lives, so that these moods can only have been achieved artificially.
(Consider soma, from Huxley's *Brave New World*.) Or consider the
happy and contented moods of the servile wife or the Uncle Tom.
Even if we acknowledge that Haybron gives a good account of what
feeling happy is, one wonders how happy *feelings* could be sufficient
for *being* happy or living a happy life.

18. Haybron 2008.

Granted, Haybron is not trying to give an account of well-being or the Good Life, which he distinguishes from happiness by claiming that the former must have morality built in; and he agrees that evil people cannot live the Good Life regardless of how happy their moods are.[19] (The move is reminiscent of Feldman's "desert adjustment".) The question, then, is how to value feeling happy per se. The worry is not that the feeling of happiness may be, for some reason, undesirable: who wouldn't rather be a citizen of A than B?

The problem is similar to problems which infect hedonism: moods and attitudes themselves do not have value in their own right, apart from that which inspires them. Whatever value they may intrinsically have, it is too flimsy on its own to serve as the foundation of a life well-lived since it can be cancelled out by being caused by something immoral or inappropriate. As with pleasure, the value of our moods is determined by what brings them about. If they are achieved naturally, as they were for the people on the island where Haybron spent the summers of his youth, then this does say something positive about the lifestyle and/or culture on the island. Unsurprisingly, it would be easier to live a Good Life on A than in a place torn by decades of war. But if the same happy moods of the people on A were brought about artificially, or if people were manipulated into having them, then we would not wish to accord them much value at all. Similarly, if these same moods were experienced by a sadistic killer or serial rapist, we would not think they are the stuff of which Good Lives are made, regardless of how "happy"

19. Haybron 2008, 155ff, is himself critical of the sort of virtue theory defended here, lumping all virtue theory in with the sort of "perfectionism" defended by Hurka 1993. These criticisms are based on the assumption that the virtues need not benefit their possessors. It should be obvious from the quote from Foot in the introduction of the present book that these criticisms do apply here: "[I]f justice is not a good to the just man, moralists who recommend it as a virtue are perpetrating a fraud". For more critical discussion of Haybron, see Lebar and Russell 2013.

they feel. Less drastically, we can also imagine another island community, perhaps with a great abundance of natural resources, in which people are childishly selfish, unfamiliar with the pleasures of sharing, or perhaps lacking in compassion more generally, where all their warm fellow feeling and "community spirit" quickly disappears on those rare occasions when the going gets a bit rough.[20]

These thoughts lead to the conclusion that what is important in one's life is not to be found in one's reactions but in the life itself. The Good Life is not to be found in our affective responses but in what we are responding to. One might nevertheless think that a feeling of self-fulfillment or even achievement might fit the bill: if moods get their value from what brings them about, then a general *sense* of self-fulfillment, well-being, or achievement might be exactly what we are looking for, especially if it allows for fallibility in the detection of self-fulfillment, coming with a significant account of objectivity built in. The literature on self-fulfillment, well-being, and achievement (SWA) is large. But even if we make out the relevant concepts, the question of the value of SWA per se remains. A general and veridical sense of them is more well-grounded, more fundamental, than pleasures or moods or attitudes, and so there is some reason to think they are better suited to be a locus for value. Unfortunately, SWA are still reactions to one's life, and so the same problem recurs: whatever value veridical experiences of self-fulfillment, well-being, and achievement may have, that value will still be derived from who one is, what choices one has made, how one has lived, and what one has accomplished.

If one is not good, then feeling good (or self-fulfilled, etc.) has little value. This is the problem with "subjectivism" in its

20. This thought was inspired by an example from Hurka 1992, which he had from Ross 1930.

most general sense. The degree to which these positive experiences or pro-attitudes are compatible with being gluttonous, cowardly, reckless, unfair, arrogant, servile, foolish, treacherous, or malicious is the degree to which they are not themselves valuable. They have only a derived value. And if self-fulfillment is only valuable when it is experienced as the result of living a good and virtuous life, we may still say of it what was said above about the value of pleasure or of a good mood: the value of the experience derives from the value of what it is an experience of. In constructing a Good Life (and using the sense of "objectivity" discussed in §2.5), we ought to stop looking for certain kinds of experiences and focus instead on becoming good people, valuing what truly deserves to be valued, namely, that which is objectively good. A stronger conclusion is that the Good Life is the result of *being good* and that goodness or excellence in human life *is* virtue.

The moral of all these stories is:

> *It's not how you feel, it's who you are.*

3.3 VIRTUE

Luckily, as noted, given the hypothesis that being virtuous is the path to the Good Life, a classical form of eudaimonism can take over. Although modern psychological concepts, such as *self-respect*, are required to properly forge the links between being moral, virtuous, and happy, the idea that virtue and happiness are constitutively related is itself, of course, quite old. If the Good Life is a realistically modest form of the Excellent Life, then we may fall back on an old, reliable literature on excellence, *virtus*, and *arête*.

Now, virtue ethics has undergone a veritable explosion in the last twenty years, and the field is now rife with new options for understanding virtue and its contribution to morality. The classical view, like the one to be defended here, harkens back to the ancient Greeks and the idea that the virtues are character traits tied to human nature, the possession of which, at least partly, constitutes a well-lived human life. Others moral philosophers huddled around this eudaimonistic campfire are Julia Annas, Neera Badhwar, Lawrence Becker, John Cottingham, Philippa Foot, Rosalind Hursthouse, Mark LeBar, Martha Nussbaum, and Daniel Russell, among others. But Alasdair MacIntyre has argued for a relativistic virtue theory in which what counts as a "virtue" is driven by cultural convention and not human nature. There are also sentimentalist versions of virtue theory, for example Michael Slote's, wherein what counts as a virtue is determined by what is fit to be admired. Consequentialist virtue theories, like those of Julia Driver and Thomas Hurka, take virtues to be those character traits which lead to the best consequences, where these are defined independently. And there are also "pluralist" views of virtue, such as those developed by Robert Adams and Christine Swanton, which do not give a univocal account of the nature of a virtue but present a virtue as simply any character trait which responds well to those items in the "field" of the virtue.

It seems, however, too close to fratricidal to present negative arguments against all these options while plumping for a favorite, and since many virtue theories are not intended to elucidate the happy life, to argue against them is to that degree at cross-purposes to the current project. Here, it will suffice to give a general understanding of eudaimonia and how a naturalistic conception of virtue is related to it.

The concept of a *virtue* is able to provide the proper values for handling the sort of moral situation with which we began in chapter 1: those in which self-regarding considerations are at odds with other-regarding considerations, since, for example, the wise or temperate thing to do in a situation is not determined solely by what is in the self-interest of the virtuous agent, nor solely by a fully impartial consideration of the matter. Notice, however, that since we can now assume the sort of re-evaluation of value and sacrifice discussed in chapter 2, the tension between self and others will arise in very different situations from those in which, say, one is tempted to cheat in order to "win" a trophy. Still, as we saw in the case of Herbert Freeman Jr. (§1.3), there are situations in which we must choose between honoring ourselves (or our loved ones) and complying with obligations to others that we see as making fair demands on us. How are we to resolve this quandary? The answer is by acting virtuously, whatever that may entail, in the circumstance. Rather than ask egoistically, "What is best for me?" or moralistically, "What does impartiality demand?", we ask instead, "What is the wise thing to do?" or "What do courage, temperance, and justice demand?"[21] We ask ourselves whether fear or desire is improperly influencing our deliberations. In this way, virtue is able to reconcile seemingly "incommensurable values"; virtue can be a "covering value" that allows for "all-things-considered" judgment.[22] The questions to ask, the values at play, are neither personal nor social, but humane. Realizing this does not, of course, make it reliably easy to know

21. The suggestion that we re-orient moral thought to revolve around the demands of the individual virtues comes from Anscombe 1958.
22. See the second footnote of chapter 1 for references to the debate about "all-things-considered" judgment.

what the right thing to do is, but it does establish a standard of correct behavior.

If "virtue" is found in demonstrations of human excellence, we are still in need of an account of why the cardinal virtues are what they are (courage, justice, temperance, and wisdom), and not some other character traits. Which ways of living count as living virtuously and which do not? We do not think a life devoted solely to the counting of blades of grass, even excellence in doing it, can count as an excellent life for a human being, absent some very special pleading. Not all forms of excellence will lead to a good life. So, which forms of excellence ought we to work to develop? The Greeks answered this question in as common-sense and natural a way as possible. They looked at the human condition and the sorts of circumstances humans inevitably face by virtue of being the biological creatures we are.[23] In particular, they noted that humans can feel either fear or confidence when confronting the world, and that we can be attracted, repulsed, or bored by things in it. Courage is excellence in managing fear and confidence; temperance is excellence in managing appetite and passion. Obviously, human beings are also largely social creatures, despite the occasional hermit, so we need to manage our relations with others, and to do so excellently is to do so fairly and with justice. And finally, human beings also have to make decisions and plan for the future and to figure out how to execute those plans. Wise people do this well, while fools do not. The thought is that, in all these sorts of situations, we can either act well or poorly and that we can train ourselves to do better at acting well. So, given the human condition, notwithstanding differences in people and cultures, the cardinal virtues remain the same.

23. See, for example, Nussbaum 1988 and Cottingham 2003.

(The claim is not, by the way, that the cardinal virtues are the only ones we can articulate individually, but that these other virtues are actually aspects or parts of the cardinal virtues. So, for example, honesty and beneficence are aspects of justice on this scheme, given they concern how to engage well with others. Resilience and endurance may require both temperance and courage. Prudence, in its narrow meaning of having foresight, is an aspect of practical wisdom. Etc. There are also intellectual virtues, which are not discussed here at all yet would be understood in terms of the proper functioning of our belief-forming mechanisms.)

Undeniably, the picture of human psychology the Greeks were working with was impoverished compared to our own, especially with regard to the role of subconscious or preconscious influences on action and the effect of social situations on behavior, but it was as undeniable to them as it is to us that some people are better than others at consistently handling well their fears, passions, appetites, and relationships; some plan better for the future than others.[24] Unless particular humans have psychological problems, we can all break our bad habits and retrain ourselves to be more like an improved version of ourselves, to better embody ideals that excellence establishes for us. The ancient Greeks appreciated this, and many of the Greek schools founded their theories of happiness on the virtues, recognizing that being courageous,

---

24. Joel Kupperman 2010, 49, reports a story he heard from the anthropologist Richard Schweder that one of the subjects who walked out of Milgram's experiment, refusing to deliver the shocks to the "volunteers", was also one of the soldiers who blew the whistle on the My Lai massacre in Vietnam.

Situationism, or the idea that how we act is due to the situation we are in and not the result of our personalities or our character traits, has become an influential criticism of virtue theory. It seems to me that the conclusions the situationists infer from their data are too strong. Given the results of social psychology, it is undeniable that a person's behavior is often influenced by the situation the person is in. But to conclude from this that humans do not possess of character traits (broad or narrow) is to ignore the fact that some people can

just, well-tempered, and wise are necessary for a flourishing life. Discussions of the first three of these are now in order; wisdom, as the ultimate virtue, will be left for the final section of the book.

3.4 COURAGE: MANAGING DANGER

If there is an incontrovertible fact about human beings, it is that we are mortal, biological creatures: we are born helpless, can feel pain, and die. Life is dangerous.[25] And, for the most part, we are frightened by the prospects of pain and death. Nevertheless, the phrase "the survival of the fittest" is an intuitively apt description of biological nature. If we are to do more than merely survive, if we are to be strong and flourish, we must learn how to respond to our fear well, since different responses to fear are certainly possible. Two natural responses are "fight" and "flight". But knowing when to stand one's ground and when to flee is at least in part a problem of self-knowledge and experience. One may give in to fear too readily and run from danger that can be overcome, which is craven; or one may be overly confident when facing danger and this is reckless. Knowing when to press on and when to retreat from danger is no easy task. Dealing excellently with fearful and/or harmful things is the stuff of courage.

Courage is, unsurprisingly, considered a virtue (and cowardice and recklessness, vices) so it may be surprising to learn that there

and do act consistently across wide varieties of situations. That situations can sometimes make most people act in uncharacteristic ways does not support the conclusion that people in general lack character and characteristic personality traits. The literature on this subject is by now large; for the best defense of situationism, see Doris 2002. For criticism of it, see Kamtekar 2004; Sreenivasan 2002; Annas 2003; and Kupperman 2001.

25. The danger of life is not something philosophers often discuss. But see Dewey 1958, chap. 2. For an analysis of "danger" and its relations to injury, see Foot 1958–59.

are theoretical disagreements over the nature of courage. One common view is that courageous people feel fear like everyone else, in all those situations which we commonsensically call "fearsome", but they do not let their fear interfere with their thinking and behavior; despite their fear, they retain the ability to assess the situation and respond appropriately. Others might object that fears which do not affect judgment in any way are like pains that do not hurt. The Stoics held a different view entirely. They thought that common sense was simply wrong about what is frightening in life and that when we understand ourselves and what is truly of value in life, as virtuous people do, we will understand that nothing in the world genuinely merits fear: the Stoic sage fears neither pain nor death. (As will be discussed in §3.7, the Stoics also thought that virtue was sufficient for happiness and that virtuous people were completely self-sufficient.) So, while pain and death are real, they are not to be feared, since fearing them would imply valuing something other than virtue, which is always a mistake. The Stoic sage may be cautious but never fearful, and relies wholly on practical wisdom, not fear, to epistemically distinguish the circumstances in which one ought to proceed from those in which "discretion is the better part of valor". On this view, neither the courageous person nor the reckless person is afraid of danger, but the former is wise in assessing his or her abilities relative to the threat, whereas the latter is foolish and either overestimates his or her abilities or underestimates both the threat and the likelihood of failure. Aristotle adopted a third position regarding the relation of fear to courage, arguing that some things in the world do genuinely merit fear and that courageous people fear only them. In this way, courageous people can use their fear epistemically to determine when to proceed cautiously or not at all; they use their fear to help distinguish courageous from reckless behavior. Despite the differences in these theories of courage, all agree that courage is excellence in responding to danger, fear, pain, and incipient death, and that, as Aristotle noted, it is easier to act bravely and step up when one has had time to prepare for a challenge; well-developed courage, on the other hand, is most clearly manifested as grace under fire in response to a "surprise attack".[26]

Of course, we cannot expect to adjudicate theories of courage here, and matters are complicated by the fact, which Plato makes clear in *Laches,* that even people who are known for their courage (in this case the general, Laches), may not understand courage per se (or qua virtue) very well at all, even if they can explain after the fact their reasons for their acting as they did in the face of danger. If being courageous requires one to have wisdom, as is likely, it need not require one to be an articulate theoretician. This means that trying to gain an empirical understanding of courage by interviewing courageous people is not straightforward, and that psychological interpretation and philosophical argumentation will be required for a full theory of courage.

Courage can also come in more than one form: there are likely to be important differences between physical courage, as we have been discussing, and moral courage and intellectual courage. Given our social nature, we do not fear only physical pain; we also fear being shunned by others. The social aspects of courage are therefore related to the virtue of justice (see below), since courage requires both making good judgments and relating well to others. If being theoretically articulate is not required for courage, being able to judge people and situations accurately is. And while moral courage and intellectual courage are generally social matters, a full analysis of courage is further complicated by the realization that completely private matters of the heart may also require courage. One can be a coward in love

26. Aristotle 1985, 1117a17–22.

as much as on the battlefield. In general, endurance, perseverance, restraint, and patience in one's endeavors, all of which may be purely private affairs, are aspects of courage and may be required to keep failure at bay. (The Wittgensteinian thought is that patience is a game played alone; the same can be said for courage when, for example, one is anticipating the worst.) As such, courage is related to temperance (see below) insofar as we can be tempted to give up on our projects when the way becomes difficult, though we should prudently avoid those places where only fools and angels tread. Knowing these differences is the overlap of courage and wisdom.

Often, discussions of courage focus exclusively on its non-cognitive elements, on how courage regulates feelings of fear and confidence or is related to anger. Notice, however, that courage is not just about excellently handling one's fears; more primarily, it is about excellently handling the things which inspire those feelings. So, it would be wrong to underplay its cognitive elements: courageous action is called for in dangerous situations or when weighing risks, so one might place courage's cognitive aspects under the rubric of "risk assessment". Courageous people will be experts at evaluating risk, even hidden risks: courageous people are good at "smelling a trap". As noted above, courage requires the self-knowledge to accurately assess one's abilities. It requires the ability to determine whether or not one can perform certain actions in one's circumstances, to see what the best course of action is, and, perhaps more importantly, to discern the possible from the impossible. Cowardly people tend to cognitively underestimate themselves and overestimate the danger they are in (cf. the note to Korsgaard 1986 in §2.2), whereas the reckless make the opposite mistake, overestimating themselves and underestimating the danger.

In making these evaluations, it is important to see the truth of the situation one faces: danger needs to be accurately represented.

Not only are there greater and lesser dangers, not all dangers are equally real. Acknowledging this and articulating the differences would also be necessary for a full account of courage. Yes, there is a sort of courage involved in facing phobias or other imagined fears. But this is similar to the sort of courage required to go to the dentist. We know that these will be difficult, even painful experiences. They are not, however, the same as facing a real threat of harm or injury, however broadly *harms* and *injuries* are conceived: there is, in fact, nothing inherently dangerous about daddy-longlegs or stepping on a sidewalk crack; even the presence of pain is not sufficient for danger; pain is, of course, unpleasant, but it is not generally dangerous insofar as it is not caused by genuine harm or injury.[27] A full account of courage must recognize that there is more to courage than what is required to face harmless insects or dentists.

Importantly, many people are capable of performing acts that appear courageous; that is, they may do what a truly courageous person would do. This alone, however, does not mean that that person or the act is actually courageous. Reckless people can get lucky and succeed by dint of luck alone; however, recklessness plus luck does not equal courage. Courage is not founded on luck but on understanding and keen judgment, and keen judgment is required to assess danger, especially in cases of hidden traps, surprise attacks, or situations in which it is hardest to maintain a cool head.

In discussing the role of "technical deliberation" in practical wisdom, Rosalind Hursthouse gives two examples of courageous behavior that are instructive.[28] The first is the case of a child wearing water-wings who "drifts out of his depth into the river current, which bears him, with increasing speed toward the weir". The well-inclined

27. Foot 1958–59.
28. Hursthouse 2006, 300–1.

but reckless person may simply run directly toward the child, dive in, and start swimming, while the truly courageous person will judge the direction and force of the current on a swimmer and run up or down the bank, diving in at the point where rescue is most feasible. The second takes off from Aristotle's comments about a surprise attack, where Hursthouse notes that one person may grab a sword and rush from the tent into the fray, while another "pauses just long enough to strap on his helmet and find his shield as well".

There is much to learn from these examples and from Hursthouse's excellent discussion, and we will attend to them more in §3.10. For now, what is most relevant are the cognitive aspects of truly courageous behavior, especially when performed "under fire". To put the point in Hursthouse's "mundane" way, courageous people are not fools, they are wise in the ways of danger; they keep a cool head in dire straits. She somewhat technically labels this a form of "calculation", and indeed, courage requires the sort of risk assessment that actuarial scientists or philosophical specialists in "decision theory" try to measure precisely. Of course, in the moment when courage is required, only "rough" calculations will be possible; and courageous people will have to reason beyond the application of what normally occurs in situations of a certain kind (e.g., a forward advance of infantry or a house on fire). There is no rulebook. Intuition may be required: people of courage appreciate the ways in which the current circumstances are "typical" of their kind and ways in which the present moment is truly exceptional; as noted, they are good at spotting traps and may become wary without even knowing what cued that reaction.[29] Indeed, these "calculations" can occur as "second nature", with a perceptual immediacy born of experience

---

29. For this sense of "intuition", see *Moral Reality*, chapter 2, and for a more general account of "intuition" consistent with this, Lynch 2006.

and reflection.[30] One must also have experience to discern (*gnōmē*) which elements of a situation to capitalize on and which to ignore. So, one way to understand courage as a cognitive achievement is as the ability to not have one's deliberative processes muddled by the "fight or flight" response: courageous people have mastered their minds enough to do what needs to be done in just those situations in which a human being's untutored responses are most likely to be panicked and lead one astray.

It may be helpful to extrapolate from three observations about courage to comments on virtue in general. First, as noted above, courage is not primarily about handling one's fears excellently, but is primarily about handling excellently the things which inspire those fears. Mutatis mutandis, this is true of each of the virtues. Consistent with what was said in §3.2 about pleasure, our feelings are reactions to events that take place in the world. While feelings are indubitably important, what is primary is managing those events well. Second, and related to this, is that virtuous people have the appropriate feelings in response to the world and these actually help them react to well to the situations they face. To the degree that emotions hinder or do not facilitate proper responses, they are "pathological" in the original sense of this term, as related to "pathos". When virtue is present, cognitive and affective aspects of mind work in concert to the best possible effect. The cognitive and non-cognitive elements of a virtuous person's psychology are responsive to, not alienated from, each other, without any duality of motivation or purpose. A courageous person acts with integrity, even in the most uncertain of circumstances. His or her emotions need not, on any account, be "reined in" by the "rational part of the mind"; rather the emotions are naturally apt; they properly fit the circumstance because

30. Hursthouse 2006; McDowell 1979.

they are the tutored responses to cognitive judgments/assessments of the situation.[31] The mind of a virtuous person functions well and calmly, in spite of the difficulty of the circumstance.

And third, courage is intimately related to the other cardinal virtues: justice, temperance, and wisdom have all been appealed to at one point or another in this section. Nevertheless, there is reason to back away from a full-blown "unity of the virtues" thesis, which holds that there is really only one virtue, that of practical wisdom, or phronesis (cf. the quote from Plutarch near the start of §2.5). There are reasons to think the importance of experience in the learning of any virtue makes it unlikely that a phronimos will ipso facto possess all the virtues: there are essential technical aspects to each virtue, which phronesis alone cannot supply. For example, full-blown courage in a surprise attack requires more than mere (!) wisdom, it requires battlefield experience. So, while there are reasons to doubt the sufficiency of practical wisdom as the one and only virtue, there are reasons to accept that it is necessary for any virtue.

3.5 JUSTICE: JUDGING FAIRLY

The personal virtue of justice, as opposed to justice as a virtue of institutions or social structures, regulates an individual's social relations. Section §1.6 contains an extended discussion of justice and how it is related to judgment, the essential thought being that treating like cases alike is necessary (but not sufficient for) fair and just judgment. In this sense justice is an intellectual virtue, a central case being the impossibility of making fair and just judgments about oneself without also making them of others. Self-knowledge, which requires

---

31. For the need of cognition to precede emotional attitude, see Alston 1968.

judging oneself fairly, also requires viewing the self fairly relative to others. So, while justice is most often taken to be an other-regarding virtue, in fact it has distinct self-regarding aspects. In the sense in which justice (ceteris paribus) entails a basic equality among people, justice can be seen as a mean between arrogance and servility.[32]

We take for granted that members of Homo sapiens are essentially social creatures, and indeed isolation from others can be used on most people as a form of torture. But some humans are not social. There are recluses or hermits who do not care to be in society, or at least care for it much less than the rest of us.[33] Of course, hermits and recluses do not self-advertise much; we obviously know nothing about the most solitary of people.[34] Hermits are not, however, exempt from the canons of justice. Being a recluse certainly does not give one a license to steal or lie. Justice is not founded on mutual material dependence, since hermits do not need us as much as we need each other. Rather than mutual dependence, justice fundamentally concerns reciprocal recognition of each other, at a crucial level, as peers or members of a kind.[35]

For these reasons, the concepts of *reciprocity, equality, desert,* and *fairness* are central to justice, and taken together as an analysis may exhaust it.[36] In this light, injustice is easily seen as unjustifiably leading to a denial of the fundamental parity among humans, as members of a kind. The Greeks named the trait that inspires

---

32. So, I disagree with Bernard Williams 1980, who claims that justice is an exception to the Aristotelian idea that virtue is a mean. Rather, I think wisdom is the only exception.
33. Hermits have not been discussed by moral and social philosophers very much at all, but see Cottingham 2010 for a rare exception.
34. For a glimpse of historically prominent hermits, see France 1997. Of course, historically prominent hermits do not seem to be very good at being hermits; the idea of a "famous hermit" is practically a joke.
35. As Rawls 1971 has famously pointed out.
36. Schmidtz 2006.

injustice *pleonexia*, which is often translated as "greed" but is better understood as the more general tendency of unjustifiably taking more than others. In this sense, we can see injustice as inspired by arrogance or by a tendency to arrogate more to oneself than is one's due. Pleonectics have a false sense of entitlement. The sort of self-deception at root here was discussed at length in chapter 1; the present point is that, when people are just, the character trait of justice mediates their relations with others, however intimate or remote, by basing those relations on an acknowledged and factually based shared status which constrains the claims we may justifiably make on each other as well as on ourselves.

The breadth of this claim might be surprising to those for whom "justice" has a peculiarly legal connotation, though a moment's reflection tells us that not everything that is unjust is against the law; for instance, not all lying is illegal. But a broader conception of *justice* may mediate all our relationships. Unsurprisingly, justice governs our relations with complete strangers, but it pervades all our personal relationships as well: if justice is always opposed to oppression, and if the latter can arise in our most intimate relationships, then justice constrains all our social interactions.[37] This broad sense of "justice" is thought by experts to be the correct way to interpret the Greek word "dikaiosyne" that figures centrally in, for example, Plato's *Republic*.[38] As noted, justice is complex, and it also often requires a sensitivity to context which eliminates the possibility of a recursive decision procedure for determining just action

---

37. An interesting discussion of how justice can figure in marriage can be found in Hampton 1993b.
38. For discussion of this broad understanding of "justice" as the meaning of "dikaiosyne", see Vlastos 1968 and Annas 1999. If one adopts the social conception of *morality*, then "dikaiosyne" can be translated as "morality", and indeed this is the case in Waterfield's 1993 translation of *Republic*.

in all cases. If pure calculation could help in the risk assessment involved in acting courageously, it is less likely that we could reduce any aspect of justice to a rote mechanical procedure; even the fairness of distributing resources in equal shares has a "ceteris paribus" clause attached to it.[39]

Nevertheless, we regularly think of justice as being determined in a cognitive way: the "scales of justice" are mechanical and the blindfold that Justice wears is meant to preclude partiality induced by prejudice or emotional connection. But to limit justice to purely cognitive resources would be unfair to it: justified resentment, righteous indignation, and empathy as well as mercy, forgiveness, and even pity can rightly figure in deliberations about what is just. If justice is a mean between arrogance and servility, it can also be seen a mean between being too draconian and too merciful in one's judgments of others. The arrogant tend to be harder on others, seeing them as inferior and deserving of punishment, while the servile tend toward leniency, seeing others as more deserving of clemency and forgiveness for their transgressions. As noted, greed is a central cause of injustice, though it is worth noting that a lack of temperance can also result in injustice: temptation and desire often cause us to commit unjust acts.[40] Recall the blindfold of Justice. So, insofar as justice moderates these non-cognitive drives, it is importantly related to temperance (which is the subject of the next section). Importantly, these non-cognitive aspects of justice (desire for one's

---

39. Medical diagnostic software is advancing to the point where we can imagine it supplanting the judgment of doctors. It is much harder to imagine software replacing a judge in court.

40. It is not always clear whether injustice or intemperance is to blame for an unjust act. Christine Swanton responds to Rosalind Hursthouse on this topic. Hursthouse 1980–81, 64, points out that if a soldier unjustly cheats his comrades out of their rations in a "pursuit of pleasure", his act is ultimately a failure of temperance not justice. Swanton 2003, 21, perhaps rightly, points out that not all unjust acts are the result of a lack of temperance; if injustice due to arrogance is a failure of temperance, it is not a normal failure.

due, proper leniency and mercy toward others) are not in conflict with its cognitive aspects: inappropriate partiality toward oneself or one's loved ones, due to feeling an emotional connection to them, is obviously in conflict with justice, whereas tempering judgment to the particular facts of the case, being sensitive to what is most humane in the particular context, taking pity where it is apt, are not in conflict with justice but are parts of it.[41]

Justice's connections to the other virtues are not hard to discern. Connections to temperance have just been noted. Being just also requires executing one's judgment, carrying it into practice, and this obviously may require courage in some circumstances. It also seems obvious that dispensing justice, or even merely arriving at a just judgment, requires wisdom in all but the easy cases. At a basic level, even children are good at detecting injustice, but to be fully just, or an expert at formulating just judgments, the nuanced sensitivity characteristic of wisdom is necessary.

3.6 TEMPERANCE: TEMPERING METTLE

Temperance has sadly become the least sexy of the virtues; even the word has taken on unfortunate connotations. Still, it is really the best option to translate the Greek word "sophrosune". Being "temperate" is more accurate than being "moderate", which is always "middle of the road" and lukewarm; "self-disciplined" connotes "rigidity", while temperate people are flexible; "strong-willed" is close to "stubborn" and no good since those who are temperate know when to compromise. In much of the English-speaking world, "temperance"

---

41. Here I disagree with George Rainbolt, who interprets mercy as a virtue which is independent of justice and in conflict with it. See Rainbolt 1990 and 1997.

smacks of temperance movements and pledges to abstain from beverages with alcohol. And probably because this family of notions (that is, being temperate, self-disciplined, etc.) has been so closely associated with astringent and self-righteous prudishness, on top of a condescending contempt for having a good time, temperance is the least well-investigated and understood virtue in moral philosophy.[42] On the ordinary way of looking at it, the only thing less sexy than temperance is continence, or the successful struggle for self-restraint. Even wantonness, or the enthusiastic embrace of what is acknowledged as inappropriate, sounds superficially better: better to be wildly and shamelessly passionate than not passionate at all. The more commonplace failure of temperance, that is incontinence or "weakness of the will" or *akrasia*, is attended to far more closely in the contemporary philosophical literature than *temperance* when conceived as the state of character in which one lives in peace with one's passions and appetites. Grit, willpower, resilience, perseverance, and the ability to delay gratification get a lot of attention in psychological literature and the media, but most of this is still discussed with little if any sense of the root character virtue which grounds them all: temperance.[43] All these dynamics are unfortunate. Somehow, it has come to look like temperance is the enemy of fun and pleasure, when this is simply false: temperance runs happily with fun and pleasure and is actually the enemy of engaging in

---

42. In January 2014, the *Philosopher's Index* lists 4626 hits for publications with the word "justice" in the title, 838 hits for "wisdom" in the title, 172 similar hits for "courage", 216 for "akrasia" and "weakness of will", and only 19 hits for "temperance". "Continence" had 9 such hits. A general search for "temperance AND (akrasia OR weakness of will)" yielded 2 hits. In Stroud and Tappolet's edited volume, *Weakness of Will and Practical Irrationality* (2003), the words "temperance", "moderation", and "discipline" do not appear once.
43. On the academic side, see e.g., Duckworth 2007 on grit; in the popular press, see Chua and Rubenfeld 2014. More citations follow below.

stupid, shameless, and regrettable behavior. Lacking passion is certainly not sexy, but neither is being desperately wanton.

It is foolish to be so "buttoned-up" or "uptight" that one can never completely relax and let go, but it is also foolish to have no control over when one loses control. On the contrary, it makes sense to think that there are indeed times in which it is wholesome and salutary to "let loose" or lose control, as long as this happens in not inapt times and places, and never with such abandon that it becomes self-destructive. Those who are temperate know when to lose control, and in such cases there is nothing inconsistent at all between temperance and passion. Indeed, there are reasons to think that one may mine a passion more deeply if one does so with restraint and patience, two hallmarks of temperance, than if one simply gives over to lustful abandon (though even this may have a time and place). Being too lazy or a workaholic are both vices of temperance. It is as much about good timing, pacing, and moving neither too fast nor too slow, as it is about quantity and avoiding gluttony and abstinence. Temperance allows one to pace oneself, it makes the good things last. Gratification delayed is often more intense. Since temperate people excel at cultivating desire for what's good, far from temperance and passion being enemies, they are symbiotic partners. Temperate people heat up fine, but only at will.

It is not mere wordplay to draw direct connections between a metal's being well-tempered and an agent's mettle being well-tempered. Tempering metal brings out its elasticity and hardness, making it both stronger and more resilient. When one's mettle is tempered, one is psychologically strong and well-grounded, resilient and better able to cope with life's trials in an energetic and effective way. Too much indulgence leads to being spoiled rotten; too harsh an environment can leave us brittle or fragile or defeated. Some people more easily "lose their temper" or have a "short fuse", some are too pliable and are more easily tempted or led astray.

Saying that "self-discipline" has inapt connotations as a translation of "sophrosune" is not to suggest that self-discipline is irrelevant to temperance. In one sense, temperance begins with the development of self-discipline, whereby one disciplines the self to want and pursue only what is good to want and pursue. For example, it is good (and sexy) to be tempted by one's beloved, assuming one's beloved is good. In contrast to this, adultery is always at best second best: it is better not to have what one wants than it is to have to lie and cheat, to engage in self-disrespecting behavior, to get it. True love comes out on top. More prosaically, whereas discipline can be taken to a self-defeating extreme, a life without self-discipline is almost certain to be similarly self-defeating. Knowing when to act like "an adult" (in the normative sense of that term), standing firm in the face of inappropriate tempta-tion, not letting one's emotions and impulses make a difficult situa-tion worse, and knowing how and when to thoroughly relax and enjoy life are necessary elements of temperance.

The first step in becoming disciplined is gaining the ability to delay gratification, in learning how to choose *when* to be gratified. Interestingly, the trick that seems to work best in helping children delay gratification is for them to distract themselves from what they are tempted by, though the technique probably works as well for adults.[44] By fooling ourselves into ignoring what we in fact want through simple distraction, we begin to train ourselves. We first learn how to do without what we want, and then practice that until it is easy. Subsequently, it becomes easier to cull those desires that we do not want to want from those we do. Discipline can be taught

44. Mischel, Shoda, and Rodriguez 1989.
    Recent data from psychology on willpower is relevant. Some have argued that willpower should be understood, literally, at least partly as a form of strength, given that glucose lev-els in the blood seem to affect one's ability to "stand firm" in the face of temptation. The hypothesis is contentious. See Baumeister, Vohs, and Tice 2007; and Gaillot et al. 2007. For a critique of this work, see Job, Dweck, and Walton 2010.

at these beginning levels, but eventually (analytically) one must be an autodidact to become truly self-disciplined. A more advanced technique concerns making "pre-commitments" which bind us in ways that constrain our future options and actions.[45] This can help us to learn how to respect our own decisions about what sort of person we want to be. So, we can take ourselves, or our desires and appetites, as items in need of training or discipline, and we can gain control over them by a variety of tricks, tactics, and techniques.

Becoming well-tempered, developing sophrosune, teaches us how to develop our willpower and to persevere. One eventually becomes resilient to the unavoidable vicissitudes in life. "Resilience" can be defined as follows: "a class of phenomena characterized by patterns of positive adaptation in the context of significant adversity or risk".[46] Judith Herman gives a more detailed description of resilience in the context of war:

> A study of ten Vietnam veterans who did not develop post-traumatic stress disorder, in spite of heavy combat exposure, showed once again the characteristic trait of active, task-oriented coping strategies, strong sociability, and internal locus of control. These extraordinary men had consciously focused on preserving their calm, their judgment, their connection with others, their moral values, and their sense of meaning, even in the most chaotic battlefield conditions. They approached the war as "a dangerous challenge to be met effectively while trying to stay alive", rather than as an opportunity to prove their manhood or a situation of helpless victimization. They struggled to construct some reasonable purpose for the actions in which they were engaged and to communicate this understanding to others.

45. Elster 2000.
46. Masten and Reed 2005, 73.

They showed a high degree of responsibility for the protection of others as well as themselves, avoiding unnecessary risks and on occasion challenging orders that they believed to be ill-advised. They accepted fear in themselves and others, but strove to overcome it by preparing themselves for danger as well as they could. They avoided giving in to rage, which they viewed as dangerous to survival. In a demoralized army that fostered atrocities, none of these men expressed hatred or vengefulness toward their enemy, and none engaged in rape, torture, murder of civilians or prisoners, or mutilation of the dead.[47]

While one might think quite rightly of courage as the first virtue of a soldier, it seems temperance is required to live through war as well as possible.

Becoming well-tempered involves managing well the affective aspects of experience that give rise to attraction, repulsion, and boredom. Attractions include the objects of our desires, appetites, and passions; repulsions include the things which we loathe or find disgusting or distasteful. (Since both fear and revulsion can lead to our turning away, the line between courage and temperance becomes thin when the right thing to do is to not turn away from something that is disgustingly horrifying.) It may seem therefore that temperance is what we need to deal with forms of stimulation, but we also need temperance to manage situations in which we are not being stimulated, when we are bored for example. Patience is a virtue because it is a form or aspect of temperance.

While temperance is typically thought to mediate the non-cognitive aspects of our psychologies (our desires, emotions, appetites, and passions), the Greeks thought of temperance as

47. Herman 1997, 59.

also having cognitive import, especially related to self-knowledge. Temperance is closely associated with the dictum inscribed over the entrance to the Oracle at Delphi: *Know Thyself*. As Plato presents it in *Charmides*, the inscription can be taken as pragmatic advice to consider when one is about to indulge in an inappropriate temptation. Saying to someone "Know thyself" is akin to saying, "Nothing in excess" or "Don't let your eyes be bigger than your stomach". Temperance is required for self-knowledge since our natural tendency to be partial to ourselves makes it hard to accurately assess ourselves. Our self-love causes us to see our own case as exceptional, to make excuses for ourselves, and to rationalize our inappropriate behavior.[48]

Above, justice was discussed in relation to self-knowledge. Teasing temperance and justice apart here is as delicate as trying to distinguish different causes of self-deception, which it may sometimes involve. At bottom, the distinction will turn on whether or not the reasons for a particular action are due to our emotions or desires getting away from us, in which case a failure of temperance is involved, or are due to the sorts of cognitive errors which make us think we are more or less deserving than others when in fact we are not; which takes us into the realm of justice. This might seem to imply that temperance is not related to epistemology, but this would be too quick. Related to the question of self-knowledge, the ancient Greeks saw temperance as important to epistemology, especially with regard to judging expertise and weighing testimony.[49] It can be

48. Butler 1900a.
49. See LaBarge 1997. For a contemporary take on the issue, see Goldman 2001.

It is worth pointing out that I respectfully disagree with the way Miranda Fricker (2007) sees these issues. She assumes all injustice is caused by the vice of injustice and takes bias in the evaluation of testimony to be a failure of justice and not temperance. As noted in the text and in footnote 40 from the previous section on justice, referencing Hursthouse 1980 and Swanton 2003, temperance and justice are sometimes difficult to differentiate. Nevertheless, prejudices like racism and sexism can be seen as psychological defense mechanisms driven by non-cognitive influences, such as fear and insecurity: we often respond to

very difficult to avoid letting one's desire for X to be true to lead one to believe that X is true. Nothing is more commonplace than "confirmation bias", the phenomenon in which we tend to trust information sources more when they tell us what we want to hear and less if we do not like what they say. We assume that one party to the debates we take part in is defending the truth or the correct position, and it just happens to turn out, quite reliably, that we think this party is us! At many levels, of course, this is no coincidence.

We tend to listen to those news sources or political experts that affirm our preconceived notions of how the world is and ought to be. We like to have our biases confirmed by the facts and dislike learning we have been wrong. So, we listen to those who tell us whatever it is we want to hear. For example, in the USA, Republicans tend to watch Fox News and read the *Wall Street Journal* and Democrats tend to listen to National Public Radio (NPR) and read the *New York Times*.

Bias or prejudice toward or away from certain perspectives is best understood by moral philosophers and epistemologists as a failure of temperance: we are discomfited to hear that things are not the way we like to think, and we tend to evaluate testimony so that people who see things as we do are in the right and those who disagree must be in the wrong. Learning to epistemically discriminate between accepting information because it is true from accepting it because it is pleasant is one way in which we develop the virtue of temperance, as is the converse: learning the difference between rejecting information because it is false and rejecting it because we do not want it to be true.

To become well-tempered we need to develop a well-honed sense of the difference between what is pleasant and what is good

our fears by deriding what causes them while simultaneously affecting feelings of superiority. Insofar as this is true, prejudice seems to be more a failure of temperance than justice. See also Bloomfield 2014.

(cf. the quote from Iyengar at the start of §1.5). Of course, many good things are pleasant, though not all are (e.g., going to the dentist). Conversely, not all pleasant things are good, some are blatantly self-destructive. We need to train ourselves to want the good things in life, not the merely pleasant ones. Part of the difficulty is that many of the things that most immediately bring pleasurable gratification are not good, and many of the pleasures of good things do not come quickly but rather must be earned by hard work and labor that is itself often unpleasant. A commonplace fact about the human mind is its attraction to what is new and novel; the mind can experience something as pleasant the first time and yet unpleasant after repeated exposure to it, and vice versa: a more striking transition is when the very same thing can go from horrible to wonderful (e.g., coffee, whiskey, exercise).[50] Some tastes are acquired, and we cannot always foresee what we will like with more experience. We can acquire some of these tastes passively through repeated exposure, but we must consciously develop others. We are born with some desires and these must be disciplined, others require cultivation.

If we consider which habits or character traits are good to develop in the long run, all things considered, we will sometimes have to overlook some initial unpleasantness because we know there is real value down the road. Here temperance is related to prudence, in the sense of making small short-term "sacrifices" for greater long-term gains. Almost always, procrastination or the avoidance of what is unpleasant, only makes things worse when we eventually do have to deal with them. Again, we must manage our reactions to the world well, so that we may manage the world itself well. We must train ourselves to do what is best, not merely what is most pleasant. Happily, what is best and what is pleasant are not

50. See Dennett 1988.

always mutually exclusive; but sometimes they are. So, we must first learn to do what is best, whether our desires naturally pull us in that direction or not. We ought to train ourselves to always do at least the bare minimum. And when our desires run contrary to what we know is best but we do what is best anyway, we do the right thing continently, which is much better than not doing the right thing at all. If next time we also favor what is best over what we desire, and if we do that again the next time, and the next, and so on, we are tempering ourselves, and over time we become acclimated to behaving this way; it will become our "second nature" to desire what is best more than what was originally more desirable.

Not only does it get easier to do the right thing, we also come to better appreciate why something is good for us or why an act is the right thing to do; experience can help us understand reasons which simply cannot be appreciated as well by the untutored. If we apply ourselves well then, ceteris paribus, we will see ourselves improving, and this, too, makes it easier to do the right thing. When we no longer have to struggle, when we are not even tempted by what is wrong, this is temperance.

Willpower is needed up front, but not as frequently in the long run. Moreover, only by experiencing over time both immediate and delayed forms of gratification, and reflecting on these experiences, can we learn what works best for us: which pleasures are immediately pleasant but ultimately unfulfilling (potato chips, cocaine), and which things are unpleasant or frustrating at first but which yield great value in the long run (e.g., learning a new skill or breaking a bad habit). This is a part of the sense in which happiness is an achievement.[51]

---

51. Annas 2004. Note, this is not about a "sense of achievement" (cf. §3.2 above), which can be had by people, like grass-blade counters, who have not really achieved anything of value.

Through such a diachronic comparison of the things which give us gratification and the kind of gratification which they give, we can see another way into the process labeled in chapter 2 as "developmental practical rationality": in the end, we seek accurate judgments about what is valuable in the world, what is good, so that we may fully bring what is valuable into our lives. By tempering our desires, appetites, and passions in the crucible of lived experience, we will subsequently not be tempted by what we do not wish to be tempted by. In the end, willpower and self-control are not required, since we no longer desire things we know we ought not to desire; we do not need to resist ourselves. If we can manage this, though it is no mean feat, then we are far more likely to live in peace.

Another diachronic feature of temperance concerns reflection or learning how to reflect well.[52] Unsurprisingly, insufficient reflection makes us likely to repeat our mistakes, while overly scrupulous, excessive, or obsessive reflection (rumination) can be psychologically damaging.[53] Being able to reflect effectively, that is, temperately, especially when we are processing negative experiences and emotions, is crucial to developing resilience. There has been some work done on effective reflecting in psychology, where it has been found that reflecting on anger-eliciting experiences can be more effective from a "cool" and "self-distanced" perspective than it is from a "self-immersed" perspective, when we ask questions about *why* something happened rather than focus on the details of *what* happened.[54]

As noted, Aristotle thought of virtue as a mean, that one can give an analysis of virtue in terms of acting in accord with a mean between

52. Tiberius 2008.
53. Summers and Sinnott-Armstrong forthcoming.
54. Kross, Ayduk, and Mischel 2005.

two extremes, and there are great similarities between choosing a mean and choosing temperately.[55] And this may seem to make temperance a necessary part of all virtue. And perhaps it is. But perhaps not. Insofar as temperance is the moderation of, or the creation of, "the mean" within our characters, such that, for example, all forms of pathological extremism are avoided, it is certainly crucial to living the Good Life. This is far, however, from taking moderation as some absolute prescription for the Good Life. While passion can be moderated, if it is overly moderated, then it will cease to be passionate. Moderation is nothing to get excited about and it is true that passion, at some level, can be understood in terms of a lack of moderation. But it is sometimes good to be immoderately passionate and to be moderate in one's moderation. As noted above, temperance will tell us to "lose ourselves" in passion when this is the right thing to do.

The temperate may be passionate. But it must be passion for what is good, and even passion for what is good ought not turn into scrupulous obsession. As familiar as we all are with weakness of will, we should also remember that people can be too well-disciplined, to the point of rigidity, brittleness, or being "uptight" or "tightly strung". It is far easier and more common to have a will which is not strong enough than it is to have a will which has become overly developed or "muscle-bound", but it can happen. Most of us err in the other way and have some weaknesses for which we should compensate by trying to indulge them less. We have already seen how taking more than one's fair share (pleonexia) can lead to immorality. Unfortunately, weakness of will is also the cause of much immorality.

Weakness of will occurs when we are tempted by something or someone, know we ought not to be, and notwithstanding this knowledge, we reluctantly give in to the temptation; it is manifest

---

55. Aristotle 1985, 1106a26–b28.

when we know we ought to successfully resist a desire, and we do resist, though we are nevertheless "overcome". When akratic, we do what we desire most, but we are simultaneously desiring not to desire it in the first place, much less to do it. A failure of resistance causes a break in one's motivational structure, such that one becomes alienated from oneself. "Weakness of the will" is really a euphemism, however, for the will is not only weak: when we succumb to inappropriate temptation, our will is broken. If the experience is habitual, it may even be hard to know which part of ourselves to identify with: we would like to identify with the part of the will which resists what we recognize as inappropriate, but our failure to resist seems to imply that we should identify with the part which surrenders. The psychology is undoubtedly complex, and difficult to parse.

Plato, or at least Socrates, did not think it possible for the will to be "weak". He thought that we always do what we most want to do, and since we cannot fail to do what we most want to do, our will is never overcome; it is always strong enough to do what actually gets done and that is what one most wants to do.[56]

Plato's position is, however, deeply counterintuitive, given that the after-the-fact claim "I couldn't stop myself" is all too common. Aristotle saw that if weakness of will were impossible, then there could also be no difference between continence (restraining one's will) and temperance (not being tempted). What is relevant to our current investigation is the way in which immorality that is the result of akrasia is due to the person's divided self. One's self is out of one's control; one cannot help oneself enough to succeed in resisting. If we see temperance as resulting from a developmental

56. *Meno* 77b-78b, *Protagoras* 358c, *Gorgias* 468c5-7. For discussion see Santas 1964; Weiss 2006.

process which begins with resisting temptation (if only by distract-ing oneself from it) and then leads to a better state in which we are not even tempted, then, again, we are describing an instance of the sort of re-evaluation of one's values and motivations dis-cussed in chapter 2. We can only gain control of ourselves after we have achieved an understanding of what is truly best for us, and then give that understanding the leading role both in the develop-ment of our character and our motivational (cognitive/emotional) structures and in our deliberations about what to do. Temperance is the effective insertion of one's best judgment into one's life: it is how to act wholeheartedly.

3.7 VIRTUE, LUCK, AND HAPPINESS

So, now we are in a position to understand the relation between vir-tue and the Good Life. And we can draw some conclusions. Early on, we saw that immoral behavior is harmful to the Good Life, implying that morality is necessary for the Good Life. It was natural to turn to virtue to find a relation of morality to the good life, since, of all the going normative moral theories, virtue theory most closely ties who we are as moral agents to the quality of our lives. If the argu-ments of chapters 1 and 2 are sound, then virtue is necessary for the Good Life. Plato had Socrates defend this necessity in various dialogues and both Aristotle and the Stoics agreed. The question that has stumped philosophers in the past is whether or not virtue is sufficient for eudaimonia, or the Good Life. A few have said it is; most have agreed it is not. Notably, Socrates, as Plato portrays him in *Gorgias*, and the Stoics argued that possessing the virtues was both necessary and sufficient for being happy and living the Good Life. They took this stance partly because of the purity it gives to the

WHY IT'S GOOD TO BE GOOD

virtuous person's self-sufficiency; they seem to be driven by the idea that, if virtue is sufficient for happiness, then one's happiness will be completely under one's control and invulnerable to any challenges or hardships life could deliver. This view was met with incredulity by some, such as Aristotle, who thought it was absurd to think that even a perfectly virtuous person could be happy while being stretched on the rack; he wrote that one could maintain that virtuous people lived good, happy lives, regardless of what disasters and misfortunes befell them, only by being committed to a theory, no matter its cost.[57] We need only consider the Bible's book of Job: regardless of how well Job bore his woes, no one, much less he, would say that he lived a happy life or a Good Life; no one would find his life choice-worthy or desirable, despite his virtuous character. To think otherwise is the very essence of being Panglossian, the parody of philosophy.[58]

The Stoics were, of course, aware of this Aristotelian criticism. Still, they stuck to their theoretical guns, saying that, once we get clear on what is and what is not valuable, the only possible position to take is that virtue is sufficient for happiness: to think otherwise is to buy into a false understanding of what is valuable in the world. To the Stoics, Aristotle's view that "external goods", such as a good birth, friends, money, power, honor, and the like, are necessary for happiness simply pandered to the opinions of the masses (*eudoxia*). If the two positions were judged merely by their nobility, the Stoics would surely win hands down.

Perhaps there are people of such strength and nobility that their Good Lives are not ruined because they end on the rack, no

---

57. Aristotle 1985, 1153b16; 1096a2.
58. For many years, I had hoped to find a way to defend the Stoic claim that virtue is sufficient for happiness. I thank Joel Kupperman for helping me see that the sufficiency claim is not something we really want in a theory of morality for human beings.

matter how painful an end this might be.[59] Or perhaps the Stoics were thinking in terms of God-like ideals, actually unattainable for normal mortal folk, perhaps they were merely letting their pro-treptic rhetoric become hyperbolic. It seems likely in any case that complete self-sufficiency requires something closer to saintliness than can be expected of any but the moral prodigies among us. But even these prodigies of self-sufficiency ought to be brought low by disasters of the greatest magnitude. Imagine a war in which all humans on the planet were killed except one, who happened to be perfectly virtuous. Are we really to imagine this person going on to happily live the Good Life? Why think that imperturbability is of so great a value that it trumps all others or is, all by itself, identical to (necessary and sufficient for) eudaimonia? This does not sound like the Good Life as much as it sounds like being shut off from life. Suppose, as legend has it, that there are hermetic monks who live excellent and perfectly self-sufficient lives meditating alone in some remote caves (there is no reason to deny the possibility); there is simply no reason to think that this sort of life would amount to the Good Life for every possible virtuous person.

There does seem to be something both right and wrong about the Stoics' point of view. On the one hand, the idea that we must *make* our lives go well is quite plausible: the Good Life will not happen on its own or by accident. It is what we *do* with our lives that makes them go well. To this degree, our happiness must be under our control: the Good Life cannot be given to one, nor can it be a passive life.[60] On the other hand, taken to the extreme, the Stoic ideal turns human life into something inhumane, or perhaps inhuman.

59. A number of such heroic stories can be found in Tec 1987. I thank Joel Blatt for the reference to this book.
60. Aristotle 1985, 1098a16–18 and 1998, 1328a37–38, 1332a7–10.

What mistake did the Stoics make that led them to such a position? Primarily, it had to do with their parsimonious view of what is of value in the world.[61] They held that only virtue is valuable, and that everything else that we would normally think of as good and valuable (including loved ones and friends, having enough to eat, etc.) is, at most, really only a "preferred indifferent": something which is not to be valued on the same scale with virtue. On this view, even the smallest consideration of virtue could outweigh (or trump or silence) even the largest considerations regarding preferred indifferents; but if there are no considerations of virtue at play, then one may choose between these indifferent items as one prefers. (Perhaps the preferred indifferents *matter* in some sense, but they are trivial compared to considerations of virtue.) So, the Stoic view that virtue is the only thing truly of value in life and that everything else easily falls into the "take it or leave it" category when stacked up against virtue, leads them to the invulnerable virtuous sage, wholly self-sufficient. The problem here is that they locate value only in virtue itself, while ignoring the value of the virtuous people themselves: the Stoics seem to see human beings as little more than possible "vessels" of virtue; qua people, we seem to be of merely instrumental value or perhaps even of no value at all.[62]

61. Julia Annas pointed out to me that the Stoics' motivation to think that virtue is sufficient for happiness might reflect an attractive egalitarianism about the Good Life which led them to think that even a slave can live happily; this is in contrast to Aristotle, for whom happiness is so fragile that it is impossible for some people, for example, those who are very ugly or those deprived of a "good birth" (1985, 1099b3-4). The Stoic position is more attractive, though this may not save them from other problems entailed by their axiology.

    Daniel Russell (2012) argues that the Stoics' narrow view of the self is the cause of the problem. See my forthcoming review of his book for a response.

62. Notorious is the following from Epictetus 1983:

    3. In the case of everything attractive or useful or that you are fond of, remember to say just what sort of thing it is, beginning with the least little things. If you are fond of a jug, say "I am fond of a jug!" For then when it is broken you will not be upset. If

The Stoics, however, get this backward. We are not mere vessels of virtue; rather, it is virtue's job to ennoble us because we are inherently worthy of both respect and self-respect.[63] Each human life, taken on its own, has a value in itself, such that we may act for the sake of living it well. And beyond the value we place on ourselves, we naturally think that those who are virtuous take romantic love, family, friendship, and community to be valuable in their own right, that their loved ones, family members, friends, and people in general, imperfectly virtuous though they may be, are not merely "preferred indifferents". Human infants are not of value merely because they are possible vessels for virtue (or rationality or agency). We may leave open the possibility of happy hermits living solitary, truly self-sufficient yet thoroughly Good Lives, conceding that relationships with others are not strictly necessary for the Good Life, but we ought not to conclude that people themselves are of no value to each other's Good Lives. To echo the theme of the first chapter, to have a view of ourselves and our lives as valuable, plus a rational commitment to judging like cases alike, without which neither self-knowledge and self-respect are possible, requires us to recognize the value of the lives of others.

So, while we recognize the value of virtue and its role in the Good Life (to be discussed more below), we must also recognize that virtue is not the only thing of value. Even if a person's virtue

you kiss your child or your wife, say that you are kissing a human being; for when it dies you will not be upset.

63. Despite how different Stoicism is from utilitarianism, the criticism here of the former is interestingly related to a criticism that Rawls 1971, 27, makes of the latter when he says, "Utilitarianism does not take seriously the distinction between persons". Singer 1993, 121, formulates the objection as follows: "It is as if sentient beings are receptacles of something valuable and it does not matter if a receptacle gets broken, so long as there is another receptacle to which the contents can be transferred without any getting spilt". See also Chappell 2013.

is invulnerable, not everything of value in a person's life is simi-larly invulnerable, and so becoming virtuous, all by itself, is not a guarantee of happiness. Let us not underplay the importance of imperturbability and resilience, and temperance in general, in the Good Life. A virtuous person can withstand and recover from more-than-normal misfortune and may even go on to be stronger than before; this is, to a large degree, an effect of the resilience of temperance and the perseverance of courage. Notwithstanding this, a misfortune of deep enough and tragic enough propor-tions may ruin any given person's life, however virtuous: we want our mettle tempered, not calloused to the point of insensitivity. Enabling one to avoid many such misfortunes may be a benefit of wisdom's forethought, but this is different than concluding that one's virtue makes one invulnerable to all the possible tragedies of life. The reasonable conclusion is that we are only mortal humans and even the best of us are far, far from perfect at avoiding misfor-tune. It would be, at least, unsuitably immodest and presumptu-ous to think one is, or could be, invulnerable to *all* possible harm. At worst, it would be self-deceptive to the point of losing touch with what makes a life go well in the first place. A fully virtuous human will be far from fragile, but there is no reason to conclude from this that the goal is to be unbreakable no matter what.

If a virtuous person's Good Life can recover from all but the worst calamities, we may conclude that, beyond virtue, the only other thing a person needs for the Good Life is a lack of tragic misfortune. This is not to say that one needs an average (normal?) amount of good luck to be happy, only that one cannot have a great deal of very bad luck. And it must be a "great deal of very bad luck" because, presumably, a resilient and virtuous person can recover from a more than average amount of bad luck.

These ideas allow us to stay true to the guiding normative principle of Stoic moral theory, namely that virtue alone makes us live as well as possible, and also to acknowledge the constraints placed upon us by human psychology: for each of us there is a limit to how much misery we can bear, after which we will begin to break down. But being as virtuous as possible allows one to withstand as much as possible. Virtue will make one as self-sufficient and resilient as one can be, and it is only by virtue of virtue that one lives a Good Life. Now, we can answer the paradox of happiness, as stated in §2.1:

> *We will be as happy as we can be,*
> *if we are as virtuous as we can be.*

In other words, we will be as happy as we can be if we always do the right thing at the right time in the right way for the right reasons, while having a correct or true understanding of the meaning of "right", however generalized or contextual it may be.

The paradox of happiness is that having the goal of being as happy as possible is self-undermining. So, what is the goal one ought to have? The answer is to live the best life one can. Which life is this? Well, there are many: any of the possible Good Lives one could live will suffice. And what makes a life good? The answer is virtue. When we are confronted with a difficult moral choice (and have time for reflection and deliberation), the question we must ask is, what is the brave, fair, disciplined, and wise thing to do? The more courageous, just, temperate and wise we are, the better our choices will be. If there is no time to think, then we will have to rely on our self-trained "second nature". The better we have been at inculcating our character with virtue, the better we will live, as a matter of course. Being as happy as possible will be a by-product or side-effect of our adopted end of excellence or virtue. The initial goal of living happily is not self-effacing since it retains its proper and considerable value and follows from being virtuous as a matter of consequence. What ought to take pride of place in practical decision-making is not being happy, but being virtuous.

Being as virtuous as possible is not, however, sufficient for happiness. Of course, it is sufficient for being as virtuous as possible. It is also sufficient for being as happy as possible, given the circumstances a person faces. This does not entail that one will be happy: as noted and to be discussed more below, some circumstances make happiness impossible. Still, one will always do as well as the circumstances allow, be as happy as possible, by being as virtuous as one can be. From a practical, normative point of view, regardless of the circumstance, doing the action which is brave, well-tempered, fair, and wise, whatever it may be, will do more to contribute to one's Good Life, considered as a whole, than any alternative. (These are facts about the practical point of view, not something to consider while deliberating about what to do.) Thus, the Good Life will come to be as virtue becomes one's final end. Even if the Stoics were wrong from an axiological point of view, they were right from a practical point of view in that all we ever need to do is act according to virtue and the rest of our lives (including friends, family, career, etc.) will turn out as well as can be. This is the sole normative principle we need to make our lives go as well as possible.

Being virtuous will make people act as well as possible, come what may. We will face minor misfortunes, setbacks, and upsets, which are part of human life, with perseverance, endurance, and determination. Again, our mettle is tempered in the crucible of life. Indeed, contrary to the life many people dream of, namely a life of ease and luxury in which pleasures and satisfaction may be plucked as easily as low-hanging fruit, there are good reasons to think that some misfortune may improve the quality of one's life: in the long run, it is best to have to work for and to earn what one has, and this requires sometimes failing in our endeavors. It is not preferable to always win, to win easily, to have everything and everyone at one's beck and call. Just as a plant that is over-watered will have weak, underdeveloped roots, always winning, always getting whatever one wants, especially without having to work for it, will make a human being weak and spoiled to the point of dissipation. Without adversity, a living thing cannot become strong and thrive.

So, we must learn to handle life as best we can, and the way to do that is to become as virtuous as possible. In this way, we will learn to take life's trials in our stride, to weather our defeats and relish our successes, and to learn from both. And barring the sort of bad luck still to be discussed, success in life will be the outcome. One will have established a solid foundation for one's character and learned to bring what is objectively valuable into one's life, while also becoming adept at keeping what is of disvalue at arm's length.

Even when experiencing a failure or when life is as bad as it gets, virtuous people can find some solace in their own good will, in their search for wisdom, probity, and rectitude; they can at least know they could not have done better given their circumstances. Virtuous people will not fail themselves or those they love; the world may fail them, but they will still know that they did as well as they could.

We must remember, however, that worldly success, when measured in terms of wealth, power, fame, or beauty, is not necessary for the Good Life. Humans may be quite poor but quite happy, taking care of themselves and their loved ones as best they can in demanding times and places: there is no a priori reason to think that a simple village life cannot afford people as good a life as is possible for human beings, rich in virtue and in love, surrounded by the warmth of community and the beauty of nature. True, such lives lack what we ordinarily mean by "luxury", but the point is that while luxurious living may be consistent with the Good Life but is certainly not necessary for it. Indeed, it may be inhibitory since it is easy to think of "highly successful", rich, powerful, and famous people who are nevertheless miserable, and sometimes made so by the very traits that others envy and covet. A simple, tranquil life can be quite excellent, quite a Good Life; indeed, practically any well-chosen and virtuous life plan, however modest it may be, can provide a sufficient basis for the Good Life.

Still, anyone may have a string of bad luck. And whether luck is a real phenomenon or not, fortune seems to smile on only a lucky few while many too many others live as miserably as Job. The fully virtuous may bear up as well as possible under the strain of a sustained bout of very bad luck, but if it is bad enough or lasts long enough then some may be broken, but no one can say about them, "they deserved it"; as noted right at the start, bad things can happen to the best of people. Even the wisest and most prudent farmer may not be able to withstand a severe drought. Natural disasters may strike, invading armies may attack, war may be declared. All over the world, children are born into hopeless conditions, and may be raised in environments that do not provide the minimum care they need for proper physical and psychological, let alone moral, development. A distressingly substantial percentage of innocent children die from easily preventable illnesses. And no one can say that their lives were cut short by anything other than the bad luck of being born when and where they were.

Some of us, who were lucky enough to have avoided natural disasters and the ravages of war, were not, however, lucky enough to be raised in a loving, caring environment. Some of those who were not so lucky will have the temperament to recover; others will tragically repeat the mistakes of their upbringing throughout their lives, sometimes inflicting on others the sort of abuse they came to see as "normal". Those whose luck is bad enough may never have the chance to live well or be happy.

Before we proceed, it may be helpful to look again at the "sacrifices" discussed in §2.3. There it was argued that, in an important sense, morality never asks us to make sacrifices because good people will always make the choice dictated by their highest values, values based on the virtues. If feeding my children is more important to me than feeding myself, I am not making a sacrifice by going hungry to feed my children. So, while morality does not require us to make such sacrifices, enough bad luck or extreme adversity can ruin our lives despite our ability to uphold our values as well as possible in difficult circumstances. We all hope to have to choose "the lesser of evils" as infrequently as possible. Nevertheless, if nature becomes "stepmotherly" (in Kant's sense) and does not afford the slightest chance of living happily, one will still live the best life possible, given the circumstances, by being as virtuous as possible, even if one will not live a very happy life at all. At least, we are able to retain self-respect.

Even this might not be possible, however, in situations of extraordinary tragedy. If choosing the lesser of two evils does not require sacrificing one's values, the chosen lesser evil is still an evil. One's choices might leave one with "dirty hands".[64] One can go to war and return to live a good life, despite the blood one may have shed. But one might be forced to make other choices that make a good life impossible; the mother in William Styron's *Sophie's Choice* who must decide which her of two children to save is just one such example, a choice from which there was no possibility for recuperation.

Virtue alone is not sufficient for happiness. But this need not interfere with the practical conclusion that it is sufficient to make a

64. Stocker 1990.

person's life as happy and good as possible; we will always do best by aiming at virtue, at what is noble and fine and good. The happiest and best life will be a composition of moments, periods, projects, and commitments in which a person says and does, as Aristotle suggests: the right thing, at the right time, in the right way, and for good reason. Ideally, we ought to hope to be or become wise people who act from good will, whose actions will have consequences that are as good as possible, given the circumstance. Of course, this is not easy, nor can it happen without a great deal of hard work and reflection, but no one ever said that living the Good Life would or should be a cakewalk.

As discussed above, mature moral people learn what is of value in the world and pursue it, and their lives are inextricably bound up with what they value, with what they care about and love. The reason there has been so much debate over the relation of morality to self-interest over the centuries is that people have assumed that self- and other-regarding considerations can be teased apart and considered independently. Answering the Question leads to the conclusion that life should be lived by taking care of both ourselves and others as best as we can, that we value to the best of our ability what is truly of value, wherever it may be, and act accordingly. We do not choose between morality and self-interest; rather we choose from among all our options to do what courage, justice, temperance, and wisdom require, all things considered, as effectively as life allows. Anything less means we live less well than we may.

When asked if he would prefer to inflict suffering on others or have it inflicted upon himself, Socrates is said to have responded that he would prefer neither; if, however, he were forced to choose, then he would prefer to suffer.[65] Similarly, Jesus preached that when

65. Again, Plato 1994, 469b–c.

we are struck on one cheek, we ought to turn the other, so that it may be struck as well. Leaving martyrdom aside, there may be limits to how much one can be asked to suffer for the sake of others but, presumably, if we suffer for the sake of what we love, there is an important sense in which we make no sacrifice: we may lament that our circumstances have forced us to make such difficult decisions, but at least we will act according to what we value most, and sometimes that is all we can do.

3.8 BENEFITS OF MORALITY

The benefits of being good are now becoming clear. As we learned in the first chapter, one benefit is the preservation of our self-respect. And in chapter 2, we saw how becoming good teaches us to recognize the value of things in the world and to learn to bring these things into our lives. And we have seen in this chapter how living well will bring us a virtuous facility (and if we are gifted, actual virtuosity) in dealing with those challenging areas of human life with which we all must grapple: managing our appetites and passions, our fears, and social relationships, and in general how to make our way successfully through a difficult world. What we learn is permanent and makes us as self-sufficient as can be, at least insofar as no one can take what we learn away from us. Barring a crushingly tragic misfortune, our well-intentioned pursuit of virtue will eventually constitute a happy life well lived, a series of choices and actions that, as nearly as possible, are all the right choices made for good reasons. In this self-consciously modest and constrained sense, virtue is sufficient for the Good Life.

As noted, the world is a dangerous place and life is not fair. Some have no chance to live a happy life, but hardly anyone in a position to read this book will be in so bad a circumstance as this. Barring misfortune, in a neutral or, with more luck, a caring environment, one may choose wisely with regard to what one does with one's life. Initially aiming directly at happiness, we learn that pursuing what is of value in itself will make a happy life a by-product of that pursuit. This value may be found in a beloved person or group, or in the development of one's natural talent into a vocation. And through this pursuit, one becomes devoted to what is of value in one's life, and in so doing, one brings its intrinsic value into one's life in a genuine, non-instrumental fashion. One's life thereby becomes more intrinsically valuable by being devoted to what is intrinsically valuable, and no one could ask for a better basis for happiness than that. Being morally good thereby justifies itself.

One may pursue a trade or art, science, or philosophy or matters of community or state, and one may do so as much in accord with virtue as one may pursue one's beloved or tend to one's family or engage with one's friends. Any objectively valuable object of pursuit can be pursued with an integrity and purity of heart not attainable by those with, at bottom, vicious, immoral, or merely instrumental ends. This allows a form of reverence or devotion to develop which is based on an objective assessment of value and not merely on convenience or selfishness.[66] Thus, we each choose to pursue what we find to be the particular embodiment of goodness that is most suitable to us, given who we are as individuals. It is famously difficult for us to know what actually motivates our actions.[67] But we can do our best to make sure that we are motivated by what we ought to be motivated by, deciding to pursue what we are most confident is truly good. If we constantly aim at the right things and are sincere and willing to learn from our mistakes, we will eventually be likely to make good choices.

66. Woodruff 2001.
67. Kant 1959, 4: 407.

Self-interest ought not to motivate us, but our good choices and our good will bring a reward that is good and also rewarding to ourselves. The successful pursuit of the good is (part of) its own reward. And the more we aim at what is good, the better we will become at finding it, at helping it flourish, and at bringing it into our lives. The successful pursuit of the good results in the Good Life.

The benefits of living morally are like those that attend good honest labor in a non-misfortunate environment. As we become practiced at bringing what we objectively judge to be of value into our lives, we will also be bringing objective goodness into our lives. In this sense, being good does pay. It does not pay if one aims *at* the pay off, if one is motivated *by* a desire for the pay off: this brings us back to the paradox of happiness. But being good nevertheless *does* pay, by one's own lights, if one is sincerely motivated by what one genuinely thinks is good.

Of course, we will make mistakes. We will get involved with the wrong people, waste our time on pursuits to which we are not suited, be deceived, be culpably and non-culpably ignorant. The more expert we become in our pursuits, however, the fewer and farther between our mistakes will be. We must never stop learning, since we are always capable of making ingenuous errors of judgment and fools of ourselves. But if we do, we will at least be well-intentioned fools and not greedy, selfish fools.

3.9 LOVE IS ITS OWN REWARD

In *Symposium*, Plato pointed out the difference between these two kinds of fool.[68] If we accept or pursue a lover because we are fooled

68. Plato, *Symposium* 1994,185a.

into thinking this person is rich, then our foolishness is shown to us when the person turns out to be poor. Regardless of how rich or poor the person truly is, our actions show us what we are worth to ourselves; they show that we are liable to disrespect ourselves by treating our love, what should be the most valuable part of us, as an instrument for the sake of access to money, which is itself only an instrument. People who do this are willing (at least sometimes) to subordinate themselves to something that has only instrumental value and this is self-disrespecting. Contrast this, however, with accepting or pursuing someone as a lover because we think this person is good, kind, and deserving, only to find out later that he or she is a scoundrel or villain. We may still be fools, but of a different sort entirely. We still learn what we are worth to ourselves: it shows that we are willing (at least sometimes) to devote ourselves to something intrinsically valuable, something good and deserving, and this does not hinder self-respect. Indeed, having values like this is the only way to preserve self-respect. We judged something to be objectively good and were mistaken or deceived. But our values were revealed to us and not found wanting.

Love is a benefit of being good. Indeed, the incompatibility of love with being bad is perhaps the best argument against the Foscos of the world. For love implies that one is willing to put the interests of the beloved before "self-interest", something the Foscos will not do.[69] Importantly, the sort of love at stake is not to be conflated with either lust or purely romantic love. While we may lust for our beloved, lust per se only seems like love to those who have never truly loved and do not know the difference. Purely romantic love is of course a form of love; it is perhaps more paradigmatic of love

---

69. Cf. the discussion from §2.2 of Stocker's argument for why egoism is incompatible with love.

than anything other than parental love. But painters may love painting; mathematicians may love proofs, and revolutionaries may love liberty and freedom. When we talk about what we love most dearly, our highest values, culminating in talk about what we would die for, we may talk broadly about whatever we pursue for its own sake and not for what it will do for us. We give ourselves over when we love. We surrender, though not in defeat; we yield, not from weakness or servility, but with our self-respect and dignity intact because we surrender to only what we revere.

We can get clearer about the view of love here by contrasting it to both a common view and one defended by David Velleman.[70] He argues against a common philosophical conception of love: to see it as a motive to benefit the beloved. Harry Frankfurt provides an example of the conception Velleman rejects: "The inherent importance of loving is due precisely to the fact that loving consists essentially in being devoted to the well-being of what we love".[71] Velleman quotes Henry Sidgwick, Laurence Thomas, Gabriele Taylor, William Lyons, Patricia Greenspan, Robert Nozick, John Rawls, Alan Soble, and a different quote from Frankfurt, all articulating this conception of love.[72]

Velleman argues effectively that this common conception misses an important aspect of love which his own captures. He notes that there are cases of divorce or particularly difficult relations in which people may love without there being a desire to benefit each other. He defends, rather, the thesis that love is a lowering of one's psychological defense mechanisms, so that one becomes "open" to one's beloved. Nevertheless, while Velleman's analysis of *love* is

70. Velleman 1999.
71. Frankfurt 2004, 59.
72. Velleman 1999, 351–52.

compelling, it does not, nor is it intended to, discriminate between good love and bad love.

At this point in the discussion of the Good Life, however, the distinction between good love and bad can be taken for granted; echoing Plato, good love is directed at someone or something that is good and bad love at what is bad.[73] Velleman may be right that all love, good and bad, requires a lowering of defenses, yet an analysis of love that fails to discriminate between the good and the bad obviously has limited practical value. Insofar as we are here considering love as benefit of being virtuous, we are only directly concerned with the love of virtuous people and that will always be good love. A complete account of *good love* will therefore involve the "opening" aspect of love which Velleman uncovers, referred to three paragraphs back as "surrendering", as well as the motivational aspect of the common conception, its "devotion" or "reverence".

This is not to imply that the common conception of *love* gets love, even good love, completely right. The reason is that it takes the motive involved in love to be a desire to benefit the beloved in the manner indicated in the quote from Frankfurt. This does not, however, accommodate the idea of loving one's vocation or loving art or science. Not without good reason, Frankfurt takes parental love as his model, but this is too narrow for a fuller discussion of how to live the Good Life. Music has no "well-being" to which musicians are devoted, nor can those who love God be motivated by a desire to benefit God's well-being (assuming they are right and God exists). Lovers are devoted to what they love, and devotion obviously has a motivational component, but it is not always a motivation to benefit the beloved's well-being: devotion can take many forms depending

73. *Symposium*, 183d.

on its object. In what follows, these manifold forms of devotion are glossed as "being good to one's beloved".

As long as we surrender to something that is worthy of our devotion, we will become better people, we will live better lives through being good to what deserves it. Of course, since we cannot love equally everything that is good, we must be selective, we must find a good match for ourselves: we want good "chemistry" with our beloved, be it a person or a vocation. Finding or choosing who or what to love is the difficult part. But, following Plato's *Symposium*, we may also say that loving what or who is good repays a lover's respect and good will, since those beloveds who are good do their best to help their lovers flourish. So, falling in love with a beloved worthy of love will be good for the lover. If the beloved is a person, the beloved will reciprocate respect for respect, good will for the same, and ultimately, if the "fit" is good on both sides, a reciprocal love will be initiated.[74] If the beloved is a vocation worthy of pursuit, if one has the requisite talent and becomes devoted to scholarship, art, children, building, or farming (as opposed to being devoted to breaking hearts, embezzling, or killing people), one will flourish through one's learning and one's achievements. If falling in love with a bad person is self-destructive, is damaging to one's self-respect, so too is pursuing a vocation that is not worthy of pursuit. (Lacking the requisite talent for a noble pursuit leads to a sort of unrequited love that should be avoided, for reasons given in the last footnote.)

So, loving the people in one's life or loving one's vocation, being good in these endeavors by making the right choices, will benefit a

---

74. One must avoid unrequited love as a self-disrespecting and ultimately degrading form of love. Why self-disrespecting? Because the non-reciprocal nature of the relation implies that the beloved is unwilling, for whatever reason, to surrender to the lover as the lover originally surrendered to the beloved. This ends up being a form of servility. See Hill 1973 and Hampton 1993a, 1993b.

person in real and substantial ways. First, if one loves truly and sincerely, with a desire to be good to one's beloved, with an eye to being a better lover, one will, in fact, become a better lover: when our goal is to love our beloved as well as possible, then we will pay attention, learn from mistakes, and come to understand our beloved to the best of our abilities and talents. We may become experts in loving our beloved and, again, assuming we have chosen our beloved well, this will lead us to make good decisions time and again, filling our lives with moments of doing the right thing for what we value most highly, thereby living as well as is possible.

The benefits of being a good, even expert lover of one's beloved do not end here, however. There are other rewards: being a good lover also makes one more deserving of being loved and to be treated with the same honor, respect, and love that one gives in the first place. What better reward could there be than to be loved well by those whom one loves well? If people only use others for their own ends, like the Foscos, then they cannot claim that those whom they call "beloved" are really beloved (just as cheaters never really win). Thus, for the Foscos, receiving love or devotion from people who are really only being used as instruments cannot feel the same as receiving love from people who are truly loved in return. Reciprocal love is mutually beneficial in a way that is not open to one-sided relationships. The pleasures of loving are often greater than the pleasures of being loved, and the pleasures of loving are pleasures that immorality cannot yield.[75] Those who aspire to the Good Life give love freely to their beloved and are rewarded with the beloved's love given freely in return. Of course, the lover is not

---

75. Since the pleasures are beyond the familiarity of immoral people, pointing them out cannot serve as much of an argument or inducement to someone who is content with their own lot; especially if this special "pleasure" comes "at the price of" having to be devoted to another as true love demands.

motivated by this reward, or by the pleasure of being loved. Again, the good lover is motivated by a genuine desire to be good to and to love the beloved. Just as happiness is a byproduct of virtue, having our love returned by our beloved is, again, a byproduct of loving well. Extraordinarily special though this may be, it is nevertheless best seen as a side benefit of loving, not its motive: lovers who are motivated only by what they can get through love are not good lovers. This is an analog of the paradox of happiness. Living a Good Life is its own reward; there is really nothing more a person may ask for. Still, one will not live a Good Life by "getting" the right things "out of it"; rather, the Good Life is the result of what one puts into it.

So, in good love, one is not motivated by the instrumental value of one's beloved to produce one's own happiness. On the other hand, one should be willing to act in a way that instrumentally promotes the happiness or thriving of one's beloved. We want to be good for our beloved. In this sense alone, one can treat oneself as an instrument without ipso facto damaging one's self-respect. Good lovers are there for their beloved, to the best of their ability, in whichever way their beloved needs or enjoys most. Good lovers attend to their beloved by being motivated by love. Good love inspires itself and in this self-generating fashion engenders flourishing: we become stronger and better by loving well.

The most important benefits of being good, like the benefits of love, are not what one gets in return for being good, but are constituted by being good itself. This is the truth behind the thesis that "virtue is its own reward". There is no better life to be lived than one in which we make good, virtuous choices and do the right thing. Yes, as Aristotle noted, there should be pleasure or satisfaction attendant upon doing the right thing, pleasure completes the activity, but pleasure is not the right reason to do the right thing; pleasure is not the motive of a good person (cf. §3.2).[76] (Indeed, "the right thing to do" cannot be motivated by the pleasure of doing the right thing and still *really* be the right thing to do; this would only be another form of the paradox of happiness.) The only motivation good enough to qualify an action to count as "the right thing done well" is the motivation stemming from a good will trying to do the right thing and expressing itself virtuously. Of course, this is not to suggest either that the consequences of having a good will are not important (this is not to favor deontology over consequentialism, or vice versa) or that one should always think about what the right thing to do is before trying to do the right thing (remembering Williams' lesson of avoiding having "one thought too many"). Rather, we must train our will to be as good as possible, to the best of our abilities, in the ways sketched out above, and then to act "in character".

3.10 WISDOM

The following is only a partly empty tautology: the actions that constitute a Good Life, or a person's best life possible, are motivated by whatever it is best to be motivated by. We ought to do what is fine and noble (*to kalon*) with fine and noble motives. Or at least we ought to do our best to do so. Sometimes we ought to be motivated by love, sometimes by respect or principle, and sometimes by consequence, whichever is best in the circumstance.[77] A large share of

---

76. Aristotle 1985, 1174b33.

77. The idea that one should have to choose up front to *always* use *either* a consequentialist or deontological approach to life is like going through life with one hand tied behind our back. The wise person will choose between these problem-solving strategies depending on the circumstance. Sometimes we should count our losses and choose the lesser of two evils, sometimes we should stick to our principles and "damn the consequences". Cf. chap. 1, note 35; for a fuller discussion of these ideas, see *Moral Reality*, chap. 2.

wisdom is knowing what is best when, and people who are virtuous are motivated to do what is most appropriate in the circumstance. Virtuous action requires at least an intuitive understanding of the underlying nature of those circumstances, a comprehension of "what makes things tick", and "how things hang together", but it also requires the practical "know-how" to apply theory to concrete cases and to determine how to proceed. Besides this comprehension, the virtuous must also be experts at deliberation and have excellent discernment, adequate native intelligence, cleverness, and creativity. Embodying these traits so that they are one's "second nature" makes one wise.[78]

This is to adopt the ancient Greek conception of wisdom, or *sophia*, as in *philosophia* or "love of wisdom", which, roughly, is broken down into practical wisdom (*phronesis*) and theoretical wisdom (*theoria*), though these interpenetrate each other: practical wisdom requires understanding theoretical matters, and, good theories must work well. The Greeks had no agreed-upon understanding of how these are related to each other.[79] One way to see their interdependence is to consider perhaps the most basic distinction in metaphysics, which is surely a theoretical discourse, and its role in practical wisdom. This is the distinction between reality and appearance. That there is such a distinction is hard to deny; indeed, it is one that even skeptics need to make in order to get their position going, despite their reluctance to accept any theoretical distinctions. Distinguishing between how things appear and how they are is certainly theoretical, insofar as it can lead us to question the nature of our world and reality: one can see it in Plato's discussion of the cave in *Republic* as well

<hr>

78. Cf. §2.5; for more on the development of this "mundane" conception of wisdom, see Hursthouse 2006; Russell 2009; and my 2014.
79. The relations of practical and theoretical knowledge are still a matter of debate. See, for instance, an exchange on the topic in Bratman 2009 and Broome 2009.

as in Aristotle's understanding of metaphysics as the study of "being qua being" which requires a distinction between how things are in themselves and how we take them to be. And yet, as theoretical as it may be, this distinction is surely of central importance to practical success in the world. One might wonder what practical wisdom is, if not the ability to see beyond superficial appearances to how the things truly are. Such a distinction is required for any practical pursuit in which appearances are possibly deceiving. Knowing the difference between appearance and reality is even basic to perception, something babies have to learn: objects may appear small because they are far away or because they actually are small. On the other hand, it takes the wisest of physicians to diagnose difficult cases in which the symptoms are not conclusive. In the moral realm, what is pleasurable may appear to be good but need not be. In general, we think wise people are those who have the perspicacity to see to the "heart of the matter". So, wisdom requires the ability to make theoretical as well as practical distinctions that allow one to see beyond appearances, below the surface. This is not to say that only metaphysicians can be wise, only that some grasp of the distinction between appearance and reality is necessary for wisdom.

Wisdom also requires the apt application of theory to practice. These theories may come in various shapes and sizes, be more or less well-developed, and more or less helpful. Aside from scientific or philosophical theories, the theory behind, for example, farming will require farmers to understand nature's ways in order to tend to their crops. Similarly, parents will require at least some understanding of what babies, children, and adolescents need, even if it is largely only implicitly understood and ineffable for most. So, there is at least an implicit and only sometimes explicit intellectual grasp of the theory, but then it must also be applied as the occasions arise. There are inevitable connections between practical theories, as both farmers and parents can spoil what they intend to help grow. And this is similar to the ways in which different areas of life may overlap and integrate, as justice may bear on courage, and discretion may be the better part of valor. The role of wisdom as the virtue that brings unity to one's life, throughout all the roles one plays and the conditions in which one lives, is one we touched on in §2.5. Seeing these connections, learning from life, and taking care to apply lessons learned aptly is the alpha and omega of wisdom.

Most of the ancient Greeks, Aristotle being an exception, thought of the virtues as forms of skill, and even Aristotle would have agreed that the virtues are all "excellences", which, like skills, must be learned and developed over time, and that virtuous people are experts or possess expertise.[80] Although it is uncommon for philosophers today to think of the virtues as skills, and the idea that morality admits of expertise is highly contentious, there is good evidence from empirical psychology that supports this thinking, about wisdom in particular. The work of Paul Baltes and the "Berlin wisdom paradigm", as well as the work of Robert Sternberg, brings modern research tools to bear in figuring out the nature of wisdom and, without seeming to appreciate the fact, they confirm a very Greek point of view on the matter.[81] Baltes and Staudinger develop the idea that wisdom is an "expert system",[82] the purpose of which is to help people navigate what they call the "fundamental pragmatics of life", by which they mean

> knowledge and judgment about the essence of the human con-
> dition and the ways and means of planning, managing, and

---

80. For contemporary accounts of virtue as skill, see Annas 1995, as well as her 2011; Stichter 2007a and 2007b; Swartwood 2013; see also my 2000 and chap. 2 of *Moral Reality*.

81. See Baltes, Glück, and Kunzmann 2005; and Baltes and Staudinger 2000; Sternberg 1998. For a philosophically informed account, see Tiberius and Swartwood 2011.

82. Baltes and Staudinger 2000, 124.

understanding a good life. Included in the fundamental pragmatics of life are, for example, knowledge about the conditions,
variability, ontogenetic changes, and historicity of life development as well as knowledge of life's obligations and life goals;
understanding of the socially and contextually intertwined
nature of human life, including its finitude, cultural condition-
ing, and incompleteness; and knowledge about oneself and the
limits of one's own knowledge and the translation of knowledge
into overt behavior.

It is perhaps surprising that Baltes and his colleagues developed
such a picture of wisdom. In contrast to much of the research done
now in positive psychology, they did not collect data about what
most people think "wisdom" is or investigate what might be called
"the folk psychology of wisdom".[83] Rather, they based their model
on "research on expertise, lifespan psychology of cognition and
personality, the neo-Piagetian tradition of adult cognitive development, as well as cultural-historical analyses of wisdom".[84] Based
on this, they developed criteria by which subjects may be trained
as judges to evaluate responses as "high" or "low" on a "wisdom
related score", when these are given by respondents who are asked
questions about "the pragmatics of life". For example, respondents
are asked a question like, "A 15-year-old girl wants to get married
right away. What should one/she consider and do?" Answers such
as the following are given a low score:

A 15-year-old girl wants to get married? No, no way, marrying
at age 15 would be utterly wrong. One has to tell the girl that

83. See Tiberius 2013 for a discussion of the relations between philosophical and psychological
methodologies in studies of wisdom and well-being.
84. Baltes and Staudinger 2000, 125.

marriage is not possible. It would be irresponsible to support such an idea. No, this is just a crazy idea.

While answers such as the following are given a high score:

Well, on the surface, this seems like an easy problem. On average, marriage for a 15-year-old girl is not a good thing. But there are situations where the average case does not fit. Perhaps in this instance, special life circumstances are involved, such that the girl has a terminal illness. Or the girl has just lost her parents. And also, this girl may be living in another culture or historical period. Perhaps she was raised with a value system different from ours. In addition, one has to think about the adequate ways of talking with the girl and to consider her emotional state.[85]

The scoring criteria are that the answers of wise respondents employ a "rich factual (declarative) knowledge" of the facts of life and understand how it is contextualized by stages of life, and they appreciate the influence of culture and society on the individual, all the while recognizing uncertainty and attempting to manage it. Much of this should seem thematically similar to the role of virtue and wisdom in the Good Life that has been developed throughout this book. Their sense of wisdom as a "metaheuristic" is just what one should expect from a character trait whose role is to play a chief guiding function in one's mental economy and in one's life as a whole. Baltes et al. define a "metaheuristic" as "a heuristic that organizes, at a high level of aggregation, the pool (ensemble) of bodies of knowledge and commensurate more specific heuristics that are available to individuals in planning, managing, and evaluating issues surrounding

85. Baltes et al. 2005, 333.

the fundamental pragmatics of life".[86] It is, unfortunately, a mischar-
acterization to call the virtues "heuristics" of any sort, given that
"virtues" are character traits that range broadly throughout one's life
while "heuristics" are generally thought of as short-cuts or "tricks
of the trade", of merely parochial use. Nevertheless, the two ideas
are united by their purpose of guiding people through their lives so
that, at the end, they can be said to have "lived well"; and if their
circumstances are not horribly unfortunate, they will persevere to
live happily, to live the Good Life.

One can never do better than doing what is wise or what is morally best, when this is understood properly. We may have to adjust
our conceptions of *morality* and *self-interest*: it may be surprising to
learn that, on occasion, morality may tell one to take care of oneself
before taking care of others, or that it may truly be best for one's
self-interest to do "the right thing" when the action involved would
ordinarily be seen as requiring a sacrifice to one's self-interest. But
it is only by having a unified system of values that our lives will go
as well as possible; we cannot live the Good Life as "houses divided
against themselves" or with a conception of *practical wisdom* in
which self-interest and morality are incommensurable. This is to
understand wisdom, and morality as a whole, as encompassing the
broadest consideration of the facts of life and figuring out what is
best (or in unfortunate circumstances what is "least worst") in light
of everything salient; the wise answer is always "all things considered". This is accomplished by people who are themselves uniquely
fit to look out for themselves (and those they care about), and so
they must act autonomously.

Once again, this brings a consideration of self-interest directly
into moral deliberation: we cannot understand what is in our

---

86. Baltes and Staudinger 2000, 132.

self-interest independently of what is going on in the world around us, nor will we act for the best, all things considered, if this is taken to be independent of the particulars of who or what is involved. And this especially includes that person for whom one is most responsible, namely oneself. As is hopefully plain at this point, the dualism of *morality* and *self-interest* was a terribly damaging theoretical turn. Doing the best we can in life, making the best decisions for ourselves and for those whom our decisions affect, will yield the best life possible. If we strive for excellence, keeping in mind that we will never be perfect, pay attention so that we do not repeat our mistakes (too many times!), take care of ourselves and those around us, then our lives will be as good as can be.

Knowing what is best from moment to moment requires wisdom in judgment, or at least requires good judgment that, over time, may become wise. Sometimes rules must be "broken"; sometimes less is more. Sometimes the courageous thing to do is resign.[87] Falling in love may require giving in to temptation. Justice errs on the side of letting the guilty go free and also sometimes requires mercy for the guilty. Particular judgments are made on whether a case is normal or exceptional and most practical lessons can only be learned through experience. The wise autodidactically acquire an intuitive and acute sense for the distinction between reality and appearance. Teaching can only go so far.

Much of modern and contemporary moral philosophy, with its unfortunate attempts to arrive at a single determinate and recursive decision procedure for solving moral problems, has flouted this elementary lesson, much to our own chagrin: there are no hard and fast absolute rules of life. This is why it is unwise to immediately conclude, based on age alone, that a 15-year-old girl ought not to

---

87. I get this example from Woods 1986.

marry. The idea that morality does *not* amount to a recursive decision procedure is still fairly radical among moral philosophers, to the detriment of moral philosophy. Not only is it unfair, but life is far too complicated to be managed well by automated heuristics handling every situation in a regimented way. Discretion, diligence, scrutiny, and courage will all be required.

In the end, all one really can to do is try, often and regularly, to do what one is doing as well as possible, assuming that it is worth doing. If one's goals are genuinely worthwhile, then having average intelligence and great perseverance will be sufficient for significant improvement, barring any prolonged strings of bad luck. At worst, all our failures will be accompanied by the satisfaction of knowing that we could not have tried harder, could not have done better, given who we were at the time and the challenges we faced.

In closing, however regrettable it may be, the sad truth is that it is naive to think that everyone has an equal chance of becoming wise. While wisdom is probably no more likely to be found in the halls of academia than it is on the farm, whether or not one becomes wise will depend on one's capacities and talents. As sad a fact as it is, it is probably impossible for someone whose intelligence is well below average to become truly wise. (If this counts as "elitism", then common sense is elitist on this point.) At some level, native talent and even some prodigal skill will likely be needed to plumb and scale the depths and heights of wisdom.

Regardless of our talents, however, we can all do better than we are currently doing, by sincerely trying and working harder to be better. Even if it may not be possible for most of us to become truly, deeply wise, hardly any of us are so preternaturally lazy and irresponsible that we have no choice but to become complacent fools or mere sheep, incapable of insight or independent thought. And, of course, we owe it to ourselves to do better than that. As long as our aim is appropriately tempered and does not lead to obsession or neurosis, then we ought to strive to do as well as possible. If we pay attention, reflect on ourselves and our behavior, and on how we should behave toward other people and the rest of the world, if we train our will to be good, our motives to be noble, and our cares to be genuine, then we will have as good a chance as any has ever had of living the proverbial "Good Life".

To know you don't know is best.
Not to know you don't know is a flaw.
Therefore, not being flawed
 Stems from recognizing a flaw as a flaw
Therefore, one is flawless.

                                        Lao-Tzu

BIBLIOGRAPHY

Adams, Robert. 1999. *Finite and Infinite Goods.* New York: Oxford University Press.
———. 2006. *A Theory of Virtue.* New York: Oxford University Press.
Alston, William. 1968. "Moral Attitudes and Moral Judgments". *Noûs* 3 (1): 1–23.
Annas, Julia. 1981. *An Introduction to Plato's Republic.* Oxford: Clarendon.
———. 1993. *The Morality of Happiness.* Oxford: Oxford University Press.
———. 1995. "Virtue as a Skill". *International Journal of Philosophical Studies* 3 (2): 227–43.
———. 1999. *Platonic Ethics: Old and New.* Ithaca: Cornell University Press.
———. 2003. "Virtue Ethics and Social Psychology". *A Priori* 2: 20–34.
———. 2004. "Happiness as Achievement". *Daedalus* 133 (2): 44–51.
———. 2007. "Virtue Ethics". In *The Oxford Handbook of Ethical Theory,* edited by David Copp, 515–36. Oxford: Oxford University Press.
———. 2008. "Virtue Theory and the Charge of Egoism". In *Morality and Self-Interest,* edited by Paul Bloomfield, 205–22. Oxford: Oxford University Press.
———. 2011. *Intelligent Virtue.* Oxford: Oxford University Press.
Anscombe, G. E. M. 1958. "Modern Moral Philosophy". *Philosophy* 33: 1–19.
Aristotle. 1934. *Nicomachean Ethics.* In *Aristotle in 23 Volumes.* Translated by H. Rackham. Cambridge: Harvard University Press.
———. 1985. *Nicomachean Ethics.* Translated by Terence Irwin. Indianapolis: Hackett Publishing.
———. 1998. *Politics.* Translated by C. D. C. Reeve. Indianapolis: Hackett Publishing.
Audi, Robert. 1985. "Self-Deception and Rationality". In *Self-Deception and Self-Understanding: New Essays in Philosophy and Psychology,* edited by Mike W. Martin, 169–94. Lawrence: University Press of Kansas.

——. 1997. "Self-Deception, Rationalization, and the Ethics of Belief". In *Moral Knowledge and Ethical Character*, edited by Robert Audi, 131–56. New York: Oxford University Press.

Ayala, Francisco. 1976. "Biology as an Autonomous Science". In *Topics in the Philosophy of Biology*, edited by Marjorie Grene and Everett Mendelsohn, 313–29. Dordrecht: D. Reidel Publishing.

Badhwar, Neera. 1993. "Altruism versus Self-Interest: Sometimes a False Dichotomy". *Social Philosophy & Policy* 10 (1): 90–117.

——. 2008. "Is Realism Really Bad for You? A Realistic Response". *Journal of Philosophy* 105 (2): 85–107.

——. Forthcoming. *Happiness as the Highest Good*. New York: Oxford University Press.

Baehr, Jason. 2011. *The Inquiring Mind*. New York: Oxford University Press.

Baier, Kurt. 1954. "The Point of View of Morality". *Australasian Journal of Philosophy* 32 (2): 104–35.

——. 1958. *The Moral Point of View*. Ithaca: Cornell University Press.

Baltes, Paul, Judith Glück, and Ute Kunzmann. 2005. "Wisdom: Its Structure and Function in Regulating Successful Life Span Development". In *Handbook of Positive Psychology*, edited by C. R. Snyder and Shane J. Lopez, 327–49. Oxford: Oxford University Press.

—— and Ursula Staudinger. 2000. "Wisdom: A Metaheuristic (Pragmatic) to Orchestrate Mind and Virtue Toward Excellence". *American Psychologist* 55 (1): 122–36.

Baumeister, Roy F., Kathleen D. Vohs, and Dianne M. Tice. 2007. "The Strength Model of Self-Control". *Current Directions in Psychological Science* 16 (6): 351–55.

Baxter, Donald. 2001. "Instantiation as Partial Identity". *Australasian Journal of Philosophy* 79: 449–64.

Becker, Lawrence. 1998. *A New Stoicism*. Princeton: Princeton University Press.

Benn, S. I. 1985. "Wickedness". *Ethics* 95: 795–810.

Blackburn, Simon. 1984. *Spreading the Word*. New York: Oxford University Press.

——. 1998. *Ruling Passions: A Theory of Practical Reasoning*. Oxford: Clarendon Press.

Bloom, Paul. 2004. *Descartes' Baby*. New York: Basic Books.

Bloomfield, Paul. 2000. "Virtue Epistemology and the Epistemology of Virtue". *Philosophy and Phenomenological Research* 60 (1): 23–43.

——. 2001. *Moral Reality*. New York: Oxford University Press.

——. ed. 2008a. *Morality and Self-Interest*. New York: Oxford University Press.

——. 2008b. "Why It Is Bad to Be Bad". In *Morality and Self-Interest*, edited by Paul Bloomfield, 251–71. New York: Oxford University Press.

——. 2008c. "The Harm of Immorality". *Ratio* 21 (3): 241–59.

——. 2009. "Archimedeanism and Why Metaethics Matters". In *Oxford Studies in Metaethics*, edited by Russ Shafer-Landau, 4: 283–302. Oxford: Oxford University Press.

——. 2010. Review of *The Reflective Life*, by Valerie Tiberius. *Mind* 119: 258–62.

——. 2011. "Justice as a Self-Regarding Virtue". *Philosophy and Phenomenological Research* 82 (1): 46–64.

——. 2012. "Eudaimonia and Practical Rationality". In *Virtue and Happiness: Essays in Honour of Julia Annas*, edited by Rachana Kamtekar, 265–86. *Oxford Studies in Ancient Philosophy*, Supplementary volume. Oxford: Oxford University Press.

——. 2013. "The Moral Point of View". In *International Encyclopedia of Ethics*, edited by H. LaFollette. Malden, MA: Wiley-Blackwell.

——. 2014. "Some Intellectual Aspects of the Moral Virtues". In *Oxford Studies in Normative Ethics*, vol. 3, edited by Mark Timmons. Oxford: Oxford University Press.

——. Forthcoming. Review of *Happiness for Humans*, by Daniel Russell. *Social Theory and Practice*.

Brandt, Richard. 1972. "Utilitarianism and the Rules of War". *Philosophy and Public Affairs* 1 (2): 145–65.

Bratman, Michael. 2009. "Intention, Belief, Practical, Theoretical". In *Spheres of Reason*, edited by Simon Robertson, 29–61. Oxford: Oxford University Press.

Brink, David. 1990. "Rational Egoism, Self, and Others". In *Identity, Character, and Morality*, edited by Owen J. Flanagan and Amélie O. Rorty, 339–78. Cambridge: MIT Press.

Broome, John. 2009. "The Unity of Reasoning?" In *Spheres of Reason*, edited by Simon Robertson, 62–92. Oxford: Oxford University Press.

Brown, Donald E. 1991. *Human Universals*, chapters 5 and 6. New York: McGraw Hill. Reprinted in Downes and Machery 2013.

Buller, David. 2005. *Adapting Minds*, 420–457. Cambridge: MIT Press. Reprinted in Downes and Machery 2013.

Butler, Joseph. 1900a. "Sermon X—Upon Self-Deceit". In *The Works of Bishop Butler*, 2 vols., edited by J. H. Bernard. London: MacMillan.

——. 1900b. "Sermon XI—Upon the Love of Our Neighbor". In *The Works of Bishop Butler*, 2 vols., edited by J. H. Bernard, section 9. London: MacMillan.

Calhoun, Cheshire, ed. 2004. *Setting the Moral Compass*. New York: Oxford University Press.

Chang, Ruth. 1998. Introduction to *Incommensurability, Incomparability, and Practical Reason*, edited by Ruth Chang, 1–34. Cambridge: Harvard University Press.

——. 2004. "'All Things Considered'". *Philosophical Perspectives* 18: 1–22.

Chappell, Richard Yetter. 2013. "Value Receptacles". *Noûs*, April 15. doi:10.1111/nous.12023.

Chua, Amy and Jed Rubenfeld. 2014. *The Triple Package*. London: Penguin Press.

Cicero. 1914. *De Finibus*. Translated by H. Rackham. Cambridge: Loeb Classical Library.

Copp, David. 1997. "The Ring of Gyges: Overridingness and the Unity of Reason". *Social Philosophy & Policy* 14: 86–101.

Cosmides, Lena and John Tooby. 1997. "Evolutionary Psychology: A Primer". Online at: http//www.psych.ucsb.edu/research/dep/primer.html. Reprinted in Downes and Machery 2013.

Cottingham, John. 1991. "The Ethics of Self-Concern". *Ethics* 101: 798–817.

———. 1998. *Philosophy and the Good Life.* Cambridge: Cambridge University Press.

———. 2002. *On the Meaning of Life.* London: Routledge.

———. 2003. "Partiality and the Virtues". In *How Should One Live?*, edited by Roger Crisp, 57–76. Oxford: Oxford University Press.

———. 2010. "Impartiality and Ethical Formation". In *Partiality and Impartiality*, edited by Brian Feltham and John Cottingham. Oxford: Oxford University Press.

Crisp, Roger. 1996. "The Dualism of Practical Reason". *Proceedings of the Aristotelian Society* 96: 53–73.

———. 2006. *Reasons and the Good.* Oxford: Clarendon Press.

Darwall, Stephen. 1977. "Two Kinds of Respect". *Ethics* 88 (1): 36–49.

———. 2002. *Welfare and Rational Care.* (Princeton: Princeton University Press).

———. 2006. *The Second Person Standpoint.* Cambridge: Harvard University Press.

Dennett, Daniel. 1988. "Quining Qualia". In *Consciousness in Contemporary Science*, edited by Anthony J. Marcel and Edoardo Bisiach, 42–77. Oxford: Clarendon Press.

Dent, N. J. H. 1981. "The Value of Courage". *Philosophy* 56: 574–77.

Devitt, Michael. 2008. "Resurrecting Essentialism". *Philosophy of Science* 75 (3): 344–82.

Dewey, John. 1958. *Experience and Nature.* New York: Dover Publishing.

Dillon, Robin. 2004. "Kant on Arrogance and Self-Respect". In *Setting the Moral Compass*, edited by Cheshire Calhoun, 191–216. New York: Oxford University Press.

Donagan, Alan. 1977. *The Theory of Morality.* Chicago: University of Chicago Press.

Doris, John. 2002. *Lack of Character.* Cambridge: Cambridge University Press.

Downes, Stephen M. and Edouard Machery. 2013. *Arguing About Human Nature.* New York: Taylor and Francis.

Dreyfus, Hubert, and Stuart Dreyfus. 1990. "What Is Morality? A Phenomenological Account of the Development of Ethical Expertise". In *Universalism vs. Communitarianism*, edited by David Rasmussen. Cambridge: MIT Press.

Duckworth, Angela. 2007. "Grit: Perseverance and Passion for Long-Term Goals". *Journal of Personality and Social Psychology* 92 (6): 1087–1101.

Eggleston, Ben. 2013. "Paradox of Happiness". In *The International Encyclopedia of Ethics*, edited by Hugh LaFollette, 3794–99. Oxford: Blackwell Publishing.

Elster, Jon. 2000. *Ulysses Unbound.* Cambridge: Cambridge University Press.

Emerson, Ralph Waldo. 2010. *Self-Reliance and Other Essays.* Edited by Stanley Appelbaum. New York: Dover Thrift Editions.

Engstrom, Stephen P., and Jennifer Whiting, eds. 1996. *Aristotle, Kant, and the Stoics.* Cambridge: Cambridge University Press.

Enoch, David. 2011. *Taking Morality Seriously: A Defense of Robust Realism.* Oxford: Oxford University Press.

Epictetus. 1983. *The Handbook of Epictetus.* Translated, with introduction and annotations, by Nicholas White. Indianapolis: Hackett Publishing.

Falk, W. D. 1963. "Morality, Self, and Others". In *Morality and the Language of Conduct,* edited by Hector-Neri Castañeda and George Nakhnikian, 25–67. Detroit: Wayne State University Press. Reprinted in Bloomfield 2008a, 225–50.

———. 1986. "Morality, Form, and Content". In *Ought, Reasons, and Morality.* Ithaca: Cornell University Press.

Feldman, Fred. 2002. "Good Life: A Defense of Attitudinal Hedonism". *Philosophy and Phenomenological Research* 65 (3): 604–28.

Feltham, Brian, and John Cottingham, eds. 2010. *Partiality and Impartiality.* Oxford: Oxford University Press.

Finlay, Stephen. 2008. "Too Much Morality". In *Morality and Self-Interest,* edited by Paul Bloomfield, 136–57. New York: Oxford University Press.

Foot, Philippa. 1958–59. "Moral Beliefs". *Proceedings of the Aristotelian Society,* n.s., 59: 83–104.

———. 2001. *Natural Goodness.* Oxford: Clarendon Press.

France, Peter. 1997. *Hermits: The Insights of Solitude.* New York: St Martin's Press.

Frankena, William. 1966a. "The Concept of Morality". *Journal of Philosophy* 63 (21): 688–96.

———. 1966b. "Recent Conceptions of Morality". In *Morality and the Language of Conduct,* edited by Hector-Neri Castañeda and George Nakhnikian, 1–24. Detroit: Wayne State University Press.

Frankfurt, Harry. 1971. "Freedom of the Will and the Concept of a Person". *Journal of Philosophy* 68 (1): 5–20.

———. 2004. *Reasons of Love.* Princeton: Princeton University Press.

Fricker, Miranda. 2007. *Epistemic Injustice.* Oxford: Oxford University Press.

Gaillot, M. T., et al. 2007. "Self-Control Relies on Glucose as a Limited Energy Source: Willpower Is More Than a Metaphor". *Journal of Personality and Social Psychology* 92 (2): 325–36.

Gardiner, Stephen. 2005. *Virtue Ethics, Old and New.* Ithaca: Cornell University Press.

Gauthier, David. 1986. *Morals by Agreement.* Oxford: Clarendon Press.

Gibbard, Allan. 1990. *Wise Choices, Apt Feelings.* Cambridge: Harvard University Press.

Gill, Christopher. 2004. "The Stoic Theory of Ethical Development". In *Was ist das für den Menschen Gute?,* edited by Jan Szaif and Matthias Lutz-Bachmann, 101–25. Berlin: De Gruyter.

Goldman, Alvin. 2001. "Experts: Which Ones Should You Trust?" *Philosophy and Phenomenological Research* 63 (1): 85–110.

Greene, J. D. 2007. "The Secret Joke of Kant's Soul". *Moral Psychology, Vol. 3: The Neuroscience of Morality: Emotion, Disease, and Development,* edited by W. Sinnott-Armstrong. Cambridge: MIT Press.

Grene, Marjorie. 1976. "Aristotle and Modern Biology". In *Topics in the Philosophy of Biology*, Marjorie Grene and Everett Mendelsohn, 3–36. Dordrecht: D. Reidel Publishing.

Griffin, James. 1986. *Well-Being*. Oxford: Clarendon Press.

Haidt, Jonathan. 2001. "The Emotional Dog and Its Rational Tail". *Psychological Review* 108 (4): 814–34.

——. 2006. *The Happiness Hypothesis*. New York: Basic Books.

Hampton, Jean. 1993a. "Selflessness and Loss of Self". *Social Philosophy and Policy* 10 (1): 135–65.

——. 1993b. "Feminist Contractarianism". In *A Mind of One's Own*, edited by Louise Antony and Charlotte Witt, 337–68. Boulder, CO: Westview Press.

Hare, R. M. 1952. *The Logic of Morals*. Oxford: Clarendon Press.

——. 1972. "Rules of War and Moral Reasoning". *Philosophy and Public Affairs* 1 (2): 166–81.

——. 1981. *Moral Thinking*. Oxford: Clarendon Press.

Harman, Gilbert. 1975. "Moral Relativism Defended". *Philosophical Review* 84 (1): 3–22.

Haybron, Daniel M. 2001. "Happiness and Pleasure". *Philosophy and Phenomenological Research* 62 (2): 501–28.

——. 2008. *The Pursuit of Unhappiness*. New York: Oxford University Press.

Heller, Joseph. 1995. *Catch-22*. New York: Everyman's Library.

Herman, Barbara. 1993. *The Practice of Moral Judgment*. Cambridge: Harvard University Press.

Herman, Judith. 1997. *Trauma and Recovery*. New York: Basic Books.

Hill, Thomas, Jr. 1973. "Servility and Self-Respect". *The Monist* 57 (1): 87–104. Reprinted in Hill, Thomas, Jr. 1991. *Autonomy and Self-Respect*, 4–12. Cambridge: Cambridge University Press.

——. 1997. "Reasonable Self-Interest". *Social Philosophy and Policy* 14 (1): 52–85.

Hills, Allison. 2003. "The Significance of the Dualism of Practical Reason". *Utilitas* 15 (3): 315–29.

——. 2010. *The Beloved Self*. Oxford: Oxford University Press.

Hull, David L. 1986. "On Human Nature". In *PSA: Proceedings of the Biennial Meeting of the Philosophy of Science Association* 2: 3–13. Reprinted in Downes and Machery 2013.

Hume, David. 1978. *A Treatise of Human Nature*. 2nd edition Oxford: Oxford University Press.

Hurka, Thomas. 1992. "Virtue as Loving the Good". *Social Philosophy and Policy* 9 (2): 149–68.

——. 1993. *Perfectionism*. Oxford: Oxford University Press.

——. 2001. *Virtue, Vice and Value*. Oxford: Clarendon Press.

Hursthouse, Rosalind. 1980–81. "A False Doctrine of the Mean". *Proceedings of the Aristotelian Society* 81: 57–72.

——. 1999. *On Virtue Ethics*. Oxford: Oxford University Press.

——. 2006. "Practical Wisdom: A Mundane Account". *Proceedings of the Aristotelian Society* 106 (1): 285–309.

Huxley, Aldous. 1970. *Brave New World*. London: Chatto & Windus.

Irwin, T. H. 1996. "Kant's Criticisms of Eudaemonism". In *Aristotle, Kant, and the Stoics*, edited by Stephen P. Engstrom and Jennifer Whiting, 63–101. Cambridge: Cambridge University Press.

——. 2005. "The Parts of the Soul and the Cardinal Virtues". In *Platon, Politeia*, edited by Otto Höffe, 119–39. Berlin: Akademie-Verlag.

——. 2008. "Scotus and the Possibility of Moral Motivation". In *Morality and Self-Interest*, edited by Paul Bloomfield, 159–76. Oxford: Oxford University Press.

Iyengar, B. K. S. 1966. *Light on Yoga*. New York: Schoken Books.

Jacobson, Daniel. 2005. "Seeing by Feeling". *Ethical Theory and Moral Practice* 8 (4): 387–409.

——. 2011. "Fitting Attitude Theories of Value". *The Stanford Encyclopedia of Philosophy*. http://plato.stanford.edu/entries/fitting-attitude-theories.

James, William. 1896. "The Will to Believe". *The New World* 5: 327–47.

Job, Veronika, Carol S. Dweck, and Gregory M. Walton. 2010. "Ego Depletion—Is It All in Your Head?: Implicit Theories About Willpower Affect Self-Regulation". *Psychological Science*, September 28. http://pss.sagepub.com/content/early/20 10/09/28/0956797610384745.

Johnson, Robert. 2002. "Happiness as a Natural End". In *Kant's Metaphysics of Morals: Interpretive Essays*, edited by Mark Timmons, 637–65. New York: Oxford University Press.

——. 2011. *Self-Improvement: An Essay in Kantian Ethics*. Oxford: Oxford University Press.

Joyce, Richard. 2006. *The Evolution of Morality*. Cambridge: MIT Press.

——. 2008. "Replies". *Philosophy and Phenomenological Research* 77 (1): 245–67.

Kagan, Shelly. 1991. *The Limits of Morality*. New York: Oxford University Press.

Kahneman, Daniel. 2011. *Thinking Fast and Slow*. New York: Farrar, Straus and Giroux.

Kamtekar, Rachana. 2004. "Situationism and Virtue Ethics on the Content of Our Character". *Ethics* 114 (3): 47–68.

Kant, Immanuel. 1959. *Foundations of the Metaphysics of Morals*. Translated by Lewis White Beck. New York: Liberal Arts Press Inc.

—— . 1999. *The Metaphysics of Morals*. Translated by Mary Gregor. Cambridge: Cambridge University Press.

Keyes, Corey, and Julia Annas. 2009. "Feeling Good and Functioning Well". *Journal of Positive Psychology* 4 (3): 197–201.

Kohlberg, Lawrence. 1973. "The Claim to Moral Adequacy of a Highest Stage of Moral Judgment". *Journal of Philosophy* 70: 630–46.

Korsgaard, Christine. 1986. "Skepticism about Practical Reason". *Journal of Philosophy* 83 (1): 5–25.

——. 1996. *Sources of Normativity*. Cambridge: Cambridge University Press.

Kraut, Richard. 2007. *What Is Good and Why*. Cambridge: Harvard University Press.

Kripke, Saul. 1972. *Naming and Necessity*. Cambridge: Harvard University Press.

Kross, Ethan, Ozlem Ayduk, and Walter Mischel. 2005. "When Asking 'Why' Does Not Hurt: Distinguishing Rumination from Reflective Processing of Negative Emotions". *Psychological Science* 16: 709–15.

Kupperman, Joel. 2001. "The Indispensability of Character". *Philosophy* 76: 239–50.

——. 2010. *Theories of Human Nature*. Indianapolis: Hackett Publishing.

Lao Tzu. 1989. *Te-Tao Ching*. Translated by Robert G. Henricks. New York: Ballantine Books.

LaBarge, Scott. 1997. "Socrates and the Recognition of Experts". *Apeiron* 30 (4): 51–62.

Lebar, Mark, and Daniel Russell. 2013. "Well-Being and Eudaimonia: A Reply to Haybron". In *Aristotelian Ethics in Contemporary Perspective*, edited by Julia Peters 85–108. New York: Routledge.

Lee, Spike, dir. 2006. *When the Levees Broke*. DVD. New York: HBO Documentary Films.

Long, Anthony A., and David N. Sedley, eds. 1987. *The Hellenistic Philosophers*. Vol. 1, *Translations of the Principal Sources with Philosophical Commentary*. Cambridge: Cambridge University Press.

Lynch, Michael P. 2005. *True to Life*. Cambridge: MIT Press.

——. 2006. "Trusting Intuition". In Truth and Realism, edited by Patrick Greenough and Michael Lynch, 227–38. Oxford: Oxford University Press.

——. 2012. *In Praise of Reason*. Cambridge: MIT Press.

Machiavelli, Niccolò. 1977. *The Prince*. Translated by Robert Adams. New York: Norton.

MacIntyre, Alasdair. 1985. *After Virtue*. London: Duckworth Press.

Mackie, John. 1977. *Ethics: Inventing Right and Wrong*. Harmondsworth: Penguin.

Masten, Ann S., and Marie-Gabrielle J. Reed. 2005. "Resilience in Development". In *Handbook of Positive Psychology*, edited by C. R. Snyder and Shane J. Lopez, 74–88. Oxford: Oxford University Press.

McDowell, John. 1979. "Virtue and Reason". *Monist* 62: 331–50.

McPherson, Tristam. 2013. "What is at Stake in Debates Among Normative Realists". *Noûs* http://dx.doi.org/10.1111/nous.12055

Mill, John Stuart. 1992. *On Liberty*. New York: Everyman's Library.

Milo, Ronald D. 1984. *Immorality*. Princeton: Princeton University Press.

Mischel, Walter, Yuichi Shoda, and Monica L. Rodriguez. 1989. "Delay of Gratification in Children". *Science* 244 (4907): 933–38.

Murdoch, Iris. 1971. *The Sovereignty of Good*. New York: Schoken Books.

Nagel, Thomas. 1970. *The Possibility of Altruism*. Oxford: Clarendon Press.

——. 1986. *Mortal Questions*. Oxford: Oxford University Press.

——. 1991. *Equality and Partiality*. New York: Oxford University Press.

Nichols, Shaun. 2004. *Sentimental Rules*. New York: Oxford University Press.

Nietzsche, Friedrich. 1989. On the *Genealogy of Morals and Ecce Homo*. Translated by Walter Kaufmann. New York: Vintage Books.

Nozick, Robert. 1974. *Anarchy, State, and Utopia.* New York: Basic Books.

———. 1981. *Philosophical Explanations.* Cambridge: Harvard University Press.

Nussbaum, Martha. 1988. "Non-Relative Virtues: An Aristotelian Approach". *Midwest Studies in Philosophy* 13: 32–53.

Parfit, Derek. 1984. "What Makes Someone's Life Go Best". In *Reasons and Persons*, 493–501. Oxford: Clarendon Press.

———. 2011. *On What Matters.* Oxford: Oxford University Press.

Piaget, Jean. 1932. *The Moral Judgment of the Child.* London: Kegan Paul.

Plato. 1952. *Euthydemus.* In *The Dialogues of Plato.* Translated by Benjamin Jowett. Chicago: Encyclopaedia Britannica.

———. 2006. *Protagoras.* In *Protagoras and Meno.* Translated by Adam Beresford. London: Penguin Classics.

———. 2006. *Meno.* In *Protagoras and Meno.* In Translated by Adam Beresford. London Penguin Classics.

———. 1993. *Republic.* Translated by Robin Waterfield. Oxford: Oxford University Press.

———. 1994. *Gorgias.* Translated by Robin Waterfield. Oxford: Oxford University Press.

———. 1994. *Symposium.* Translated by Robin Waterfield. Oxford: Oxford University Press.

Plutarch. 1987. *On Moral Virtue.* In *The Hellenistic Philosophers*, edited by Anthony A. Long and David N. Sedley, 1: 377–78. Cambridge: Cambridge University Press.

Price, Richard. 1787. *Review of the Principle Questions of Morals*, 3rd revised edition. London: T. Cadell.

Prichard, H. A. 1912. "Does Moral Philosophy Rest on a Mistake?" *Mind*, n.s., 21 (81): 21–37.

———. 1952. "Duty and Interest". In *Readings in Ethical Theory*, edited by Wilfrid Sellars and John Hospers, 690. New York: Appleton-Century-Crofts.

Quine, W. V. O. 1956. "Quantifiers and Propositional Attitudes". *Journal of Philosophy* 53: 177–87.

Quinn, Warren. 1994. "Putting Rationality in Its Place". In *Morality and Action*, 228–57. Cambridge: Cambridge University Press.

Rainbolt, George. 1990. "Mercy: An Independent, Imperfect Virtue". *American Philosophical Quarterly* 27 (2): 169–73.

———. 1997. "Mercy: In Defense of Caprice". *Noûs* 31: 226–41.

Rawls, John. 1957. "Symposium: Justice as Fairness". *Journal of Philosophy* 54 (22): 653–62.

———. 1971. *A Theory of Justice.* Cambridge: Harvard University Press.

Robertson, Simon, ed. 2009. *Spheres of Reason.* Oxford: Oxford University Press.

Rosati, Connie. 2009. "Self-Interest and Self-Sacrifice". *Proceedings of the Aristotelian Society* 109: 311–25.

Ross, W. D. 1930. *The Right and the Good.* Oxford: Clarendon Press.

Russell, Daniel. 2005. "Aristotle on the Moral Relevance of Self-Respect". In *Virtue Ethics, Old and New*, 101–24. Ithaca: Cornell University Press.

———. 2009. *Practical Intelligence and the Virtues*. New York: Oxford University Press.

———. 2012. *Happiness for Humans*. Oxford: Oxford University Press.

Santas, Gerasimos. 1964. "The Socratic Paradoxes". *Philosophical Review* 73: 147–64.

Scanlon, T. M. 1982. "Contractualism and Utilitarianism". In *Utilitarianism and Beyond*, edited by Amartya Sen and Bernard Williams, 103–28. Cambridge: Cambridge University Press.

———. 2000. *What We Owe Each Other*. Cambridge: Belknap Press.

Scheffler, Samuel. 1982. *The Rejection of Consequentialism*. Oxford: Clarendon Press.

———. 1992. *Human Morality*. New York: Oxford University Press.

Schmidtz, David. 1996. *Rational Choice and Moral Agency*. Princeton: Princeton University Press.

———. 2006. *Elements of Justice*. Cambridge: Cambridge University Press.

———. 2008. "Because It's Right". In *Morality and Self-Interest*, edited by Paul Bloomfield, 79–101. New York: Oxford University Press.

Seeskin, Kenneth. 1976. "Courage and Knowledge". *Southern Journal of Philosophy* 14 (4): 511–21.

Seneca. 1995. *On Anger*. In *Seneca: Moral and Political Essays*, edited by J. F. Procopé and John M. Cooper, 1–116. Cambridge: Cambridge University Press.

Setiya, Kieran. 2007. *Reasons without Rationalism*. Princeton: Princeton University Press.

Shafer-Landau, Russ. 2003. *Moral Realism: A Defense*. Oxford: Clarendon Press.

Sidgwick, Henry. 1907. *The Methods of Ethics*. 7th edition Indianapolis: Hackett Publishing Company.

Singer, Peter. 1993. *Practical Ethics*. New York: Cambridge University Press.

Sklar, Larry. 1995. *Physics and Chance*. Cambridge: Cambridge University Press.

Slote, Michael Anthony. 1964. "An Empirical Basis for Psychological Egoism". *Journal of Philosophy* 61 (18): 530–37.

Sowell, Elizabeth R., et al. 2001. "Mapping Continued Brain Growth and Gray Matter Density Reduction in Dorsal Frontal Cortex: Inverse Relationships during Postadolescent Brain Maturation". *The Journal of Neuroscience* 15 (22): 8819–29.

Sreenivasan, Gopal. 2002. "Errors about Errors: Virtue Theory and Train Attribution". *Mind* 111: 47–68.

Steinberg, Laurence. 2004. "Risk Taking in Adolescence: What Changes, and Why?" *Annals of the New York Academy of Sciences* 1021: 51–58.

Sternberg, Robert J. 1998. "A Balance Theory of Wisdom". *Review of General Psychology* 2 (4): 347–65.

Stevenson, Charles Leslie. 1937. "The Emotive Meaning of Ethical Terms". *Mind* 46 (81): 14–31.

Stichter, Matthew. 2007a. "Ethical Expertise". *Ethical Theory and Moral Practice* 10: 183–94.

——. 2007b. "The Skill Model of Virtue". *Philosophy in the Contemporary World* 14: 39–49.

Stocker, Michael. 1976. "The Schizophrenia of Modern Ethical Theories". *Journal of Philosophy* 73: 453–66.

——. 1979. "Desiring the Bad". *Journal of Philosophy* 76: 738–53.

——. 1990. *Plural and Conflicting Values*. Oxford: Clarendon Press.

——. 2008. "Shame and Guilt". In *Morality and Self-Interest,*edited by Paul Bloomfield, 287-303. New York: Oxford University Press.

——. and Elizabeth Hegeman. 1996. *Valuing Emotions*. Cambridge: Cambridge University Press.

Strawson, Peter F. 1962. "Freedom and Resentment". *Proceedings of the British Academy* 48: 187–211.

Stroud, Sarah, and Christine Tappolet, eds. 2003. *Weakness of Will and Practical Irrationality*. Oxford: Clarendon Press.

Summers, Jesse and Walter Sinnott-Armstrong. Forthcoming. "Scrupulous Characters and Mental Illness". In *Character: Perspectives from Philosophy and Psychology*. Edited by Iskra Fileva. New York: Oxford University Press.

Sumner, L. W. 1996. *Welfare, Happiness, and Ethics*. New York: Oxford University Press.

Svavarsdòttir, Sigrún. 2008. "The Virtue of Practical Rationality". *Philosophy and Phenomenological Research* 77:1–33.

Swanton, Christine. 2003. *Virtue Ethics: A Pluralistic View*. New York: Oxford University Press.

Swartwood, Jason. 2013. "Wisdom as an Expert Skill". *Ethical Theory and Moral Practice* 16 (3): 511–28.

Tec, Necama. 1987. *When Light Pierced the Darkness: Christian Rescue of Jews in Nazi-Occupied Poland*. New York: Oxford University Press.

Telfer, Elizabeth. 1968. "Self-Respect". *Philosophical Quarterly* 18: 114–21.

Thomson, Judith Jarvis. 2003. *Goodness and Advice*. Edited by Amy Gutmann. Princeton: Princeton University Press.

Tiberius, Valerie. 2008. *The Reflective Life*. New York: Oxford University Press.

——. 2013. "Well-Being, Wisdom, and Thick Theorizing". In *Thick Concepts*. Edited by Simon Kirchin. Oxford: Oxford University Press.

——. and Jason Swartwood. 2011. "Wisdom Revisited: A Case Study in Normative Theorizing". *Philosophical Explorations* 14 (3): 277–95.

——. and John D. Walker. 1998. "Arrogance". *American Philosophical Quarterly* 35 (4): 379–90.

Timmons, Mark. 1999. *Morality without Foundations*. New York: Oxford University Press.

——, ed. 2002. *Kant's Metaphysics of Morals: Interpretive Essays*. New York: Oxford University Press.

Tooby, John and Lena Cosmides. "On the Universality of Human Nature and the Uniqueness of the Individual". *Journal of Personality* 58: 17–67. Reprinted in Downes and Machery 2013.

Vaish, Amrisha, Malinda Carpenter, and Michael Tomasello. 2010. "Young Children Selectively Avoid Helping People with Harmful Intentions". *Child Development* 81 (6): 1661–69.

van Roojen, Mark. 2010. "Moral Rationalism and Rational Amoralism". *Ethics* 120: 495–525.

Velleman, David. 1999. "Love as a Moral Emotion". *Ethics* 109 (2): 338–74.

Vlastos, Gregory. 1968. "The Argument in *The Republic* that 'Justice Pays' ". *Journal of Philosophy* 65 (21): 665–74.

Walsh, Denis. 2006. "Evolutionary Essentialism". *British Journal of the Philosophy of Science* 57: 425–48.

———. 2008. "Teleology". In *Oxford Handbook of the Philosophy of Biology*, edited by M. Ruse, 113–37. Oxford: Oxford University Press.

Watson, Gary. 1983. "Virtues in Excess". *Philosophical Studies* 46: 57–74.

Wedgwood, Ralph. 2013. "The Weight of Moral Reasons". *Oxford Studies in Normative Ethics*, edited by M. Timmons, vol. 3, 35–58. Oxford: Oxford University Press.

Weiss, Roslyn. 2006. *The Socratic Paradox and Its Enemies*. Chicago: University of Chicago Press.

Wheeler, Samuel. 2014. *Neo-Davidsonian Metaphysics: From the True to the Good*. New York: Routledge.

Whitman, Walt. 2007. *Leaves of Grass*. New York: Dover Thrift Editions.

Williams, Bernard. 1973. "A Critique of Utilitarianism". In *Utilitarianism: For and Against*, co-written with J. C. C. Smart, 77–150. Cambridge: Cambridge University Press.

———. 1980. "Justice as a Virtue". In *Essays on Aristotle's Ethics*, edited by Amélie O. Rorty, 189–200. Berkeley: University of California Press.

———. 1981. *Moral Luck*. Cambridge: Cambridge University Press.

———. 1985. *Ethics and the Limits of Philosophy*. Cambridge: Harvard University Press.

Wolf, Susan. 1982. "Moral Saints". *Journal of Philosophy* 79 (8): 419–39.

Wong, David. 2006. "Moral Reasons: Internal and External". *Philosophy and Phenomenological Research* 72 (3): 536–58.

Woodruff, Paul. 2001. *Reverence*. New York: Oxford University Press.

Woods, Michael. 1986. "Intuition and Perception in Aristotle's Ethics". *Oxford Studies in Ancient Philosophy* 4: 145–66.

Wright, Crispin. 1992. *Truth and Objectivity*. Cambridge: Harvard University Press.

Zagzebski, Linda. 1996. *Virtues of the Mind*. Cambridge: Cambridge University Press.

Zimmerman, Michael. 2001. *The Nature of Intrinsic Value*. Lanham, MD: Rowman & Littlefield.

INDEX

achievement, 49, 61, 87–8, 169–71, 183, 197, 219
Adams, Robert, 110n15, 173
agency, 64, 65, 67, 93–4, 161, 205
agent-centered prerogative, 22–3, 115n21
agent-centered restriction, 23–4
akrasia, 189, 200. *See* weakness of will
Alfred, Katherine, 139n41
Allen, Woody, 151n51
all-things-considered judgment, 11, 18, 32, 35, 40–2, 94, 145, 174, 196, 212, 228–9
Alston, William, 184n31
appearance/reality distinction, 51, 54, 223–4, 229
appraisal respect, 61–2, 88
appropriation, Stoic, 126n33, 136n36
arête, 159, 172. *See* virtus
Armstrong, Lance, 50n46, 59, 90
arrogance, 48–51, 78, 82, 154, 172, 185–7.
    See *also* greed, pleonexia
Aquinas, 12n4
Annas, Julia, 11n1, 12n2, 26n27, 30n32, 49, 103n9, 110n15, 126n33, 136n36, 165n14, 173, 177n24, 186n38, 197n51, 204n61, 225n80
Anscombe, G. E. M., 12n4, 174n21
Aristotle, 11-2n2, 27n29, 48, 51n49, 56n54, 58n55, 61n58, 110n15, 136n36, 162,

178–9, 182, 185n32, 198–9, 200–3, 204n61, 212, 221–2, 224, 225
Audi, Robert, 50-1n48
authority of morality, 12–4, 22, 24–5, 40–2.
    See also queerness
Ayala, Francisco, 161n10

bad luck, 154, 206, 209–11, 230
Badhwar, Neera, 52n51, 54n53, 58n55, 75n72, 119n25, 120n28, 173
Baier, Kurt, 20n17
bait and switch, 85–8
Baltes, Paul, 225–8
    and J. Glück, U. Kunzmann, 225n81
    and U. Staudinger, 225n81
Barnum, P. T., 62
Baumeister, Roy, K. Vohs, and D. Tice, 191n44
Baxter, Donald, 18n14, 68n67
Becker, Lawrence, 12n2, 26n27, 126n33, 173
Benn, S., 151n52
betrayal, 46, 57, 64
bias, 73–5, 144–50, 194–5
biology, 65–7, 157, 160–2, 168, 177
Blackburn, Simon, 2–3, 30n31
Blatt, Joel, 203n59
Bloom, Paul, 136n36
Bloomfield, Donald, 39

Bloomfield, Paul, 5n7, 26n27, 30n31, 137n37, 156n6, 163n12, 194–5n49. *See also, Moral Reality*
boredom, 175, 180, 190, 193
Bradley, Ben, 166n16
Brandt, Richard, 120n26
Bratman, Michael, 223n79
Brink, David, 58n55
Broome, John, 223n79
Brown, Donald, 66n65
Buddhism, 82
Buller, David, 66n65
Butler, Jospeh, 19–20, 51n48, 97–9, 109, 130–1, 144n45, 194n48

Callicles, 13, 47
cardinal moral virtues, 38, 155, 159–61, 165, 175–6, 184, 207–8
Catch -22, 94–5
Chang, Ruth, 12n2, 107n14
Chapman, Tracy,
Chappell, Richard, 205n63
character trait, 5, 17, 61, 134, 162, 173, 176n24, 188, 177, 189, 192, 196, 227–8. *See also*, moral character
cheating, 1, 46–50, 57–9, 70, 90–1, 116, 119, 150, 154, 174, 187n40, 191, 220. *See also*, "winning"
children, 20, 65, 71, 90, 115, 116, 120–2, 132, 139, 142, 150, 163, 188, 191, 204n61, 210–1, 219, 224
Chua, Amy and J. Rubenfeld, 189n43
Cicero, 58n56, 90, 126n33, 136n36
Cleinias, 45
Cobb, Craig, 71
Collins, Wilkie, 47
common sense, 40, 66, 106, 124, 138, 175
common-sense morality, 31–2, 38
community, 4, 16, 113, 154, 171, 205, 209, 214
confirmation bias, 194–5
Confucius, 48
consequentialism, 24, 34n35, 103n9, 115n21, 117, 173, 222
considerations, see other-regarding considerations, self-regarding considerations
constitutive value, 51, 109, 127, 131, 164, 172
continence, 189, 197, 200

contractualism, 17
Copp, David, 12n2
Cosmides, Lena, 66n65
Cottingham, John, 92n1, 104n18, 173, 175n23, 285n33
courage, 38, 61n58, 67, 134–6, 139n41, 162, 162, 176, 177–84, 187–8, 193, 206, 225, 229, 230
cowardice, 91, 107, 172, 177, 179–80
Crisp, Roger, 20n17, 21n20
Cyreniacs, 166

Dalai Lama, the, 48
Darwall, Stephen, 20n17, 21n20, 61
Davidsonians, 65. *See also* agency
de re/de dicto attitudes, 76–7
Dennett, Daniel, 196n50
deontology, 24n25, 34n35, 222
desire, 1, 10, 19–20, 44–5, 50–1nn47-8, 59n57, 86, 104, 113, 168, 174, 187, 188–201, 215, 217–21
Devitt, Michael, 66n65
devotion, 175, 214, 216–20. *See* reverence
Dewey, John, 177n25
dignity, 19, 64, 85, 217
Dillon, Robin, 48n42, 51n48
dirty hands, 120n26, 211
discretion, 178, 225, 230
Donagan, Alan, 65
Don Juan De Marco, 51
Doris, John, 177n24
Driver, Julia, 173
drugs, 51–2, 53, 168–9
dualism, 18, 19, 20n17, 22n21, 23, 24, 28, 31, 42, 110, 156–8, 229
Duckworth, Angela, 189n43
dupes, 14, 45, 48n44, 50, 54, 58, 62–3, 78, 88, 89, 91, 99. *See* fools, suckers
dutiful daughter, 32–4, 35, 39, 117, 133

Eggleston, Ben, 94n4
egocentricism, 100, 122, 147–9
egoism, 3nn3–4, 28, 30, 30n31, 44, 58n55, 103, 108, 113–4, 216n69. *See* Fosco, immoralism, solipsism
   ethical egoism, 13
   psychological egoism, 97–8

egoists, 3n3, 4–5, 13–5, 16, 19, 21, 23, 24–7,
  30–1, 37, 43–4, 46–7, 81, 93, 99–102,
  111, 113–4, 129, 137n39, 148–9, 174. *See*
  immoralist
  Fundamental Paradox of Egoistic
  Hedonism, 97. *See* paradox of happiness
Elster, Jon, 192n45
Emerson, R. W., 3
emotion, 22, 39, 120n28, 135, 142n44, 144,
  158–60, 63, 183–4, 187–8, 191–4, 198,
  201, 227
end in itself, 79, 85, 109, 125–6, 129–33, 142.
  See final end, intrinsic value
endurance, 135, 176, 180, 208. *See*
  perseverance
Engstrom, Stephen, 18n13
Enoch, David, 156n5
Epictetus, 204n62
Epicurus, 97, 166
equality, 12, 17, 60, 68, 74, 83–4, 185, 187, 219
essential properties, 63–4, 66n65, 69, 71, 78
eudaimonia, 4, 11, 11n1, 12n4, 30n32,
  54, 103n9, 163, 172–3, 201, 203. *See*
  flourishing, happiness, the Good Life
Euthyphro contrast, 27, 52-3n52
evil, 29, 47, 65, 170,
  gleeful evil, 151–2
  necessary evil, 2, 6, 17, 25, 94, 152
  lesser of two evils, 106, 119–23, 211, 222
existential commitment, 105–7
experience machine, 52

Faber, Ginny, 120n27
fairness, 1, 34–5, 50, 58, 72–9, 90–1, 115,
  124, 147, 174–5, 184–8, 213
Falk, W. D., 5, 20n17, 26n27, 29, 32, 35,
  116–7, 133, 139
fallibility, 7, 47, 136, 141n43, 171
family, 4, 7, 15, 23, 36, 43, 48, 66, 69, 121,
  149, 205, 208, 214
fanaticism, 15, 150. *See* racism, sexism
Feldman, Fred, 166–8, 170
fellow-feeling, 15, 19, 93, 113, 171, 205
Feltham, Brian, 92n1
Fields, W. C., 62
final end, 109, 114, 128, 131, 137, 142, 161,
  163, 208. *See* end in itself

Finlay, Stephen, 20n17, 39n39123n32
flourishing, 14, 67, 157, 161–3, 177, 215,
  219–22. *See* eudaimonia, happiness,
  the Good Life
foolishness, 3, 39, 45, 50, 56, 58, 63, 91, 98,
  129, 134, 146, 159, 172, 178, 180, 190,
  191, 216
fools, 1, 2, 14, 45, 50, 52, 78, 90, 175, 182,
  215–6, 230. *See* dupes, suckers
fool's paradise, 52
Foot, Philippa, 2, 26n27, 30n32, 110n15,
  136n36, 156n6, 161–2, 170n19, 173,
  177n25, 181n27, 229. *See also*, dualism
formal conception of *morality*, 28–31, 37,
  42, 43
Fosco, Count, 47–57, 61–63, 67, 68, 71–9,
  79–91, 94–6, 98–103, 107–14, 118, 123,
  129–30, 130n34, 144, 216, 220
France, Peter, 185n34
Frankena, William, 29, 30n31, 41n40, 139
Frankfurt, Harry, 20–1, 121n29, 217–8
free-rider, 13–4, 25, 30n31
Freeman, Herbert, Jr., 35–7, 116–7, 174
Fricker, Miranda, 194-5n49
friendship, 4n6, 58n55, 70, 113–4, 202,
  204–5, 208, 214
Fundamental Dualism of Practical Reason,
  19, 20n17, 24, 28, 31, 42, 110, 157
Fundamental Paradox of Egoistic Hedonism,
  97, 125–6. *See* paradox of happiness
fundamental pragmatics of life, 225–8

Gaillot, M., 191n44
Gandhi, Mohandas, 82
Gauthier, David, 17, 20n17
Gibbard, Allan, 105n12
Gilbert, Margaret, 39n39
Gill, Christopher, 126n2004
Glaucon, 1, 16, 81, 94
God or gods, 4, 7, 48, 155–6, 203, 218
Goldman, Alvin, 194n49
Good Life, the, 4, 7, 10–1, 14, 17, 26, 30–1,
  34, 38n37, 45–59, 61n58, 63, 68, 73, 79,
  80, 86, 88, 90, 111–2, 119, 134, 147n47,
  153–65, 166–8, 170–2, 199, 201–15,
  219–21, 227–8. *See also* eudaimonia,
  flourishing, happiness

good will, 17, 209, 212, 215, 222
grass blade counting, 105, 168, 175, 197n51
greed, 186–7. *See also* arrogance, pleonexia
Greene, Joshua, 158n7
Greenspan, Patricia, 217
Grene, Marjorie, 66n65, 161n9
Griffin, James, 21
guilt, 37–40, 58, 77, 148, 162–3, 229
Gyges, 2, 14

haecceity, 83–4
Haidt, Jonathan,
Hampton, Jean, 33n34, 58n55, 117n24, 186n37, 219n74
happiness, 4, 6–7, 17–20, 21, 44, 45, 51–3, 66, 78, 80, 83, 92–6, 97–104, 107–12, 114, 125–34, 142, 146–7, 153, 159, 163–4, 165, 168, 170, 176, 197, 201–13, 213–5, 221. *See* eudaimonia, flourishing, Good Life
    and self-deception 52–3, 89–91
    and self-respect, 4, 6, 85–9, 94
    and servility, 23, 96, 124
    as by-product, 51n49, 207, 221
    feeling happy, 51–2, 168–72
    fraudulent happiness, 38n37, 110, 147
    paradox of, 92–6, 125–34, 153, 207, 215, 222
    virtue as sufficient for, 6–7, 178, 202–9, 211–3
Hare, R. M., 30n31, 73n70, 120n26
Harman, Gilbert, 17, 20n17
Hartright, William, 48–57, 68, 74, 75, 78, 88, 89, 91
Haybron, Daniel, 21n20, 52-3n52, 168–71
hedonism, 10, 51n49, 89–90, 166–8
Heller, Joseph, 95
herd mentality, 13, 48n44, 89, 230
Herman, Barbara, 18n14
Herman, Judith, 192–3
hermits, 175, 185, 203, 205
Hierocles, 15.
Hill, Thomas, Jr., 17, 23, 41n40, 169, 219n74
Hills, Alison, 3n3, 20n17, 31n33, 81n76
Hinduism, 59n57, 82
Hobbes, Thomas, 16–7, 87, 162
Homo sapiens, 7, 65, 67–8, 155, 157, 161, 163, 181. *See* human being, humanity

honor, 49, 56, 60, 96, 174, 202, 220
horse and rider, 22n21, 158
house divided against itself, 24, 100, 111, 228
Hull, David, 66n65
human being, 5, 7, 15, 45, 63, 65, 66, 69, 75, 79, 84, 93, 102, 160–5, 175, 183, 205n62, 209. *See* Homo sapiens, humanity
human nature, 65–8, 135, 153–65, 173
humane morality, 7, 24, 40, 44, 67, 83, 115, 124, 154, 174, 188, 203
humanity, 15, 61, 64–6, 70–2, 83, 86, 92n1, 93, 162. *See* Homo sapiens, human being
Hume, David, 13, 47, 60, 85, 104–7, 137
Humean, 85, 137
Hurka, Thomas, 103n9, 170n19, 171n20, 173
Hurricane Katrina, 35
Hursthouse, Rosalind, 110n15, 136n36, 138, 156n6, 161–2, 173, 181–2, 183n30, 187n40, 194n49, 223n78
hypocrisy, 38, 151, 155

immoralist, 4, 31
immorality, 3–6, 15, 25, 31, 39, 42, 48, 53n52, 55–7, 57–72, 79, 80–1, 83, 89, 92–4, 146–52, 199–200, 220. *See also* egoism, evil, fanaticism, racism, sexism
    self-righteous/malicious immorality, 5, 150–2.
impartial point of view, 24, 28, 93, 118
impartiality, 5, 15, 17, 24–5, 28, 40, 43, 57, 66, 92–4, 110–1, 114, 116, 118, 124, 144n46, 145, 147, 174. *See also* partiality
    proper or improper partiality, 5, 93, 110–1
instrumental value, 26–7, 44, 62–3, 65, 68, 78–9, 80, 83–4, 86–8, 99–102, 109, 111, 114, 126–31, 133, 138, 142, 146, 204 214, 216, 220–1
instrumental reason, 99, 105, 137, 139, 148
integrity, 22n21-2, 26, 38, 49, 160, 183, 214
intrinsic value, 27, 49, 100, 102–3, 126–7, 131, 138–9, 142, 170, 214, 216. *See* constitutive value, end in itself, final end, noninstrumental value
intuition, 66, 154, 158, 180, 182–3, 207, 223, 229. *See also* second nature

irrationality, 3–4, 25, 55, 58n55, 107, 148–52
is/ought distinction, 60
Iynegar, B. K. S., 59n57, 196
Irwin, T. H., 12n4

Jacobson, Daniel, 159n8
James, William, 121n29
je ne sais quois, 83, 102
Jesus Christ, 51, 82, 212
Job (Biblical), 202
Job, Veronika, C. Dweck, and G. Walton,
    191n44
Johnson, Robert, 18n12-3
Jones, Todd, 83n78
Joyce, Richard, 20n17
justice, 2, 35, 40, 57, 73n69, 74, 92, 93, 115,
    134–5, 150, 170, 176, 184–8, 195n49,
    225, 229. *See also* treating like cases alike

Kagan, Shelly, 20n17
Kahneman, Daniel, 154n1
Kamtekar, Rachana, 177n24
Kant, Immanuel, 4, 17–8, 111–2, 137, 148,
    156–7, 164n13, 211, 214n67
Kantians, 17–8, 64, 73
Klingons, 67
Know Thyself, 54, 194
Kohlberg, Lawrence, 136n36, 149n50
Korsgaard, Christine, 3n4, 58n55, 65n60,
    106n13, 148n49, 180
Kraut, Richard, 161n10
Kripke, Saul, 63n59, 66
Kross, Ethan, O. Ayduk, and W. Mischel,
    198n54
Kupperman, Joel, 94n3, 176n24, 177n24,
    202n58

LaBarge, Scott, 194n49
Laches, 179
Lao Tzu, 232
Lebar, Mark, 173
    and Daniel Russell, 170n19
Lee, Spike, 36
Long, A. A., and D. Sedley, 15, 126
love, 35, 113–8, 191, 205, 213–23, 229
luck, 154, 163, 181, 201–14, 230. *See also* bad
    luck, misfortune, tragedy

Lynch, Michael, 52n50, 182n29
Lyons, William, 217

MacIntyre, Alasdair, 173
McDowell, John, 183n30
McPherson, Tristam, 155n4
Machiavell, Niccolò, 13, 47, 54
Mackie, John, 40
Mafioso, 37–8
malice, 5, 18, 150–2, 172
Mandela, Nelson, 48
Masten, Ann, and M. Reed, 191n46
mercy, 187–8, 229
metaethics, 27, 53n52, 65n61, 103n10, 141,
    156, 163
metaheuristic, 227–8
Mischel, Walter, Y. Shoda, and M.
    Rodriguez, 191n44
Milgram, Stanley, 158, 176n24
Mill, John Stuart, 18–9, 115n19
Milo, Ron, 151n52
Milo the wrestler, 164
misfortune, 7, 59, 132, 154–5, 201–14. *See*
    also bad luck, tragedy
moderation, 135, 187–9, 199
moral character, 29, 39–40, 70, 88, 189, 199,
    209, 222. *See also* character traits
Moral Reality, 34n35, 160n9, 161n9, 182n29,
    222n77
moralism, 12n4, 24–5, 28, 31, 174
moralists, 2, 5, 12, 14–5, 16, 24–5, 27, 30–34,
    37, 43–4, 46, 48, 57, 100, 111, 114,
    170n19, 174
mortality, 7, 68, 177, 203, 206
More, Sir Thomas, 48
motivation, 6, 41, 99, 104, 131, 135, 183,
    200–1, 204n61, 218, 222
Murdoch, Iris, 110n15
My Lai massacre, 174n24

Nagel, Thomas, 3n4, 20n17, 55n58, 122n31,
    139n42
naturalism, 66n65, 155–65
Nichols, Shaun, 158n7
Nietzsche, Friedrich, 13, 30n32, 47
noninstrumental value, 68, 99–102, 126, 131
non-naturalism, 155–61

Nozick, Robert, 3n4, 52, 217
nutrition, 164–5
Nussbaum, Martha, 156n6, 173, 175n23

objectivity, 27, 53, 103–4, 110, 128, 133, 140–
    9, 153–4, 171–2, 209, 214–5, 216
    weak form of, 110
obligation, 7, 12, 18, 23, 67–8, 174, 226
one thought too many, 93, 114, 118, 222
overridingness, 5, 12, 29, 31–2, 41, 84, 96,
    99, 106, 153
other-regarding considerations, 16, 18, 21–2,
    25, 28, 31–8, 40–4, 79, 81, 146, 174,
    185, 212
ought implies can, 67–8

pain, 66n65, 89, 166–8, 178–81, 195–7, 203
paradox of happiness, 94–100, 109, 112, 124,
    125–34, 146, 153, 207, 215, 221, 222
parenthood, 32–3, 35 39, 63, 66, 71, 117,
    122–3, 132, 138–9, 217–8, 224–5, 227
Parfit, Derek, 20n17, 21n20, 58n55
partial identity, 68n67
partiality, 4–5, 15, 48, 92–3, 108, 110–1,
    114–8, 132, 145, 147, 187–8. See also
    impartiality
    proper or improper partiality, 45, 93, 108,
        110–1, 114–118, 132
passion, 18, 22n21, 66n65, 67, 98, 104–7,
    175, 176, 189–90, 193, 198, 199, 213
pathology, 9, 151–2, 183, 199
patriotism, 4, 93, 149
perfectionism, 22n22, 170n19
perseverance, 59, 180, 189, 192, 206, 208,
    228, 230. See endurance
Philosopher's Index, 167n17, 189n42
phronesis, 26, 134–8, 184, 223. See practical
    wisdom
Piaget, Jean, 136n36, 149n50, 226
Plato, 1–2, 14, 22n21, 26n27, 45, 55, 81,
    121n30, 154n3, 158, 179, 186, 194, 200,
    201, 212n65, 215, 218, 219, 223
    Charmides, 194,
    Euthydemus, 45, 154,
    Gorgias, 121n30, 148, 200, 201, 212
    Laches, 179
    Meno, 148, 200

Protagoras, 148, 200
Republic, 1–2, 14, 22, 26n27, 55, 81, 186,
    223
Symposium, 50n47, 215, 218, 219
pleasure, 41n47, 51, 56, 59, 89–91, 96,
    97, 113, 122, 152, 154, 165–72, 183,
    187n40, 188–201, 208, 220–2, 224
    propositional/sensual pleasure, 166
pleonexia, 19, 186, 199. See arrogance, greed
Plutarch, 135, 184
Polus, 121n30
practical rationality, 24, 26, 28–9, 31, 37,
    41, 43, 67, 111–2, 134–46, 148, 151,
    156, 198. See also phronesis, practical
    wisdom
practical wisdom, 21, 34n35, 134–46, 176,
    178, 181, 184, 223–4.
preferred indifferents, 204
prejudice, 28, 110, 140, 141–50, 163, 187,
    194–6. See bias
Price, Richard, 12–3
Prichard, H. A., 12–3
proper function, 26, 161–2, 176, 184, 227
prudence, 12, 15, 19, 26, 135, 137n39,
    139n41, 176, 196
Pruitt, David, 38n37
psychic harmony/disharmony, 55, 81

queerness, 40. See also authority of morality
Question, the, 6, 10–1, 14, 24–5, 28–31,
    42–5, 53n52, 94, 95, 153, 212
Quinn, Warren, 26n27

race or racism, 4n4, 15, 71, 93, 150, 162,
    194n49. See fanaticism, sexism
Rainbolt, George, 188n41
Rawls, John, 73n69, 74, 93, 143, 185n35,
    205n63, 217
Rand, Ayn, 13
rationalism, 22n21, 148
rationality, 13, 17–8, 21, 22n21, 24, 25, 26,
    28–31, 37, 41, 43, 64–7, 93, 105n12,
    111–2, 134–46, 151, 156–9, 198, 205
realpolitik, 14, 54, 89, 111
reciprocity, 185, 219–20. See also recognition
    respect
recklessness, 172, 177–82

recognition respect, 61–2, 64, 68, 78, 185
rectitude, 5, 13, 48, 93, 150, 209
re-evaluation, 108, 126–34, 138, 144–6, 163, 174, 198, 201
   genuine/ersatz, 129–30
reflection, 11n2, 144, 183, 198, 212
relativism, 17, 103–4, 164–5
religion, 4, 12, 43, 93, 123, 147
reproduction, 67, 157, 162
repulsion, 193
resentment, 19, 76–7, 187
resilience, 138, 176, 189–92, 198, 206–7
respect, 43, 59–72, 72–79, 79–91, 100, 122, 137, 145, 192, 205, 219, 222. *See also* disrespect, self-respect, self-disrespect
responsibility, 138–9
reverence, 214, 217–8. *See* devotion
risk assessment, 180, 187
Robinson Crusoe, 38
Rosati, Connie, 119n25
Roosevelt, Eleanor, 48
rules, 13, 90, 117–8, 143, 160, 182, 229
Russell, Daniel, 12n258n55, 61n58, 136n36, 170n19, 173, 204n61, 223n78

sacrifices, 2, 13, 14, 25, 42, 49, 54, 55, 82, 86, 94, 96, 108, 112, 116–8, 118–23, 125, 129, 130, 137n39145, 174, 196, 211, 213, 228
sainthood, 49, 82, 123, 203
Santas, Gerasimos, 148n48, 200n56
Scanlon, T., 20n17, 21n20
Scheffler, Samuel, 12n3, 20n17, 22–4, 26n27, 41n40, 115n21
schizophrenia, 24, 44, 114
Schmidtz, David, 13n7, 136n36, 185n36
Schroeder, Andrew, 115n20
Scotus, 12n4
second nature, 182, 197, 207, 233. *See also* intuition
self-abnegation/derogation, 12, 75, 96, 124, 144. *See* servility
self-deception, 48, 50–5, 58, 75, 77–9, 86–8, 90, 100, 110, 151, 186, 194, 151, 206
self-discipline, 38, 188–92, 196, 199
self-disrespect, 4, 23–4, 46–7, 57, 63–4, 69–72, 93–4, 115, 191, 216, 219n74

self-effacement, 103, 112, 132–3, 208
self-hate, 46
self-interest, 2, 4–5, 10, 12–4, 15, 16–7, 21–6, 28, 31–2, 35, 36–7, 40–2, 43, 46, 49, 58n55, 68, 81, 86–8, 92, 96, 97, 101n8, 108, 112, 114–7, 119–23, 125, 137n39, 146, 174, 212, 215, 216, 228–9
self-knowledge, 53, 72–9, 144, 163, 177, 180, 194, 205
self-fulfillment, 171–2
self-regard, 5, 18–9, 28, 38, 40, 79, 81, 174, 185
self-regarding considerations, 16, 21–2, 25, 31–4, 43, 44, 174
self-respect, 4, 6, 13, 17–9, 22n22, 23, 27, 35–6, 38, 43–50, 55, 60–3, 71, 72–9, 80–91, 94, 96, 112, 147, 151–2, 153, 155, 163, 168, 172, 192, 205, 211, 213, 216–9, 221.
   fraudulent self-respect, 50n46, 63, 78, 89–91
self-sufficiency, 141, 178, 202–7, 213
selfishness, 15, 30, 48n44, 121, 145, 171, 214, 215
semantic reshuffling, 40–1
Sensible Knave, 13, 24, 30n31, 42, 47, 148
sentiment, 13, 22n21, 127, 141n43, 156n6, 158–9
servility, 17, 23, 32, 38, 47n41, 67, 82, 93, 96, 154, 169, 172, 185, 187, 217, 219
Setiya, Kieran, 26n27, 156n6
sexism, 15, 93, 150, 162, 194n49. *See* fanaticism, racism
Shafer-Landau, Russ, 156n5
shame, 38–40, 162–3, 167, 189
shamelessness, 46–7, 50, 114, 167, 189
Sidgwick, Henry, 19–20, 28, 96–8, 110–2, 125–6, 128–9, 137n39, 217
Singer, Peter, 205n63
situationism, 176-7n24
Slote, Michael, 113n17, 173
Smith, Matthew Noah, 76n74
Soble, Alan, 217
social conception of *morality*, 13, 16–21, 24, 30–4, 35–40, 43, 80–2, 123–4, 174
Socrates, 30n32, 45, 47n41, 48, 52, 54, 121n30, 147–8, 151, 200, 201, 212

Socratic paradoxes, 148, 200
solipsism 13–4, 30n31, 103
Sowell, Elizabeth, 139n41
spoiling, 58, 124, 190, 209, 225
Sreenivasan, Gopal, 177n24
Steinberg, Laurence, 139n41
Stepmotherly Nature, 211
Sternberg, Robert, 225
Stevenson, C. L., 20n17
Stocker, Michael, 4n6, 24n25, 39n38, 66n66, 113–4, 120, 142n44, 211n64, 216n69
    and E. Hegeman, 142n44
Stoics, 7, 15, 126n33, 136n36, 178, 201–8
Strawson, P. F., 76n73
Stichter, Matthew, 225n80
stringency, 12, 15, 20n17, 22, 31, 42, 49, 95, 115, 124, 144n46
Stroud, S. and C. Tappolet, 189n42
Stryon, William, 211
subjectivism, 47n41, 52, 52–3nn51-2, 85, 103–4, 171
sucker, 14, 25, 62. See dupes, fools
sufficiency for happiness, 6–7, 51, 169, 178, 201–13. See also self-sufficiency
suicide, 38
Summers, Jesse and W. Sinnott-Armstrong, 198n53
Sumner, W. L., 21n20, 22n22
supernaturalism, 155–8
supervenience, 73, 85. See also treating like cases alike
swallows and summer, 48, 70
Swanton, Christine, 136n36, 173, 187n40, 194n49
Swartwood, Jason, 225n80

Taylor, Gabriele, 217
Tec, Necama, 203n59
teleology, 66, 160–1
Telfer, Elizabeth, 20n17, 61n58
temperance, 38, 67, 134–5, 139n41, 176, 187, 188–201, 206
theoretical wisdom, 223–4
Thomas, Laurence, 217
Thomson, Judith, 26n27, 156n6
Thrasymachus, 13, 21, 23–4, 30nn31-2, 42, 47, 52

Tiberius, Valerie, 18n14, 21n20, 53n52, 163n12, 198n52, 226n83
    and J. Swartwood, 225n81
    and J. D. Walker, 48n43
Timmons, Mark, 18n14, 53n52, 141n42
tragedy, 36, 52, 145, 155, 165, 206, 210–1, 213. See also bad luck, misfortune
treating like cases alike, 63, 72–5, 78, 184. See also supervenience
Tooby, John, 66n65

Übermensch, 47, 54
Uncle Tom, 23, 169
unity of virtues, 135, 184
universalizability, 13, 30n31, 73
unfairness, 1, 7, 33n34, 56, 72–4, 79, 90, 110, 123, 147, 172, 187, 230. See also immorality, pleonexia

Vaish, Amrisha, M. Carpenter, and M. Tomasello, 136n36
value, see constitutive value, instrumental value, intrinsic value, noninstrumental value
van Roojen, Mark, 148n49
Vayrynen, Pekka, 83n78
Velleman, David, 217–8
vestigial traits, 162
veterans, 192–3
villains, 15, 47, 49n44, 148, 216
village life, 49, 209
virtue, 2, 7, 12, 18, 34, 38, 67, 96, 134, 135–6, 137, 159–65, 172–7, 178, 179, 183–4, 185, 188–9, 193, 195, 198–9, 201–2, 211–2, 213–4, 221, 225–8
virtue theory, 103n9, 134, 159, 170
virtus, 159, 172. See arête
Vlastos, Gregory, 186n38
Vulcans, 67, 155

Walsh, Denis, 66n65, 161n9
wantonness, 152, 189–90
Waterfield, Robin, 186n38
weakness of will, 29, 39, 64, 128n42, 199–200. See akrasia
Wedgwood, Ralph, 13n6
Weiss, Roslyn, 148n48, 200n56

well-being, 21, 22n22, 80, 170–2, 217–8, 226n83
Wheeler, Samuel, III, 61n65, 116n22
Whiting, Jennifer, 18n13
Whitman, Walt, 3
Williams, Bernard, 24n25, 39, 66n66, 92–3, 114, 137n38, 185n32, 222
willpower, 189, 191–2, 197–8
winning, 58, 98, 119, 147, 154, 209, 220
"winning", 58, 90–1, 174, 220. *See also* self-respect (fraudulent), Lance Armstrong
wisdom, 7, 14, 21, 34n35, 53n52, 45, 53, 86–7, 90, 134–5, 136, 138, 152, 154, 155, 159, 161, 164–5, 175, 176–7, 178–80, 181–2, 184, 188, 189n42, 206, 207–31. *See also* practical wisdom, theoretical wisdom
Woman in White, 47, 48
Wolf, Susan, 20n17, 49, 82, 123n32, 144n46
Wong, David, 136n36
Woodruff, Paul, 214n66
Woods, Michael, 229n87
Wright, Crispin, 27n28

Xavier and Yves, 69–70, 76–7
Xena and Yvonne, 127–9

Zimmerman, Michael, 38

CPSIA information can be obtained
at www.ICGtesting.com
Printed in the USA
BVOW08s1356250118
506159BV00001B/1/P